THE ULTI

SH*T HITS

THE FAN

SURVIVAL GUIDE

THE ULTIMATE
SH*T HITS
THE FAN
SURVIVAL GUIDE

HOW TO LIVE THROUGH ANY CATASTROPHE

LEN McDOUGALL

Skyhorse Publishing

A PERSONAL NOTE FROM THE AUTHOR

At some point in this book, you're likely to be offended by something I've written as I attempt to make a point. With all due respect, dear reader, think of it as tough love.

There are so many misconceptions, so many myths—many of them surprisingly recent in origin—that a scarred, gray-bearded old woodsman who's learned many a lesson the hardest of ways (short of actually dying) could go nuts just trying to dispel them all. Forget about trying to teach someone to survive; you could spend weeks just debating beliefs that are not only untrue, but often dangerous. In the more than quarter-century I spent teaching survival classes to people who came from all over the country, I turned away most clients who said "I already know a lot . . ." during our pre-contract telephone interview. I'm a survival instructor, not the captain of a debate team.

I've spent my entire life—almost sixty years—learning the nuts and bolts of staying alive under adverse conditions—both in urban and wilderness conditions—and it often was not my choice. My own education didn't stop during the more than thirty years I took money in exchange for teaching the wilderness skills I'd learned to others.

My foray into the world of survival began as a way of life; I grew up the eldest of seven children in a dirt-poor household. Not in a metropolitan ghetto (although I did spend my infancy there), but in the Michigan northwoods. During the summer, you'd swear that the bugs would carry you away. In the winter, when the weather can (and sometimes does) kill a person just for doing nothing at all, you sometimes go into the root cellar just to see dirt.

The turning point for me, personally, came in the winter of 1964–65. We lived two miles outside of a tiny burg named Carsonville. When the blizzard hit, it was my mother (always a frail woman), sister, three brothers (two of them—twins, who were less than a year old), and me, the eldest. My stepfather was away, driving a truck, and nobody who would have cared could get to us down the snow-choked dirt road.

Days passed, then a week. The cupboards went bare and the powdered milk needed to be saved for the babies. We were eating rolled oats three times a day. Then the sugar ran out, and mealtimes truly became drudgery. We were surviving, but that was all. By the time a farmer who lived a mile down the road came putting through the snowdrifts that choked our hundred-yard driveway on his John Deere A tractor to check on us, we were on our second day of eating nothing at all.

That experience left a mark. My brothers and sister don't remember, but my mother did, and for me it definitely left a lasting impression. I vowed that we would never go without food again, and we never did. There were hard times again, but I made sure there was always meat, fish, and fowl on the dinner table. Sport hunters who've never killed for more than some kind of fun have demonized my actions as somehow offensive to their magazine-instilled ideals, but my younger siblings never went without a meal. They'll probably never appreciate that the good health they've enjoyed as adults is likely a result of eating more natural than "store-bought" foods, not just wild game, but from the truck garden and livestock we raised. We learned to can, dry, smoke, and jerk just about everything you could consider food.

I've often attracted people who want to prepare for the end of the world—or at least, the end of the world as *they* know it. They're usually surprised that I don't think in those terms. I doubt the world will end in a fiery Armageddon, but I'm sure that times can get tough—and then, they'll get tougher yet. I remember the Associated Press photo of an old man, several days dead, in a wheelchair, desiccating under a hot sun, while a pair of toddlers played on the sidewalk next to him—and that wasn't in Ghana or Peru, it was in New Orleans, Louisiana. After the 2010 Earthquake, decaying corpses were stacked like cordwood in Haiti, because there were neither resources nor a place to remove them from public view. Finally, for the sake of public safety and hygiene, those babies, wives, and grandfathers were unceremoniously bulldozed into a big hole, and covered over. How "civilized" a person might be is entirely dependent on how tough conditions are.

Because lessons are, by definition, stories, I've elected to illustrate some of those that I've learned with factual anecdotes. Some of these lessons have scarred me—a painful lesson is one that you'll probably remember. I was fortunate to have absorbed many lessons vicariously, while on a few occasions the people who should have learned from their experiences haven't survived to exploit the learning. It is my most sincere and fervent hope that by relating events from my own life, I can pass on information that I've obtained the hard way without costing you the blood and pain that I've paid. Sometimes, there are numerous pieces of wisdom to be gathered from a single misadventure.

No, I don't believe that the world will end, per se—at least, not in the glorious and mercifully quick fireball that so many hope it will. But it's a given that *your* world will end. A biblical proverb says that no man can know the time, but, according to the Department of Homeland Security, every one of us can expect to face some form of widespread catastrophe in our lives. It might be human-caused, it could be one of the increasingly common (and increasingly extreme) weather-driven calamities. Or, even something as improbable, but maybe not so impossible—according to some big names in computer design—as machines that get smart enough to become dangerous. Or maybe even a conquering army from another planet. The possibilities for our complete or partial destruction are almost endless.

Whatever the cause of a disaster, your objective is to live through it, if for no other reason than to continue our species. And it is the stated objective of this book to enable you to achieve that goal. However you choose to use the knowledge and wisdom I've worked hard to put into this book is up to you. Either way, good luck.

CHAPTER ONE

PHILOSOPHIES OF SURVIVAL

"**A** human being should be able to change a diaper, plan an invasion, butcher a hog, conn a ship, design a building, write a sonnet, balance accounts, build a wall, set a bone, comfort the dying, take orders, give orders, cooperate, act alone, solve equations, analyze a new problem, pitch manure, program a computer, cook a tasty meal, fight efficiently, die gallantly. Specialization is for insects."

—Robert Heinlein

Attitude and Philosophy

A sudden screech of tires next to my open window sent ice water down my spine. It was a Friday afternoon in July, and the highway was bumper-to-bumper, jammed mostly with tourists who were fleeing their urban neighborhoods.

The reversed image in my mirror showed a Ford LTD sedan, brakes locked and tires smoking, skidding sideways in a desperate attempt to avoid the stopped traffic ahead. The driver missed the other vehicles, but his car slammed broadside into a molded concrete curb. The big car rolled onto its side like a mortally wounded beast, its exposed underside unsettling to me, and it continued over, impacting hard onto its roof before sliding to rest in a deep, grassy ditch.

I parked, then grabbed my truck's on-board first-aid kit and ran toward the inverted car while my wife used our sideband CB radio to call a local REACT (Radio Emergency Associated Communication Teams) base station operator on Emergency channel 9. That operator in turn called the police from his home (there was no 911 in those days). From a hundred feet the air was thick with gasoline fumes—I could hear dripping fuel sizzling onto hot exhaust pipes.

On the passenger side, a thirty-year-old-looking man, one of the passengers, was pulling the right arm of a plump woman who was suspended upside-down from her shoulder belt. The driver was lying on his belly inside the opposite window, pulling on her opposite arm. Neither man was cognizant enough to understand the lady's repeated complaints that she was stuck, unable to reach the belt's release button.

When the man on the passenger side ignored my repeated comments to that effect, I grabbed his shoulder with enough grip to get his attention, and pointed out the problem. He released the woman's arm and began yanking against the seat-belt strap. The woman, who could smell and hear sizzling gasoline, began to panic and wriggle wildly against her restraints.

This was stupid, and I lacked the courage to spend a second more near that car than I had to. I flicked open the large blade of my Buck CrossLock folding knife and told the man to move his fingers. He ignored me, pulling mindlessly against the strap until I laid the Buck's polished edge against the belt next to his fingers. The man jerked his hands back automatically. A single slash later, the woman dropped heavily onto the car's ceiling, scrambling out the passenger window even before she landed.

The woman ran to a little boy and a girl who were already out of the car. The three of them hugged and wailed uncontrollably while I tried vainly to ascertain if everyone was out. All three adult occupants were in a daze, and all had slipped away from reality for the moment. I smelled beer.

Terrified that the sizzling LTD might burst into flames, I ran back and tried to look inside. The front windows were open, but the car's roof was crushed down onto the front seat's back. (That meant that both of the kids outside had probably been in the front seat.) The back windows were not only closed, but tinted, and I could see nothing of the interior.

I grabbed the handle and pulled, but the latch was wedged tight. At least thirty motorists had gathered to gawk, their cars lining the highway on either side, so there seemed to be plenty of muscle available. I called out for a couple of big, strong guys to lend a hand and, incredibly, not one bystander even blinked. Like a herd of ruminating cattle, every one stared blankly, and I had the nauseating impression that they regarded what they were witnessing as reality television.

I braced a foot against the LTD's quarter panel and heaved. The door opened. Huddled on the car's ceiling was a little girl, about ten years old, with wide brown eyes. She was scratched and bruised, but seemed to have no real injuries.

"C'mon Honey," I said, more calmly than I felt, "Your Mom's right here waiting for you." She took my hand, and I pulled her from the wreck. Without a word she ran over to the woman and two children, and now all four were sobbing hysterically. The driver and the other man were milling around in a stupor, but everyone was out of the car.

The overturned Ford was cloaked in a stench of gasoline and hissing like a Hognose snake. The mob of motorists who'd gathered to watch the show were within fifty feet of what I feared might become a fiery explosion at any second. When I pointed out the danger to them in a loud voice, the crowd backed up in unison (like a school of minnows, I thought), but only about ten feet. Disgusted, I dismissed them all with a wave of my hand.

A fleet of fire trucks immediately screamed onto the scene, so I shouldered my first-aid kit and headed back to where my wife sat, still talking with the REACT operator who had called them. Rubber-clad firemen hosed down the Ford as we pulled back onto the highway. I tried not to think about the toxins they were washing into the groundwater that ultimately fed into my house's well.

There are several lessons to learn from that story—like how valuable it might prove to carry a first-aid kit and a fire extinguisher in one's vehicle at all times. Or how having a sharp folding knife on your belt can make possible feats that would otherwise be impossible. I also made a mental note that today's improved braking systems might not always be a good thing if the car behind yours doesn't also have them.

The most disappointing lesson came from those motorists who had stopped to do nothing except witness tragedy, vicariously seeking a thrill they could use to remind themselves that they could still feel something in their numbed lives. However psychologists might try to explain the reluctance of this crowd of people to help, the bottom line is that not one person at the scene lifted a finger to aid a family who was clearly in need of immediate assistance. I pray that none of my loved ones are ever the victim in a similar circumstance.

Reality and Glory

Since "survivalist" became a byword of the late 1970s (ironically, about the same time that the song "Macho Man" appeared on the music charts), I've seen a whole spectrum of survival experts and heard more survival philosophies than I care to recall. In those days of the Cold War, there existed a universal social unease. Natural disasters seemed far-fetched; more likely were invading armies from that supposed pit of Hell, the Soviet Union. Or, worse, the appropriately coined acronym MAD—for Mutually Assured Destruction—by nuclear ICBMs, enough of them to bathe the globe in radioactive flames. Only in recent years, with the de-classification of governmental documents, do we realize how very close we came to incineration a couple of times. When the USSR collapsed, fear shifted to invasion by United Nations troops. Then Chinese . . .

Meanwhile, in Monroe County, Michigan, near Detroit, the Fermi II fast-breeder plutonium reactor's core experienced a Chernobyl-style meltdown in 1966, and nobody noticed. In 1969, the Cuyahoga River and Lake Erie were so polluted with petrochemicals that the water caught fire. In 1978, the super-polluted Love Canal in New York literally exploded under the community built atop it. In 1979, the Three Mile Island nuclear power plant near Middletown, Pennsylvania, partially melted down. And so on.

At the time of this writing, a legislative boondoggle by Michigan's Governor Snyder has poisoned the drinking water of Flint, Michigan, turning it urine-yellow, even after treatment. It is not paranoid to maintain a survivalist attitude; it is naive not to.

Many people perceive the world around them as going to hell in a proverbial handbasket, and they feel powerless to make any effective changes to its progress. Their collective psyche needs to feel like it is not entirely vulnerable; they need to believe that a catastrophic situation that might not have yet happened—or even been identified—isn't entirely hopeless.

So, people choose to prepare as they believe is wisest. Along with socially normal people, every neurotic with a psychological axe to grind is attracted to the "cause" of survivalism, or prepping, or whatever the most faddish catchphrase is for that week. The hard truth is that preparing to survive a disaster whose form and severity are unknown must be a theoretical exercise—in part, at least.

Not nearly as theoretical as some make it, though, because there exists a whole library of empirical fact—how knowledgeable any survivalist might be is in direct proportion to how willing he is to study. In the twenty-first century, there is no reason—and no excuse—for a survivalist to not know the boiling temperature of water, how many yards are in a mile (or meters in a kilometer), how to navigate from Orion's Belt, or any number of commonly known empirical values. Although there are certainly individuals (sadly, maybe the majority) who live up to Hollywood's image of the redneck ne'er-do-well who sits on a case of canned goods with a shotgun and a bad attitude, the genuine survival expert is indistinguishable from any good neighbor. He doesn't sport a rebel flag or bring attention to himself unnecessarily, and he is generally well-versed in most topics. Not necessarily because he is a genius, but because staying alive, no matter what, is no less serious than studying to be a lawyer, and a genuine survivalist appreciates that knowledge is, indeed, power. The best part is that education, like good hygiene, is free for the taking.

A survival expert also knows that there will be nothing glorious or romantic in keeping themselves and their loved ones alive during a real-life catastrophe. That conclusion isn't theoretical or hypothetical, but based on actual events from the past, present, and certainly future. For the Jews in Hitler's Germany in 1939, there was nothing romantic, nor for refugees in Serbia and Bosnia when First World Yugoslavia suddenly descended into bloody anarchy, with caveman mentalities and twenty-first-century weapons. Even in the United States. The most amazing thing about the aftermath of Hurricane Katrina in New Orleans, Louisiana, was the speed at which that city plunged into lawless chaos.

There will be no sudden burst of heroic magnificence, followed by a quick and painless end. Imagine those things that your mind refuses to think of. Watching your wife or daughter being gang-raped, then beaten to death, their eyes cut out with a knife, while you can do nothing but watch. Envision the slow death of a small child who's been burned so horribly that her skin sloughs off, and you can do nothing, except pray that death comes like a merciful angel.

Are you thinking, "Oh my God, what is wrong with the SOB who wrote this book?" Good. Because as bad as you might think I am, I freaking assure you that if supermarket shelves go bare and amenities that we think of as necessities start disappearing, there are people out there who make me look naive.

This is not to invoke fear unnecessarily. *Mad Max* movies notwithstanding, the small percentage of people who have a sociopathic mental bent have never survived for long in a human society that has always striven to rebuild itself after an apocalypse. But be aware that they will exist; a minority of desperate, need-driven people who have always congregated together to form a common spine, as it were. They will be driven by fear, maybe hopelessness, because they have no survival strategy. They pose little danger to a well-organized party, but history has shown that they might present a danger to loners, and to groups smaller than their own.

As a whole, people will band together for the good of their communities, because that's what human beings do. After the 2011 earthquake in Fukushima, Japan, and the subsequent tsunami that breached a large nuclear reactor there, citizens were remarkable in their communal display of calm. There was no looting, no one rioted, and no one martyred themselves before television cameras. Residents just quietly picked up and helped their neighbors do the same and, working together, they gave news broadcast crews—who thrive on tears, pain, and drama—little reason to even be there.

The earthquake/tsunami/nuclear disaster that triple-whammied Japan in 2011 is but one recent example of how planetary changes can destroy a person's world between breakfast and lunch. (Photo courtesy API)

Toughness and the Survivalist

And that brings us to another truism that seems to be especially frightening: The toughest man who ever lived was pretty fragile. All of us like to believe that we're able to withstand abuse on a superhuman scale, but the simple fact is that humans are pretty easy to kill, and not especially difficult to take out of action.

Even mentally, humans are easy to break. Every person who ever successfully served a hitch in the US military has been broken—most reduced to tears—and that especially applies to elite special forces. Military SERE (Survival, Evasion, Resistance, Escape) trainers are experts at reducing the toughest man to a blubbering mass, and the only soldier who might not have been broken is the one who washed out in boot camp. To quote *Dirty Harry*, "A man's got to know his limitations."

Gladiators of Old Rome trained hard so they would not kill an opponent, because gladiatorial exhibitions were, above all, entertainment.

A soldier, battle-hardened—which is to say, experienced and still alive—knew that the secret to walking off any battlefield lay in taking an opponent out of the fight immediately. It didn't really matter if the other fellow died, so long as he was incapable of inflicting harm. If that translated into a quick thrust and slash that left an enemy struggling to scoop his own entrails back into his abdominal cavity, so much the better. A gladiator knew that people were easy to kill.

A gladiator also knew that genuine sword fights were concluded in a matter of seconds, usually with a single blow; so the gladiator's objective was to thrill a crowd, and that meant showmanship took precedence over combat skill. An uprising of gladiators in the Third Servile War (73–71 BC), led by the infamous Spartacus, easily swept aside the Roman Guard (police force); but Spartacus's army fell to returning legions of battle-hardened soldiers who did not know how to sword fight, only how to eliminate an enemy.

Over the centuries, gladiators morphed into different types of less-deadly sport fighters. The bare-knuckled brawlers of John L. Sullivan's day were still too dangerous to one another, so boxing gloves were adopted; not to protect fists, but faces. A friend who'd recently earned his black belt in Tae Kwon Do asked his sensei to demonstrate what he might expect in a street fight—the sensei knocked him down immediately.

The enemies most likely to lay low a survivalist aren't big. They don't even have teeth or claws. Mosquitoes and black flies have brought down the strongest of men—and not just in the woods; the worst epidemic of Yellow Fever in America occurred in New York City. A few years back, one of my friends actually knocked himself unconscious because of mosquitoes during a hurried midnight trip to the outhouse. Among lumberjacks of old, there was malady known as "swamp madness," during which victims (primarily of exhaustion) temporarily lost their minds until they were returned to town.

In that same vein, some survival authorities have gone on record saying that it's preferable to drink untreated water from a stream or pond, and to subsequently contract an aquatic parasite, than it is to be dehydrated. That is, to put it bluntly, some of the worst advice ever dispensed—and under the water section in this book, you'll learn how to do neither. A case of cryptosporidium might not kill you (it does do just that in a few instances), but the diarrhea, stomach cramps, fever, and generally crippling flu-like symptoms that accompany the intestinal parasite are definitely not conducive to fending for oneself in life-threatening circumstances.

The crux of my message in this section up to now has been to convince you how tough you are not. Now, let's address how tough you are—the real world proves that a typical human is tough enough to accomplish some pretty awesome things. When Lt. Ian MacHorton and his unit of British *Chindits* forged deep into Japanese-held territory in Burma during WWII, they accomplished their mission of destroying enemy rail lines. But in doing so, the unit was scattered throughout some of the most feared jungle on Earth. Thanks to their training and ingenuity, many of the lost *chindits* made it back to British-held India after surviving months in the bush. Lt. MacHorton was missing-in-action for 100 days before he walked out of the jungle, almost none the worse for wear.

During the decade of excavation before the 42-mile-long Panama Canal officially opened in 1914, malaria, yellow fever, dengue, and other insect-borne ailments ranked as the most feared hazards in the jungle. More than half a century later, the most advanced, best equipped soldiers the world had ever seen were being brought down by parasites in Vietnam. Even today, malaria is much-feared in places like Africa.

Yet, human beings have thrived in such "inhospitable" places for millions of years—without quinine, inoculations, and white-coated doctors. Survival isn't about Kung fu and midnight firefights, it's about being strong enough to resist the minuscule, everyday threats that are immediate dangers.

One secret to doing so is to remain healthy and physically strong, and that means that you do not tough-out any situation that you don't have to. It's imperative that you remain well-fed, hydrated, that you get sufficient sleep, and that you do nothing that might compromise or weaken your immune system. It isn't about being tough, it's about being healthy. Achieve that seemingly simple goal and you'll find that you're tougher than the guy who denies needing those things.

Why Survive?

In the aftermath of widespread devastation—a suffering on a global scale that, with today's inflated human populations, results in a death toll the likes of which has never been seen in history—would you even want to survive? Do you want to raise your children and grandchildren in a world that is devoid of happiness, where the simplest pleasures—like clean water to drink and enough food to fill your belly—might be just fond memories of past generations?

The answer is yes. A fundamental of human survival, on an instinctual, even cellular level, is that you must continue the existence of your species. This is insect strategy; an instinctive reaction that goes beyond instincts like fear, love, and anger. It's a soul-deep desire that drives us to continue the existence of our bloodline. It is why wolves began to take coyotes as mates at least two decades ago. It's the reason that the Jews, Asians, and the American Indians, like every other conquered people, capitulated to their masters, rather than have their entire genealogies erased. When all else has failed, when a situation has fallen to that single-celled animal level, and you know beyond a doubt that doom and extinction are the inevitable results, the ultimate solution is to survive—scientists call that *evolution.*

The insect-level survival instincts operate all around us. It's the instinct that makes locusts swarm over places where there is food, even though birds and small carnivores eat them until they can't eat any more. The same force that drives mating fish to school upstream, in disregard of fish-eaters who massacre them by the thousands. The same impetus that compelled Japanese soldiers trapped on Guadalcanal Island to throw themselves at Marines who they thought were there to annihilate their race. Often mistaken for heroism, it's the force that drives adults to shield children from harm with their own bodies. Even the "suicidal" migrations of lemmings are actually a representation of the drive to sacrifice some to ensure survival of the species.

So, when someone asks, "Why would I want to survive in a world that's radioactive, or where the cities are in ruins?" The answer is: because that's what we're wired to do. No one wants to die—that's our personal survival instinct—but if just one human being lives through whatever it is that's trying to kill off our species, then we've satisfied our most profound drive to survive.

Misanthropy versus Conscience

Misanthropy is the hatred of one's own kind. This cognitive feeling runs counter to our cell-deep, insect-like instincts. But like so much about the human condition, our species has evolved a hodgepodge of emotions that have created a whole industry of psychology and self-help from people who claim to understand what's going on in our heads better than we can.

Being humans, we are cursed with mental processes that other animals have been spared. It has been argued that to be self-aware on the level we are is the very definition of hell on Earth. Our minds can translate what would be an idyllic life to those who are less blessed as a damnable existence.

Misanthropy is common in a catastrophic event. Someone must be to blame. Everyone else is to blame. You need to look out for number one. You need to make hard decisions, and to hell with anyone/everyone else.

But unless you truly believe that whatever is happening to you is indeed the end of the world, then it's imperative that you maintain a positive attitude. That's not a cliché. You need to have a plan to survive, and you need a clear head to form an intelligent plan. To have a clear head, you need to believe that there is a reason to live through another tomorrow.

Biased against that, you might be required to make tough decisions. If you have only enough water to keep your own family alive, you might have to watch while your neighbor's children die of thirst. That's only one of a thousand horrible, unthinkable dilemmas that can, have, and might occur.

There is no correct answer to such problems, there are no proper solutions. There is only the recognition that horrid things none of us like to even imagine might happen. Like survival itself, what a person does in response to any set of conditions will vary according to circumstances.

The best you can do is be aware and be prepared to meet as many contingencies as you can. Whether you will sacrifice humanity for continuation of life for yourself—or for a loved one—is a choice you could face, and you need to at least recognize that as fact.

Trust, Secrets, and Need to Know

The aim of survival is to be prepared to meet problems whose form you can't prepare for. Put simply, that's impossible. In today's world, the potential problems are legion. More than that, the challenges might be very different from one region to another.

Begin with the generics. In most instances, you'll need to establish a safe haven. Maybe not a place in which to spend the rest of your life, but a hideout where you can escape to at a moment's notice with those you choose to take with you, and regroup until you can fully assess a situation. Leaping before you look is an age-old mistake, and life could well depend on having a respite in which to strategize.

Take, for instance, the turn of the millennium. It didn't take a master in computer assembly language to know that the presumed Y2K bug was never going to be a problem in itself (most personal computers never even noticed), but AM radio scaremongers had half the country ready to panic over passenger planes falling from the sky, medical records disappearing, 401Ks vanishing, and Wall Street collapsing.

In reality, forewarned is forearmed, and every industry had been aware of the potential flaws in the 2-digit date system for more than fifteen years—time enough to ensure that any critical digital data was transferred onto an updated machine. Nobody was going to lose anything.

Still, I distrusted the generalized fear that I was hearing from friends and neighbors—or even overhearing in conversations between other people in supermarket checkout lines and elsewhere. I decided that it would be prudent to have an escape plan; a ready place to go to, should widespread panic ensue because of a glitch or two in somebody's computer. It probably wouldn't need to be a long-term haven—although I sure wasn't going to rule that out by being unprepared for an extended stay—the fist-fights, riots, and even unsubstantiated rumors of investors jumping out of high-rise windows on Wall Street in 1929 stand as proof that panic by itself can be mindlessly lethal.

Since part of my job entails backpacking, no one thought anything of it when I left for a weekend in a million-acre state forest. When I got to where I was going, at the end of a miles-long, 4-wheel-drive-only 2-track, I took the 55-gallon open-head plastic barrel from the covered bed of my truck and hauled it a couple more miles back into the woods. When I reached the high-ground glacial ridge I wanted, in the midst of a deep swamp, I buried it deep enough that bears (hopefully) wouldn't find it, and partially filled it with the contents of my backpack. Over the next few months, that barrel became a pretty impressive emergency cache.

Y2K passed with barely a hiccup, but that retreat site later became the place where I built a log cabin for my book *The Log Cabin*. It proved to be a good site because, although many have looked for the place since I moved out in 2002, no one has yet found it.

And it's unlikely that anyone else will ever find it—especially since the forest has naturally changed to erase what little sign I'd left when I was living there. A well-stocked hideout like this one might be a lifesaver one day, but only if its location—indeed, its very existence—remains absolutely unknown. It has been said, validly, that two people can keep a secret if one of them is dead.

Best friends, lovers, wives, husbands, kids—none of these people need to know where your safe house is located. Not until the time comes when it is needed. For every head that contains this information, the value of the place decreases geometrically until it might very likely become useless. A drunken, angry, even innocent slip of the tongue can undo a decades-worth of planning and preparation, and it's human nature to demonstrate one's importance by revealing a secret—the bigger the secret, the more important its keeper must be.

But one cannot divulge secrets that one doesn't know in the first place. And, as Butch Cassidy once observed about his famed Hole-in-the-Wall hideout, the only reason it hadn't been found was because it wasn't worth the trouble for lawmen to come a-lookin' for it. Remember, a secret is not a secret if someone else knows about it.

CHAPTER TWO

THE NOT-NAKED APE

Tools and Equipment

One of the romantic, and patently unrealistic, notions of what constitutes a genuine survival expert is his or her ability to be dropped off naked into the backcountry, where they will not only thrive, but build a Wal-Mart Superstore.

It doesn't work that way, folks. It has never worked that way. Since the appearance of *Homo habilis*—the "Handy Man"—in the evolutionary line of primates, humans have prevailed through the manufacture and use of tools. Denied the senses, natural tools, and weapons of so-called lesser animals, people owe their origins—and their continued survival, even (and perhaps, especially)—in the twenty-first century to an innate creativity. That, combined with opposable thumbs and long fingers, enables us to manufacture superior replacements for teeth, claws, and an infinite spectrum of other tools.

It's true that a genuine survival expert, armed with thousands upon thousands of hours—not just an occasional weekend—might make his way, Rambo-style, with almost nothing. But that's only because he possesses the experience and tactile know-how to create tools from whatever materials are at hand. No Apache, Bushman, or Aborigine ever willingly went into the wilderness without packing along as many comforts and necessities as circumstances would allow. An Athabascan wouldn't even think about it.

Why You Need a Knife

"Can I borrow your knife?" I've heard that question with increasing frequency for the past thirty-five years, and often from people in a work environment, where a knife is needed on a daily basis; for everything from opening boxes and cutting tape to stripping wire and scraping away a layer of paint. You don't need to be a back-assward woodsman to regard your knife as an invaluable tool of everyday life.

When I ask the would-be borrower why they don't carry their own knife, the inevitable answer is "I don't need one." I won't even address the hypocrisy of that statement. I say *would-be borrower*, because my answer to their requests is, also inevitably, "no." That's not to say that I won't perform the necessary cutting task for them—if it's not a ridiculous job that would damage or break my knife. But don't expect my help when you ask for a knife in the same breath that you say you don't need one.

You wouldn't believe how many people will break your knife, if you let them, in part because not enough folks carry a knife these days to understand the tool's limitations. It is not a prybar or a screwdriver, although I have sometimes pressed a knife into service for those tasks when necessary (I can do that with my own knife). I've personally seen too many sometimes expensive knives broken in the hands of a borrower who clearly neither knew nor cared about the blade's almost religious value to an experienced woodsman.

Another reason that I refuse to loan my knife is that my personal knives are sharp enough to shave off a beard, and they're kept that way. That's not a boast, it's a point of fact. A dull knife is a piece of scrap metal, a poorly designed prybar. I've lost count of the people who, before I was eighteen, had literally flayed themselves with one of my knives after I'd conferred upon them the customary warning to "be careful, that's sharp." Predictably, on their way to the Emergency Room, they blame me, saying something ridiculous like, "You don't need a knife that sharp."

The bottom line is that I sincerely recommend against handing your knife to anyone who asks to use it, or even to look at it. There's no dividend, and there may be serious repercussions—especially if I'm successful in the following pages of conferring on you the ability to create a keen edge. An artery-deep gash is serious under the best of conditions; slashing oneself in the filth and rubble after a Magnitude 8 Earthquake is nothing short of calamitous.

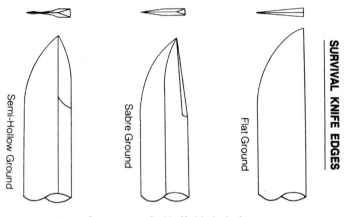

Common survival knife blade designs.

Ground Edges

How a knife blade is ground—sometimes called its geometry—has a lot to do with how it performs. In general, the thinner a blade the sharper its cutting edge can be made, and so the longer it will retain its sharpness. A wider blade enables a longer, narrower, and sharper grind. A longer blade flexes more than a shorter blade. A narrower blade penetrates more easily than a wide blade, and has historically been the choice for stabbing tools and weapons. A heavier blade generates more inertial force, and is better for chopping. A wider radius at the tip of a blade—called its "belly"—provides a longer cutting surface and is the choice for skinning knives.

There is no "wrong" knife, and the best survival or skinning knife is the one you have. Some knives have features that simply make them mechanically better suited for some tasks, but the ability to sever a rope, et al, is the important point. I once had to skin and quarter a deer with only a folding electrician's knife; it was far from the ideal, but I made it work.

"Blood Groove" or Fuller

A fuller, known colloquially as a "blood groove," isn't necessary for draining blood. Nor is it needed to break the suction that urban legends claim makes it difficult to withdraw a blade from a stabbing victim (any knife that can cut its way in will also cut its way out). But a fuller, known as a "strongback" in the metal stamping industry, effectively increases the surface area, and makes a blade stiffer, stronger, and less likely to flex under pressure. With today's stronger, tougher, more homogeneous steel alloys, and a variety of space-age hardening (tempering) methods, a fuller isn't needed. Some knives, like the classic USMC Utility Knife, carried by American GIs in both World Wars and Vietnam, still feature a fuller, but it has become noticeably absent on most models since the 1980s.

All of the manufacturing and design options available today have resulted in a glut of readily available knives that make Jim Bowie's legendary Iron Maiden look like a framing nail by comparison. State-of-the-art steels of yesteryear are being used in department store knives today, and steel alloys that used to be used to cut steel are themselves being blanked out as knife blades by modern dies. Even cheap knives boast an edge retention that would've impressed hunters of a couple generations ago, and the finest blades would have been the stuff of science fiction to our grandfathers.

Cutting Edges Defined

Like different sized or differently shaped spoons and forks, there exists a variety of blade shapes and types that are specifically designed to perform certain tasks better than the others. Recently, I happened upon a YouTube video in which a youngster claimed to start a fire "in the pouring rain." It wasn't raining, but that's beside the point. My biggest exception to his purportedly instructional process was that he was using an Ontario-made Old Hickory kitchen knife as his outdoor knife—and he was beating it with a club through a section of green sapling to split it. This is exactly the wrong knife for the job on more than a dozen levels, and its manufacturer will tell you that (we won't address the absurdity of attempting to make fire with green wood here).

The best knife can break under ordinary conditions, but equipping yourself with the best choice for the most anticipated jobs helps to ensure that you'll always have this most critical of survival tools at hand, and ready for action, not broken, chipped, and too dull to cut a clothesline.

Saber-Ground

A saber-ground blade is ground to a cutting edge halfway down the width of its blade, leaving half of its width at full thickness for greater strength. As its name implies, this grind has been especially common for sabers and dirks, whose primary use might be as a weapon as well as for hacking, stabbing, or deflecting blows from another weapon. It is not the sharpest edge and it doesn't retain its edge well enough to be preferred for, say, skinning an elk—although it can, and has, performed that task. What it can be counted on for is maximum blade strength.

Flat-Ground

The cutting edge of a flat-ground blade begins at its spine, tapering evenly down from there on a single plane to its cutting edge. Speaking generally, a flat-ground edge can be made very sharp, it resharpens easily, and retains its edge well. Drawbacks include an inherently weak cutting edge that can chip easily, but today's stronger alloys have made flat-ground blades quite popular for field knives.

Hollow-Ground

A lot of knives nowadays are mistakenly referred to as hollow-ground when they are, in fact, semi-hollow ground. An actual hollow-ground design would be a straight razor, with deeply concaved edges that begin at the spine and extend down to the sharpened edge. This configuration results in an extremely thin and sharp cutting edge, but one that's also very fragile and easily chipped or broken.

Semi-Hollow Ground

Semi-hollow ground is the classic hunting knife blade. Probably older generations recognize it as the classic Skagel-style hunting knife, with a handle made from stacked leather washers, a small, usually brass, finger guard, and a pinned- or screwed-on knob pommel. The edge can be made shaving-keen, it holds an edge well, resharpens easily, and has good prying strength because half the blade's width remains at full thickness.

Double-Edge

Better known as a dagger, a typical double-edge knife has a slender, sharply pointed blade that has a sharp edge on both sides. There are, of course, various configurations—like the surprisingly versatile CUMA Tak-Ri from TOPS Knives. Designed by my friend Kung-Fu Sifu Johnny Tsai, this knife bears mentioning, because this broad, unconventionally-shaped, double-edged blade actually took me by surprise with its ability to perform remarkably well for everything from skinning deer and filleting fish to whittling tool handles and self-defense. Most double-edged blades are not so generic, however (or so ruggedly built), and they're generally classed more as stabbing weapons than field knives.

A note about double-edged knives: These knives can be dangerous to their users; pressing down onto a blade's spine to increase shearing pressure is a common practice with working knives, but this isn't possible when both sides are sharp. Too, adding a second edge literally takes the spine out of it, halving its strength. For those and other reasons, a dagger-style isn't a good choice for field use.

Types of Knives

Dirk

This is the traditional knife of a Scottish nobleman. Born in an era of violence, it takes the slender, penetrating power of a dagger, but usually has only one sharpened side, leaving its opposite (spine) at full thickness and strength. This enables it to be pressed into service as a skinning and butchering knife, but with the muscle to penetrate armor, usually with the length to "run through" an opponent. A dirk was the original side-arm, deft enough to be used in close quarters, where a full-length sword was unwieldy and it was decidedly lethal enough to be outlawed by name in some municipalities. Before creation of the knife that still bears his name (but might never have actually been owned by him, in the form we recognize), a dirk was the preferred weapon of James Bowie; used by him in the infamous "Vidalia Sandbar Fight."

Stiletto Edge

Best known as the edge on a classic switchblade, a stiletto incorporates a narrow penetrating blade with a sharpened edge near its point that extends about one-third the length of the blade, leaving a full-thickness spine from there to the choil. This allows a slender, pocketable blade to maximize its stabbing power without sacrificing strength. Most popular as the folding switchblade of the 1950s used by James Dean in *Rebel Without a Cause*, the stiletto configuration has been used for designs like Gerber's Silver Trident, but retains the air of weapon more than tool.

Serrated-Edge

If you aren't skilled at resharpening your knife, a fully or partially serrated blade might be the answer. Unlike a "straight" or "plain" edge, a serrated edge delivers superior cutting power for some materials—like a rubber garden hose. The coarse, ripping cuts of a serrated edge more resemble the action of a saw than a knife. With about double the cutting surface, it seems that a serrated surface stays sharp much longer. That makes it a better choice for people who aren't skilled at resharpening.

A problem with serrated edges is that they're difficult to resharpen. With both protruding and recessed cutting edges, on two different planes, rehoning demands a conventional flat-surfaced hone for the former, and a round hone for the latter. As a manager in one hone-making company told me (off the record, because his company makes special round hones for resharpening serrations), the main objective is to sharpen the outermost "teeth" of a serrated blade, so most experienced sharpeners just use a conventional flat honing surface.

Steel Alloys

Most steels bear an SAE—Society of Automotive Engineers—number designation, because SAE was the original standard for identifying different metal (and plastic) formulae. In many cases, the same numerical and alphabetical designators have been carried over by the more recent

American Iron and Steel Institute (AISI), which also recognizes designators for the same proprietary alloys made by other countries, as well as the growing number of metallurgical alloys that simply didn't exist for previous generations. There is often considerable overlap. For example, Chinese-made 8Cr13MoV is a mirror of Japanese AUS-8, which is virtually identical to SAE 420J2. Try not to get too lost in the numbers.

It's difficult to imagine these days, but production-manufactured steel is a product of the early twentieth century; before that, steel products were individually hand-forged by blacksmiths, and many tools were simply cast from iron—either cast iron, which is hard and brittle, or malleable iron, which is soft and bendable, depending on whether its mixture has a high or low carbon content. There are ancient tales of battles in which a warrior had to halt the fight long enough to step on his sword to straighten its soft blade—which was preferable to having a sword that was brittle enough to break in two.

Steel quality was entirely dependent on the skill of the blacksmith, his forging know-how, the impurities he added to his iron, and his hardening (or tempering) process. As with many manufactured materials, steels of yesteryear were, in fact, not all that great. Nostalgic myths aside, the famed Marine Corps KaBar was a rusty nail compared to many inexpensive blades of today.

The three general qualities of a steel are hardness, toughness, and strength.

Hardness determines the ability of a knife to take a sharp, polished edge. Too soft and the potential sharpness is limited; too hard and the steel tends to become brittle.

Toughness describes a steel's ability to resist abrasion—that is, to hold an edge. Hard, tough steel is preferred for skinning knives, because nothing takes the edge off a knife like cutting through fur. Cast iron is very hard and it can be made very sharp, but it doesn't resist friction well and dulls easily.

Strength is an alloy's resistance to bending or breaking. Brass (an alloy of tin and copper) was the original cutting blade because it takes less heat to forge but flexed or broke easily. As a weapon, brass blades lost power through flexing when stabbed at even light armor, or they broke in two.

Steel was a great incentive for Romans, armed with brass-bladed Gladius swords, to try to conquer Celtic peoples, who had learned the arts of smithing steel tools and weapons. Even with steel, the line between strength and hardness has always been hard to maintain.

Common Blade Alloys

SAE 1095

The original modern knife steel. Known colloquially as "spring," or sometimes just generically as the original "high-carbon" steel, 1095 made its real debut as a fighting knife in WWI, and it's still one of the most popular blade steels today. Hard, tough, and strong, it will oxidize swiftly, especially around salt water, and nearly all outdoor-type knives made from it come from the factory with protective coatings. DO NOT sand off this coating, as so many neo-survival experts are wont to do. It was put there because a knife made to be subjected to the elements needs a protective coating. If it matters, a black or gray blade is also less reflective and harder to see.

SAE 440

The original stainless knife steel. Famed survival knife designer Blackie Collins told me, just before his tragic death, that if he had to choose just one knife to do it all, the blade would be made of ". . . one of the four-forties." I personally would not make the same choice, but I'm far from qualified to argue with this master knife maker, and the fact that he made such a statement says a great deal about the capabilities of this alloy. There are variations in 440: A, B, and C grades, with harder and tougher—but more brittle—C being the most preferred choice for knife blades. Most flatware and steak knives are made from 440.

SAE 420

This alloy is essentially a variation of 440, insofar as its capabilities as a knife blade. The main difference is that 420 is suited to hammer-forging; meaning that, instead of being "blanked" from a sheet of room-temperature steel then ground to shape, it's stamped under tremendous pressure while the steel is red-hot. The result is a blank that comes from a die nearly finished with little grinding or polishing needed to make it a finished product.

The 420 is often quite brittle (for example, the original M9 Field Knife, issued by the US Army), so knives made from it are kitchen cutlery, or, if it is used to make a field-grade knife, the spine is extra-thick to provide added strength. Blackie Collins was also a fan of the 420.

D2

This is a high-carbon (the general meaning of which is that it will rust) alloy that was once restricted to "tool" steel applications, like the dies that cut out parts from softer grades of steel. Problem was, it was too hard and too tough for dies of the time to blank-out into production knives until the late 1990s. So blades made from D2 were individually smithed, which ultimately meant that exploiting the real potential of this fine steel was dependent on the skill of the smith, and knives made from it were prohibitively expensive.

D2 is unmatched for edge retention, but is not a good choice for the typical survival kit. D2 is deucedly hard to resharpen when it dulls. It has been said that if you laid a dull D2 blade and $100 down in front of any roomful of people, few could ever collect the reward for making the blade sharp again. Even good knife-sharpeners have a tough time getting this steel to a keen edge—as one expert put it, "D2 takes a lousy edge and holds it forever."

But it *can* be made razor-sharp—D2 is one of my favorite blades, and I won't keep a knife that can't be made shaving-sharp. Later, techniques will be discussed for resharpening this alloy, but since most of the necessary skill is tactile and must be learned, I don't expect to deliver much success in this endeavor. Better just to stick with more easily sharpened alloys.

ATS-34

This stainless-steel alloy is only slightly less tough to sharpen than D2. Again, it holds an edge beautifully and offers the added advantage of being rustproof. Knives like Buck's Strider are excellent examples of putting this fine steel to its optimum use, but they make poor field knives for most folks because ATS-34 is so darned hard to sharpen.

A1 (and A2)

These traditional tool and die steels can be made extremely hard without becoming unacceptably brittle, and they aren't inordinately difficult to resharpen. I have several of these, all of them beautiful examples of what a field knife should be.

My main gripe is that most knives made from A1 are collectibles (or "tactical," which generally means the same thing these days), not actually made for hard field use but rather as a status symbol for sport hunters who'll never do anything more strenuous with them than gut a deer.

S30V

This is my favorite stainless steel alloy, and one of my all-around favorite steels. Like any alloy, it depends on who made the steel—especially how it has been hardened—but a quality S30V knife—like Benchmade's extensively used, and sadly discontinued, RUKUS folder—is nothing short of incredible. As difficult to dull as you could ask, easy to sharpen, and extremely strong, properly hardened S30V is as near to ideal as you could get.

Protective Coatings

Probably most field-grade knives sold today have some type of Teflon-like coating applied to their blades. Although many stainless-steel blades are coated (more for esthetic than practical purposes), the protective coating on a high-carbon (i.e., rust-able) alloy is as necessary a feature as any found on the knife. DO NOT sand off or otherwise remove this coating. The "natural patina" that some buckskin-clad traditionalists claim offers protection is actually just a discoloration caused by oxidation (rust) and is essentially the same as the bluing on a firearm. Like bluing, it offers no protection against red rust that can quickly leave a polished blade pitted from corrosion. Knife manufacturers apply a protective coating to their high-carbon blades for good reason. Again, do not remove this coating; it does not contaminate food you cut.

Handle Materials

Bear in mind that your knife is likely to be wet, perhaps coated with animal fat and blood, maybe petrochemicals, and that it will probably be subjected to abuse and the forces of nature. Maybe you'll need to pound on it, to drive the blade like a nail into some material. No knife handle is indestructible, but a survival knife worthy of that title must be tough enough to withstand abuse.

Typical Survival Knife

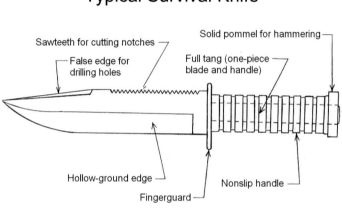

Typical survival knife anatomy.

Molded rubber like Kraton is grippy when wet and resistant to weather extremes. Stag and bone are hard but textured, and these materials (even their molded plastic look-alikes) can be chipped, cracked, or broken. Hytrel is virtually indestructible. Grivory is a recent man-made molded material that has proven to be impressive. The smooth ebony of some popular hunting knives has proven to be downright slippery.

Traditional bone or antler handles—often molded from a resin these days—are usually limited in ergonomics and toughness, and they tend to be a bit brittle.

Rubber-like handles, like Kraton or Hytrel, are excellent for knives that are expected to see tough, even abusive use. These molded materials are unbreakable, chemical and corrosive resistant, and provide good grip under all conditions.

Fiber-reinforced plastics, like Micarta and G10, are pretty much state-of-the-art, tough, almost unbreakable, textured, and impervious to all but prolonged exposure in a campfire.

Never throw a knife—that same advice is usually included with the handling instructions of a new knife.

Replacing a Broken Handle

A broken handle is serious, because depending on the length of its tang (where blade becomes handle), it can make the knife useless. If the tang is full length (recommended), the quickest fix is to wrap it in multiple layers of tape. Or you can place a piece of wood on either side (perhaps with a little whittling and shaping), then wrap the wood in place with tape.

Alternatively, and especially if the blade has a tang narrower than its blade, washers cut from leather, flooring vinyl, wood, or even plastic can be slid onto the tang and stacked, a la the old KaBar Marine Corps knife. Use your ingenuity, but don't make it complicated. Primitive peoples have been fashioning handmade hilts to knife blades for many millennia—the project is not beyond a modern human's capabilities.

Sheaths

The sheath of a field knife is also very important. Carrying a sharp blade Tarzan-style, without encasing it, just stuck into a waistband is incredibly dangerous—especially to its owner. A knife without a sheath is very much akin to a firearm without a safety catch, except that the knife is always loaded.

More than that, a field knife's utility is tremendously enhanced by its sheath's ability to contain numerous small items. Add a disposable butane lighter and an inexpensive compass and your knife transforms into a full-blown survival kit. Add ten feet of monofilament fishing line and a couple of hooks—their barbs made safer by a layer of cellophane tape—and the knife becomes a fishing kit.

The sheath of an emergency knife needs a retaining strap to hold it securely. A few years ago, while I was a field editor for *Tactical Knives*

Magazine, I worked with bona fide genius John Moore of *Mission Knives* on the Beta-titanium-bladed Katrina Rescue Knife. The ballistic nylon sheath, with integral gear pouch and snap-down retaining strap, passed field trials. But the friction-fit, molded Zytel sheath allowed the blade to slip free during normal activities that might be demanded during rescue operations—like belly-crawling through rubble. A good many friction-fit sheaths cannot be trusted, and a missing knife is like losing a loved one in a survival scenario. A word to the wise.

Moreover, retaining straps should be sited to encircle a knife's handle low down, just above the blade's choil. Most handle designs are naturally narrower there so that the strap secures tighter, with less allowance for that annoying—and potentially hazardous—rattle of blade against sheath that so many knives exhibit while walking. Positioning the retaining strap here also lets a knife "break" at your hip joint, making it feel less stiff during normal movements while keeping the hilt more exposed and easier to quick-draw without looking when needed. I'm not a fan of hook-and-loop (Velcro) retaining straps for numerous reasons; an old snap-type is most trustworthy.

As an FYI, keeping a blade from rattling in its sheath might be considered a survival technique, because any combat veteran can affirm that rattling gear can get you killed under the right circumstances.

There are numerous methods of causing a blade to fit tightly in its sheath. A plastic juice or milk bottle, scissored into a sheet, that is then folded until it can be inserted into a sheath liner serves to take up space and hold a blade securely; when the correct size is determined, a few drops of Gorilla Glue on the outer surface of the plastic holds it in place.

Alternatively, glue dripped into the mouth of the sheath and allowed to run down inside might be enough to take up excess room. Like everything: use your imagination.

Replacing a Sheath

Replacing a lost sheath isn't an especially complex process, and some of the finest sheaths I've carried a knife in have been something that I fashioned. I've written about making replacement sheaths in the past, and some of the most prized comments I've ever received came from readers who told me that they appreciated being told how to make them.

The easiest, and perhaps best, replacement sheath for most knives is made from a discarded automobile seat-belt strap. Fold over about 4 inches on one end of the strap and sew or, easier, staple the end to itself using two heavy steel staples to form a belt loop.

In the same manner, bend the other end of the strap upward on its opposite side to form a pocket deep and long enough to accommodate the knife's blade. Fasten the two longitudinal sides of the blade pocket together with steel staples. The staples ensure that a sharp-edged blade won't cut through the sheath.

A retaining strap is necessary to make certain that your knife stays in its sheath during rough-and-tumble activities. This can be as simple as a cord tied around the handle, low on the hilt, just above the finger guard. If you're the handy type, secure a strap to the sheath's belt loop (see illustration) with Velcro-type hook-and-loop fasteners, or a snap set available at crafts stores—it's a good idea to have one or two snap sets on hand in the home survival kit.

Knife-Wearing Options

Lately, primarily because of movies, I think, urban Rambos have taken to wearing fixed blades horizontally on their belts, ostensibly because this orientation somehow turns one into a knife fighter. There are even shoulder rigs that allow a blade to be carried handle-down suspended in a spring-release holster, similar to a concealed handgun.

In an anything-goes survival environment, where you might be doing everything from swimming in muck to belly-crawling through rubble, the best way to carry your knife is the old-fashioned way: hanging from your belt. Adding to the ease with which a fixed-blade knife can be drawn and resheathed, without looking at it, are tie-downs at the bottom of a sheath, near the knife's tip. Tying down a sheath with a cord around your thigh (a simple square knot has always sufficed) keeps it steadier. Now maybe it's a personal affectation, but I draw and resheath my belt knife fifty times a day, and the more natural and effortless that activity is, the better my day goes.

Primitive and Makeshift Knives

One of the favorite murder weapons among heavily romanticized gangland-style murder novels is an ice pick. A hard, pointed length of spring steel rod inserted into a wooden dowel handle. Despite claims of expertness, forensic examiners admit that they have no idea how many murders slipped by them, because a victim was stabbed through the top of his skull with a 6-inch ice pick. The pick, driven forcefully through a "soft spot" (usually the *anterior fontanelle*) of the skull, penetrates the cerebral cortex. Death is usually instantaneous but the exterior wound is tiny, evidenced by just a small spot of blood that dries and often falls off, leaving a wound that resembles a mole. Only because some victims have been blond, and some coroners especially sharp-eyed, do forensic experts understand how many murders have probably escaped their notice.

This illustrates that a knife can take many forms. You can't slice salami with an ice pick, but you can't drill another adjustment hole in a leather belt with an *Ulu*. The ideal knife cuts, stabs, pries, picks, drills, and shaves.

Those necessary uses can be derived from a number of materials. Traditionally, primitive peoples without metallurgical skills have crafted cutting/stabbing/scraping tools from antler, bone, and stone. Today, functional knives can be made from plexiglass, styrene-type hard plastic, and even shards of metal. In generations past, many a fine fillet and kitchen knife was cut from a carpenter's saw blade, and the first Buck-brand knives were ground from old files. Gurkhas were famed for making the trademark Kukris knife that beheaded many a Japanese soldier in WWII from old truck leaf springs.

As any prison convict can assert, abrading a knife-to-be under pressure against a rough surface—like concrete or sandstone—can form and sharpen anything from a plastic toothbrush to a steel coffee can lid. Whatever it's made from, any knife is better than no knife.

Much has been made of "pressure flaking," that is laying a relatively flat stone onto another stone surface and then striking its intended edge with a usually rounded stone hammer. The objective is to remove small chips of stone until a narrow, irregular cutting surface has been formed.

Despite what you might have read, pressure flaking isn't exactly rocket science. A small child can do it using a variety of types of stone. The trick is to practice using different variables: smaller or larger hammers, different types of stone, harder or softer strikes. Most types of rock can be pressure-flaked to create a very sharp skinning or scraping edge; some types of stone are better than others for flaking, but most varieties will work. With a bit of experience, you'll soon find yourself creating spear heads, even arrow heads. These tools are brittle and can easily be broken, but may also be sharpened more or less conventionally, as you would an ordinary blade.

Folding Knives

The purpose of a folding knife—that is, a knife whose blade is on a hinge pin so that it can be folded into a recess in its own handle—is not only the compactness that has caused it to become generally known as a "pocket knife," but for reasons of safety. A sharp, pointed blade without a cover for its cutting edge and tip is akin to carrying a loaded firearm without a safety mechanism.

Today, most folding knives are one-hand openers, with an integrated clip that enables the closed knife to be carried clipped to its owner's pocket, where it is more quickly accessible than ever. With a little practice and familiarity, the typical pocket knife of today can be deployed in the blink of an eye.

In the first years of the new millennium, it became almost standard to fit folding knives with thumb studs—or holes in their blades—just behind the choil (the usually reinforced portion where blade is hinged to handle). Either of these features gave the user's thumb purchase against the blade, allowing it to be pushed/rotated to its open position.

Even at the first, there was dissension among the utopians; the omnipresent nirvanists who believe that a perfect world would result from simply outlawing anything that might be employed as a weapon. They complained that the same one-handed speed of deployment that enabled a folder to be brought into perhaps lifesaving action against a rope or strap, or for an uncountable number of other tasks, somehow defeated the Federal Switchblade Act of 1958.

The anti-weapon ranks became downright noisy in 2007 when a few knife makers started experimenting with spring-assist mechanisms that snapped a blade into its open and locked position by simply rotating it a few degrees from its closed state. This time, the proposed legislation to ban them was brought before Congress by US Customs Agency, under the guise of banning—to begin with—cheap imports under an amendment to the 1958 Switchblade Act. To his credit, President Barack Obama vetoed this latest attempt at restricting tool rights.

In reality, spring assist is a pretty cool toy; there's no denying that it's kind of fun to see your blade snap into its open position of its own accord. But so far as speed of deployment, there's no discernible reduction in the time it takes to draw and bring a folder with either system to its ready position. Under real-world conditions, a thumb-stud opener is every bit as fast, and even some 1970s-era knives would open under inertia with a forceful flick of the wrist. More important than gunslinger speed is an ability to get a knife into action with one hand while the other hand is occupied holding or doing something else.

Several anecdotes from my own life bear that out, but the one that comes foremost into my mind happened during one of my first jobs in the early 1970s. We were hauling mostly-empty barrels on a straight truck, 144 fifty-five-gallon steel drums per truckload. It was one of those invisible industries that no one gave a thought to—and the world is paying dearly for that today. We'd pick up the drums, take them to a refurbishing plant where they were washed with caustic solution, repainted, and sold to a chemical company for refilling.

It was a dangerous job in the best of times. On that day, we'd off-loaded part of our mixed load at one end of the storage yard and my partner had secured the unstable remainder, stacked three high, and four across, with a quick turn of rope around the racks. He rode in the back while a yard worker drove our International truck to a pile where the rest would be stacked.

Somehow my partner got between the rope and the barrels. The truck hit a rut and the load shifted, pinning him at the abdomen between several tons of steel and a multi-ton, half-inch nylon rope. Almost before he had time to say "ow!" I'd drawn my stainless-steel Silver Falcon folder from its homemade open-top belt sheath and snapped it open with a flick of my wrist. A single slash of its shaving-keen edge parted the rope. Barrels fell booming to the steel deck all around us, but they posed less danger than the rope had.

Another fairly recent innovation for folding knives is a "pocket clip" that permits a closed knife to be carried clipped, ink-pen style, to a hip pocket. Many better knives offer an option to mount the usually spring-steel clip to either side, at either end of the knife. This arrangement means that you can carry your knife tip-up (blade), tip-down, on either the right or the left side, so there's no reason to learn to accommodate a knife—you can carry it in the orientation that seems most natural to you.

An inherent weakness in pocket clips is that most are screwed in place with several tiny screws that tend to come loose at inopportune times, and many require a specialty screwdriver bit to retighten them. While it's great that you can mount a clip in different positions, it's unlikely that you'll ever need to reposition it again. For that reason, I use an instant glue or, better I think, the newer Gorilla Glue to more or less permanently affix a clip in my desired location.

A couple of generations ago, most pocket knives had no lock to keep a blade from folding back onto a user's fingers. We adapted, but a whole lot of old-timers are sporting scars from having their flesh scissored between a sharp blade and the handle.

Which locking mechanism is best is largely a matter of conjecture, but bear in mind that no folding knife is meant for hard use: if the job requires an effort on your part, it's probably too heavy a task for a folder. The lock-back style—with an indentation in the top of the handle that must be pressed inward to release the blade—has been field-proven for generations, but it's a bit clumsy today.

"Liner-locks," in which a piece of spring steel blocks blade closure until moved aside by a user's thumb, are renowned for being strong and secure. These are a favorite, but some users find it a bit uncomfortable to unlock, especially one-handed.

Slide-locks, like Benchmade's award-winning Axis lock are superb, and they can be operated easily with only one hand. Likewise, Gerber's tough, but less-expensive, push-button lock 06 Combat Folder.

Discontinued, and probably obsoleted by a half-dozen later models, the Schrade "Bomb Tech" is the author's favorite survival knife.

Sheath Knives

I knew that no camping was allowed where I'd made mine, at the end of a forgotten logging road in northern Michigan's Jordan Valley. For the past day I'd been observing a newly mated pair of beavers that had dammed a nearby stream. Their youthful enthusiasm made them oblivious to my camera, and I spent several days photographing their activities.

I wasn't surprised when a large green 4 × 4 roared toward my camp, blue strobe and headlights flashing and skidded to a halt just feet from where I stood. I grinned when the conservation officer jumped out, looking a little disappointed, and said, "Oh, it's you." Conservation officers cut me slack because I wrote about outdoor activities and showed my gratitude by erasing my campsites.

I poured the CO a cup of coffee and we squatted next to the fire. He sipped gingerly from the hot metal cup while his eyes wandered over my backpack, leaning against the rear tire of my truck.

"Geez, Len. Do you think you've got enough knives?" His question referred to the fixed-blade survival knife and the working-class jackknife on my belt, but especially to the heavy, short machete that was strapped onto my backpack.

I laughed and replied, "I have as many as I need."

It would be hard to find a survival instructor, or any experienced outdoorsman, who didn't believe that a good knife is the cornerstone of every survival kit in any environment. With a strong, keen blade you can cut a rope, fashion other tools, and perform countless chores that would be tough to impossible without one.

But experience has proven that no single knife is ideal. The trustworthy fixed-blade that friends say is welded to my hip in the woods suffices for everything, but it isn't the most effective tool for delicate tasks, like filleting bass or digging out slivers. Neither does it deliver the chopping power or leverage to efficiently clear brush and chop wood. I could get by with only a survival knife, but this versatile trio of working knives is worth the weight when quality of life depends on the gear in my possession.

Today, two decades after having coffee with my conservation officer friend, I still carry three good knives whenever I backpack or kayak into wilderness areas where it pays to be self-reliant. But while the principle remains unchanged, the knives themselves have undergone many improvements.

The beefy machete that had captured my friend's attention was handmade from quarter-inch SAE 1060 bar stock, with a twelve-inch blade that was short enough to swing in heavy brush, but six inches wide to give it the chopping power of a hatchet. I'd been forced to make my own, because machetes of the day were not heavy enough to handle northern hardwoods, especially in subzero temperatures, and I deemed a hatchet too limited in function for backpacking.

The machete on my pack these days is factory-made, with stronger steel, a more comfortable handle, and a nicer sheath, but with the same heavy construction and cutting power. Among big knives—suitable for everything from skinning to machete work—my current favorites are the Armageddon knife from Tactical Operations Products (TOPS) Knives, and the outstanding Mah-Chete from Columbia River Knife and Tool (CRKT). Made from SAE 1095 (hard) and 1075 (tough) steels, respectively, both have proved themselves capable tools in the field.

Numerous fixed-blade knives have ridden my hip over the years. Some have been better than others, but all have been the single-most valued tool in every wilderness outfit. This is the do-everything knife, and it never leaves my belt except when I sleep. It must provide a secure grip under the most slippery conditions, it has to handle nimbly, hold an edge, resharpen easily, and it may never break. Beyond that, it should be as multi-functional as possible, able to hammer, drill, and notch, and to carry other survival tools onboard. That's a tall order, but any knife deserving of the title "survival" knife in the new millennium will meet those requirements.

And many do. The multi-functional SCHF1 Schrade Extreme Survival Knife is a one-piece toolbox, with coarse saw-teeth along the spine of its SAE 1070 spear-point blade, and a strong hollow handle packed with assorted tool bits. A large gear pouch on its sheath accommodates fire starting, fishing, and orienteering tools.

Probably most improved in this trio of essential working knives is the folding knife that performs light tasks where a keenly polished edge is more important than strength—like cleaning squirrels or just slicing food. My folder never leaves my side, even when I'm sleeping. Today's folders boast the finest blades ever fitted to a jackknife: the surest locks, the most grip-friendly handles, and a pocket-clip that negates the need for a belt sheath.

Favorites among working folders are the 06 Combat Folder from Gerber and the classic 2-blade Muskrat Trapper from Case Knives. Both are beefy, hand-filling knives with strong, sharp blades that have proven themselves equal to the job of quartering a whitetail yet nimble enough to fillet a fish.

The beauty of this triad system is that, with some limitations, any one of these knives can perform every task. A hardcore backcountry

The biggest survival advantage a human has is an ability to make and use tools;
a multi-tool has become a necessity for every survival kit, in every locale.

backpacker will find plenty of uses for all three around camp, but will probably carry only a survival knife and folder for day hiking. At night, or for in-camp activities like fishing, the belt knife might be left in a tent while the handier folder serves to cut fishing line, clean a bass, or open a new blister-packaged casting reel. This three-knife outfit ensures that you will always have the most ideal blade for the task at hand, and it guarantees that you will have a functional knife on your person at all times.

Multi-tools

A knife is one piece of equipment that must be carried by race drivers in Alaska's Iditarod, Michigan's U.P. 200, Minnesota's John Beargrease, and any other sanctioned long-distance dogsledding competition. Rule 33 of the Iditarod states that a musher who kills a moose, caribou, or buffalo "in defense of life or property" (moose are infamous for attacking dog teams) must gut the animal. Other racers who come upon the scene must help, because "no team shall pass until the animal has been gutted, and the musher killing the animal has proceeded." Most uses a musher might find for his knife are less dramatic, but veterans of the sport unanimously agree that it's an indispensable tool.

Not any knife will do in temperatures cold enough to crack spring-steel snow plows and turn most liquids to solids. It's a world where LCD screens can be destroyed by subzero temperatures, fresh batteries can go dead in hours, and keeping drinking water from becoming a block of ice is a challenge. A musher's blade must not become brittle; it should be glove-friendly and operable with cold-numbed fingers; and it has to withstand abuses like severing steel cables inside the "gangline" that connects dogs to sled. There's also the need to retighten panhead screw-and-nut fasteners that steady a dogsled's flexible joints when they work loose on a rugged trail. Or unscrewing an iced-up threaded locking sleeve on the carabiner between gang-line and sled frame.

Counterbalancing those needs is a universal compulsion by racers to keep the weight of their trail-ready rig as low as possible. Every piece of gear has to be something they can't do without, and each of those items needs to be as multi-functional as possible. To find out what cutting instrument best serves the array of needs a dogsledder might encounter when he or she is many miles from the nearest checkpoint, I went to the experts; the weather-hardened veterans of what some say is the toughest racing sport in the world.

Maybe not surprisingly, every veteran musher interviewed elects to fulfill the knife requirement with a multi-tool that can perform as many tasks as possible. Bill Borden, the first musher from sunny Georgia to complete the 1,151-mile Iditarod, told me how he once used a multi-tool to drill a hole through the hard white ash of a sled runner to repair it on the trail.

The late Jim Warren, a dear friend and veteran of several Iditarods, also preferred a multi-tool, and experience made him insist on a model with one-hand operation. In 2008, while training his team in Michigan's untracked Betsy Lake Wilderness Area, his dogs became tangled in dense underbrush. One of the dogs got the cable-reinforced gangline (the common pulling rope) wrapped around its neck, and with panicked huskies pulling in all directions, only Warren's desperate grip on the rope kept the stricken dog's neck from breaking. Having one hand occupied as he was violently jerked and dragged meant that he couldn't get to the multi-tool zipped into his parka pocket (that's a lesson in itself). Luckily, two other mushers appeared and helped Warren to extricate the throttled dog before it sustained any real injury.

Racer Mike Murphy is adamant about never being without his multi-tool "on or off the sled." Murphy says that he's carried numerous folding and fixed blades from the Iditarod to the Tahquamenon Country Sled Dog Race and numerous races in between, but hard experience forced him to adopt a multi-tool as his all-around knife. Like most seasoned mushers we interviewed, he hedges his bets by carrying two; one zipped into an anorak pocket and another in the "dog bag" of his sled. Murphy says he doesn't trust sheaths enough to carry his vital multi-tool on a belt, but prefers to secure it in a pocket.

The same sentiments are echoed by most other mushers, even those (like myself) who just feel more secure having a full-sized working blade. Today's multi-tools have evolved to offer a variety of choices that can deliver when the job is tough, help isn't available, and a good knife just isn't enough. No survival-minded person should be without one of these essential tools.

Food Processing Knives

Not all uses for a knife involve backwoods survival, and a big, heavy knife isn't always the best choice for processing vegetables or butchering. This point is proved by the existence of butcher and food processing knives. But if you ask the typical survivalist or prepper, you might find that a good many of them have overlooked this necessary chore. A blade heavy enough to lop off a large tree branch might not be ideal for cutting steaks or dicing stew meat, and might be so unwieldy as to pose a danger to its user when employed for such chores.

If you're bugging out, and all of your worldly possessions are in a backpack, a kayak, or a Dodge Neon, you might be restricted as to how many blades you include (although I'd sure try to include at least a boning knife in any long-term survival kit).

But if we're discussing a home or cabin outfit, you'll want a good block of cutlery that includes, at minimum: a chef's knife, carving knife, boning knife, and paring knife—some sets include a large pair of meat scissors, too. Kitchen cutlery has been a separate class of knives in homes and cabins since medieval times.

The thinner blades of kitchen-class knives are easier to sharpen, they tend to retain their edges longer, and they're more nimble for delicate work. Meat hunters have traditionally boned larger, deer-sized game, so that it takes up less room and is easier to butcher—no mouthful of meat ever contains a bone. There is a clear delineation, visible as an irregular white line between muscle masses; cutting down to, then around the bone separates large, roast-size (if the game is large enough) masses of meat and leaves nothing but a skeleton. This task, and others like it—like filleting a fish—demands a keen, agile blade.

Likewise, fine kitchen cutlery is not suited to hardcore survival or backwoods work. Many a kitchen drawer contains knives with bent-over or broken tips. Never use a piece of fine kitchen cutlery as a screwdriver, prybar, or for anything else but slicing through food.

Batoning

In the past decade or so, there has arisen the apparently previously undiscovered practice of "batoning" a knife blade lengthwise through a piece of wood; using a larger piece of wood as a bludgeon to split it into smaller pieces.

I mention the practice here only to say that it is not only entirely unnecessary, but stupid to hammer the blade of what is perhaps your most vital survival instrument into a chunk of wood. In half a century of living in the wilderness, I have never found occasion to commit this act of abuse, and neither did any of the past masters of woodcraft—including Daniel Boone, Jedediah Smith, and Davy Crockett. Batoning is the invention of neophytes who, in the twenty-first century, have none of the legitimate uses for their knives, like butchering meat and making tool handles that made a blade a part of daily life for our forebears. Some method of determining how good or bad a knife is had to be created, so the practice of batoning firewood was invented.

And that wouldn't matter, except that driving a knife blade through wood with a heavy club will break it. Maybe not the first few times, but no knife alloy can withstand that level of abuse for long without a large, usually half-moon-shaped chunk of its blade breaking away. Ironically, the poorer the knife (i.e., softer and less able to keep a sharp edge) the longer it can typically survive being hammered, so if the practice is supposed to be evidence of good quality, it usually proves the exact opposite.

Manufacturers of working-class lumberjacking axes specifically recommend against pounding the tool's head into wood, and if batoning is considered a bad idea for an axe, it's definitely not a smart thing to do with a far more lightly built knife.

Should it become necessary to split a piece of wood into smaller strips using a knife blade, there is a way to do it that won't destroy your knife: place the cutting edge atop the end of the wood to be split (it doesn't matter if the end is sawed-off flat or broken jaggedly) and press it down into the grain with a wiggling motion. When it's embedded a quarter-inch or so, rocking the blade back and forth while twisting it sideways is sufficient to cause a split to develop in the wood.

Using only hand pressure, push the blade deeper into the split and rock the knife's blade to widen the separation. At this point, the wood will usually split in two. Do not try to split off too large a strip—maximum size is largely dependent on the size of the knife being used and the leverage it provides. When splitting kindling to make a fire, narrower and thinner is better in any case. Be especially cautious to not drive the sharp edge down into your skin.

The definition of an axe is a very strong, very heavily built tool that can cut and hammer its way through almost anything—beware status-symbol axes that are too light to be of service in a survival scenario.

Axes and Hatchets

When it comes to doing the tough stuff—anything from splitting and chopping logs to busting through a wall of concrete blocks or opening a locked steel door—an axe is the tool made for the job. After a rock and a wooden club, an axe is the oldest tool known to humankind and still ranks as the most effective.

Simply described, an axe is an elongated, very thick and heavy steel (originally stone) "head," affixed to the end of a long shaft in a "T" configuration. When swung, the weighted head generates tremendous inertial power. With the ends of the T flattened, the tool is called a sledgehammer. With strong spikes on both sides of its head, it's a pickaxe. With a cutting edge formed into one or both sides, it's an axe, generally made for manipulating wood; put a stout spike opposite the cutting edge and you have a Pulaski, or Firefighter's axe, which is still standard equipment on fire engines today.

There is a trend today toward lightweight, lightly constructed axes and tomahawks, but these, in fact, defeat the inertial power that gives an axe its advantage as a survival tool.

Beyond those, there are numerous configurations that date back to a time before mass-produced steel was introduced, at the beginning of the twentieth century. Most of the variety of configurations have disappeared, except for the Michigan-type crosscut (chopping) axe, which is still made in single- and double-edge types, and some latest-generation splitting axes.

A typical axe head weighs 3.5 pounds, with a 33.5-inch handle, but some "timber cruiser" heads might weigh up to 5 pounds with hafts of 36 inches or longer. The longer the handle, the greater the inertia it can generate at the head. The same can be said for a heavier head.

Shorter models, with handles in the 24–26-inch range and heads of about 2 pounds, are a favorite of survival hobbyists (mostly because they feel insecure with a bigger axe). In days' past, these abbreviated axes were sold in catalogs as "Boys' Axes," because they possess neither the heft nor the length (i.e., power) of a full-sized axe, nor can they—according to their own sales literature—withstand the hard use that's likely to be required of a full-sized axe.

Smaller yet, with handles of 14–18 inches, and heads weighing about a pound, are hatchets. From the Old French, *hatchette* is the diminutive of hache, or axe, and describes a one-handed axe made for lighter jobs.

For "light/heavy" tasks, like chopping through bone, and cutting frozen meat, nothing beats a good, sharp hatchet.

In this author's opinion, the mid-sized "Boys' Axe" is the lesser choice of the two, being too large and long for light hatchet jobs and too light for axe work.

As a tool or a weapon, a full-size axe has little respect for anything, and there are very few objects that can stand up to it. It knows no equal for knocking holes in walls or smashing down doors, and as a weapon it historically defeats any armor the strongest man can carry. Aramid fibers, like Kevlar, have shown themselves to be poor defense against a sharp cutting edge; a "trauma plate" inside the vest might withstand the cutting action of an axe, but the man wearing it is likely to suffer internal hemorrhaging and broken bones.

Maintaining an axe blade is relatively simple. Probably the oldest, most time-honored method of keeping its edge in keen, unrusted condition is merely to bury it into an upturned section of log. Unfortunately, a log-splitting block isn't always present or feasible. Slip-on leather, plastic, or folded steel (I use flattened cans) covers that tie in place are easy to make. If your axe isn't going to spend its life standing in a tool shed, a cover to protect its edge and to protect the unsuspecting from its edge (my axes are sharp enough to skin a deer) is vital.

Tightening Loose Handles

An axe handle does a lot of work. I once had a lady describe, almost poetically, how the lovingly-cared-for axes she'd seen in the barns of old-timers often had wooden handles that were polished by sweat and use. I respectfully submitted to her that maybe those axes weren't so well-used, because I've always broken about two axe handles a year.

Because of the twisting and hard hits an axe is designed for, sometimes a handle loosens in its head. This is extremely dangerous, because a heavy lump of sharpened steel flying uncontrollably across a yard is always a bad thing.

Most hardware stores and aisles carry serrated metal wedges designed to be pounded down into wooden handles where they protrude from the top of their heads. These wedges spread apart the wood, thereby causing it to press more tightly against the sides of a tool's head.

A similar good ol' boy trick was to use nails to accomplish the same end; just pounding them into the top of the handle until it fits tightly. Alternatively, drywall screws can be used and seem to work even better.

A trick that I've found useful since my childhood has been to drill a small (about 1/8-in.) hole through the side of an axe head, with its handle inserted, then drive a nail through, bending over the portion that sticks through the other side with a hammer so that it can't come out. I've never

Author Robert Heinlein said "Specialization is for insects." As this new-whittled replacement axe handle demonstrates, the skills that a survivalist needs are endless.

reasoned why such a good retainer hasn't been adopted as a regular safety feature by the axe-making industry.

Making an Axe Handle

I believe that it's an essential part of being capable of taking care of one-self to be able to make, fabricate, adapt, and modify whatever materials are at hand to meet whatever the needs are at a given time. Hence the title of my first wilderness survival book, *Practical Outdoor Survival*. Primitive, modern, conventional, unconventional—it doesn't matter, so long as it works, and it gets the job done. Right and wrong are meaningless words when it comes to surviving; all that matters is that it does or doesn't work.

Making an axe, or any other tool's, handle is a more or less critical project, because a tool—especially an inertial tool, like a hammer or axe—may be all but useless without one.

Begin by cutting a suitable haft from a green sapling. Length should be at least as long as the original handle, but remember that a longer handle enables a more powerful swing and greater leverage. Diameter should be at least an inch greater than the widest point of the original handle, because you can always whittle more off, but it's a lot tougher to *add* thickness or width.

If at all possible, select a handle that already has the desired curvature to reduce the amount of shaping you'll need to do. This means that you might have to do a little hunting to find a suitable candidate. There are advanced procedures for steaming or boiling green wood to make it pliable enough to form fairly elaborate shapes in a jig, but those are beyond the scope of most survival needs.

Other Tools

As any DIYer will tell you, a handyman cannot have too many tools. Pliers, wrenches, screwdrivers, hammers—these exist because there's a need for them. So whether you live in a high-rise apartment building or far off the beaten track, the need for tools is as great.

But if you've had to bug-out, the odds of not having a toolbox are pretty good. That's why a good multi-tool is important. Unfortunately,

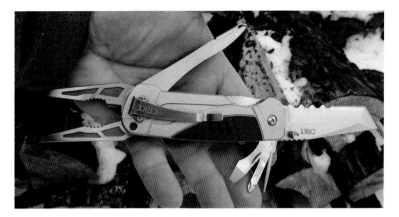

Long-distance dogsled racers are required, by rules of the sport, to carry a knife in their equipment bag, and many of them are opting for the incredible versatility of a good multi-tool, like this BIVY model from Columbia River Knife and Tools. (Photo courtesy of CRKT)

a multi-tool, regardless of quality, is what you use when you don't have proper tools. Once, when my truck fell into a log-skidder hole that was concealed by tall grass, I pulled a long-handled shovel from its box while my companion proudly unfolded his entrenching tool—within a minute he understood the difference between the two.

But proper tools are heavy, so a multi-tool has got to substitute for as many of them as it can, just as an e-tool substitutes—albeit poorly—for a shovel. The most workable strategy is, as one of my more astute survival students observed from my pack, for everything to serve multiple functions.

One of the more useful multi-purpose examples of that philosophy is the Schrade Company's Demo Tool. A prybar, chisel, shovel, nail-puller, hatchet, and ice-axe, this model also incorporates a wire stripper/cutter, an O2 bottle wrench, a gas shut-off wrench, and several yards of parachute cord. It has earned a place on my backpack.

More important than this tool is the philosophy behind it. Envision multiple uses for every component in your survival kit; fishing line can also work for snares, sewing, and many jobs that demand cordage. A nail can work as a punch, or an awl . . .

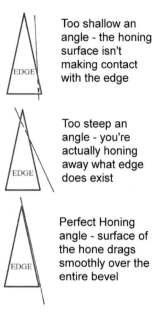

Too shallow an angle - the honing surface isn't making contact with the edge

Too steep an angle - you're actually honing away what edge does exist

Perfect Honing angle - surface of the hone drags smoothly over the entire bevel

A pointed bevel is the definition of a keen cutting edge; this illustration depicts the most common mistakes.

Knife and Tool Sharpening

A cutting tool with a dull edge is worthless; like a rifle without sights or a car without tires. A dull axe, scythe, or machete forces you to work harder; to strike more often and more forcefully to accomplish the same amount of work. Moreover, a dull knife is dangerous to its user, as it requires you to press harder to drive its edge through a given material. Applying more force means that there's a greater likelihood of slipping, and human skin cuts far more easily than rubber or hemp rope. Many a hunter wears a long scar from a skinning knife.

But honing an edge onto a cutting tool, particularly by manual means—that is, with an abrasive stone and hand pressure—is a disappearing, increasingly arcane skill, whatever an individual might claim. I've often issued this challenge: open any kitchen drawer, pull knives from any cutlery block, and count how many sharp blades you find. If you bet money on not finding any, you'd win more than you'd lose.

This is one of those areas, dear reader, where some of you are going to be offended. Too bad. My intention is to pass along what I know about sharpening; my own knives—and I have dozens, literally, all of them used hard—are keen enough to shave your face. Even my axes, many of which have been employed for cutting meat, are sharp enough to make you need stitches if you run your hand across their blades. I place great value on a cutting edge, and if it's meant to slice, then, by God, mine will slice.

Getting the Edge

My grandpa used to say that he knew just six people who could sharpen a knife, and that he'd taught that skill to five of them.

As I approach the sixth decade of my own life, I find that Grandpa was more right than wrong. Pick a knife from any kitchen drawer or cutlery block and run your thumb across its edge (it is a mark of intelligence that you NEVER run a thumb lengthwise down a cutting edge). If everyone I've issued that challenge to had bet me ten bucks that they'd find a sharp knife, I could buy a new car with cash.

Putting a keen edge on any cutting tool isn't difficult. Neither is sending Morse code with a telegraph key; but both skills have all but disappeared as they aren't needed in our daily lives. Gone are the days when every schoolboy carried a jackknife for everything from cleaning fish to cutting binder twine on hay bales—having a pocket knife today will get a kid suspended from school. In the way-past-politically-correct atmosphere of today, there is genuine cause to fear for the safety of children who haven't the slightest idea of how to operate a sharp knife beyond slasher movies and video games.

Skilled honesmen have gone the way of shade tree mechanics. Farmers, housewives, and home-cooked meals are evolving out of existence, and with them the need to have a cutlery block of knives sharp enough to process food without making a mangled mess of it.

Sharpening any cutting instrument isn't rocket science, but it is a science and it does take hands-on skill to do well. There's no shortage of opinions on this subject, but opinion is very often the refuge of ignorance; if you *know* something, that's not an opinion, it's a fact. The fact is that there are physical characteristics which must be established before that elusive quality known as sharpness can emerge. Logically, achieving those requisite features is a lot easier if you first know why an edge is keen or dull.

All-Important Bevels

Most important, whatever a blade's design, alloy, or features, is the edge bevel on either side of the cutting edge (one side on some Asian grinds). Seen end-on, these bevels *must* come together at a very pointed apex, or else a keen edge is impossible to achieve. The more pointed and polished the V formed by their joining, the sharper the blade. The angles of the bevels don't matter, and are, in fact, dependent on blade thickness, and profile (saber-ground, hollow-ground, flat-ground, etc.), as well as other factors.

In fact, the fixation with angles is probably the greatest reason that honing an edge seems to be so complex. I was recently berated by a fellow who actually owns a small knife-making company in Michigan's Upper Peninsula because, despite a video that proved otherwise, he stated, in no uncertain terms, that I didn't know how to sharpen a knife—I'd accomplished the task using methods that were unknown to him, therefore I'd done it wrong. That the blade sliced paper in the video was of no consequence.

Regardless, applying bevels to a blade isn't as complicated as some experts would like it to appear. My editor at *Tactical Knives* magazine used to lament that it wasn't really fair for either of us to evaluate a new sharpening gadget, as we could get a shaving edge from a chunk of concrete. It doesn't matter how you establish the bevels—whether you do it with a file, a honing stone, or an end mill—just so long as the inclines meet at a sharp point. That is the *only* feature of any importance.

A dulled, previously sharp knife already has the necessary bevels, but the apex where they meet is no longer pointed: it has been blunted, rounded by friction and wear—in a word, dulled. In the phraseology of old-timers, the apex where the bevels meet needs to be "stood up"; brought back to a sharp point by removing just enough metal from the bevels to restore it to its original keenness.

One reason angles don't matter is because you'll be "setting" them yourself on a never-sharpened blade—creating bevels where there were none. In the case of previously sharp blades, you'll be matching existing angles against whatever honing surface you're using. Depending on the width of the bevel and the thickness of the blade and the grind, honing angles may vary considerably from one blade to another.

Sharpening Tools

A new generation of tools resolves that problem by fixturing a blade so that it cannot move, then similarly locking-down the honing surfaces so that they cannot deviate from the angle at which they're set. Fixtured hones enable anyone to get a razor-edge on almost any knife; their main disadvantage is that the simplest of them is a multi-part kit, which makes them less feasible for in-the-field sharpening jobs.

More portable, and simpler, are pull-through sharpeners, which incorporate carbide or diamond cutting surfaces on either side of a pre-set-angled V-notch. As a blade is pulled, heel-to-tip through that notch, its sides are literally scraped off until the bevels of its cutting edge are identical to the angles of the notch and the apex meets in a sharp summit. Again, the angles of your bevels are determined by the angle of the carbides.

Either sharpening tool allows the greenest beginner to get a sharp edge on a knife, but remember that you're essentially milling hard to very hard steel from a blade to make its edge terminate at a pointed apex. The duller a knife, the more metal will need to be removed to restore its edge, so begin with your coarsest hone.

Hand Honing

Sharpening a knife manually, with no other tool except an abrasive surface in your hand, is at the very heart of the self-reliance philosophy. No skill is more representative of self-sufficient ideals than the ability to hone a dull knife back to keenness using nothing more complex than an abrasive rock. This is the knife-sharpening skill that everyone wants, and the one that my grandfather referred to as being almost extinct.

It's not that the skill is especially difficult to understand, even if it does take a bit of practice to develop real skill. The biggest cause of ineptitude that I've seen is attributed to poorly written sharpening instructions. Forget everything you've heard about maintaining a precise angle. It's important that your honing angle match the angle of the edge bevel; but you cannot visually determine, then manually hold a blade at an exact angle.

That does not mean that abrading the bevels at the correct, matching angle is less important with a hand-held sharpener. Again, apex is everything and you cannot achieve a sharp apex unless you hone the bevels at matching angles, just as you cannot make a circle without arcs. But maintaining angles with machine-like precision by eye alone just isn't possible when holding knife against stone. Such immobilization is beyond human muscle-control.

It's easiest to begin with a knife that has previously been sharp, even though it's dull when you start. Most knives today come from the factory with a sharp edge, which means that proper-edge bevels have been applied—as opposed to the unsharpened condition (for reasons of presumed liability) of blades manufactured prior to the 1990s. It's easier to learn the feel of an edge bevel against a honing surface if the correct bevel is already there.

You can see these bevels. To quote Meatloaf in his song "Paradise by the Dashboard Light," they're "glowing like the metal on the edge of a knife" if they've been applied correctly. They'll appear as an even-width line of flat, polished steel extending from choil (heel, next to the finger guard) to a blade's point. The flatter and more polished the bevels, the keener the point where they join and the sharper the cutting edge.

Achieving polished bevels by hand requires a little work and patience. Begin by laying the blade against the honing surface, then slowly rotating the cutting edge against it as though you were trying to slice a thin layer from the hone. The rotational motion is easier to control and enables you to evenly abrade the same amount along the entire length of a blade.

Feel the Bevels

F-e-e-l the blade drag against the abrasive surface; an uneven bevel or an improper honing angle will slip jerkily as you rotate. A proper angle and an even bevel produces a steady, smooth drag as you drag the blade against the stone, beginning at the choil, and pressing downward with an even (not hard) force as you draw the blade back toward its tip.

Geometry dictates that you raise the knife's handle slightly as you pass a blade's rounded belly. You'll see for yourself that it's necessary to do that to maintain the same angle and width of the bevel toward the blade's point.

For the sake of efficiency, most practiced honesmen learn to rotate a blade against a honing surface. Doing that covers more ground, faster, than simply dragging a blade from choil to tip. Start at the cutting edge, next to the choil, and move the blade into the stone as though you were trying to cut a thin slice from the stone. When the blade has reached as far as it can go without falling off the stone, drag it back—while never losing touch with the stone's surface—in a circular movement. Drag the blade back as you inscribe circles against the stone, from choil to tip. When you've reached the tip of the blade, remove it from the stone and placing it against the stone at its choil, begin the series of rotations again, circling from choil to tip.

With a bit of practice, you'll soon find yourself smoothly rotating the blade as you draw it back, choil to tip on one side, then flipping the knife and doing the same to the opposite side.

If honing doesn't produce a noticeable increase in sharpness, one of two things is happening: you're honing at the incorrect angle and the bevel isn't flat against the honing surface, or the bevels aren't yet meeting at a keen apex—the edge isn't sharp yet.

The former is the most common problem, but will reveal itself as a line running longitudinally along the length of the bevel. Look closely and you can see this line which indicates that the bevels are being honed on two different angles, with the line delineating those planes.

The latter is shown by a similar line—this one always near the very edge. It indicates that the honing angle is correct, but the apex, rounded from wear, hasn't yet been brought to a keen point. The solution in this case is to continue removing metal at the same angles until the bevels meet.

Keep your hones clean. Every type of hone needs to be clean to work efficiently. Plain water is the only honing solution you'll ever need, but liquid soap is ideal for cleaning away residue that will eventually glaze and degrade a hone's abrasive ability. Barring that, scrub the surface of your hone with sand, water, and a rag.

An Unconventional Shortcut

For very dull knives, or knives that have never been sharpened and need considerable metal abraded off to form edge bevels, I often do something that isn't suggested in honing instructions. I use a very abrasive instrument, sometimes a file, sometimes a coarse aluminum-oxide stone, cleaned frequently with clear water, and grind forcefully back and forth, against, then with, the edge, up and down the length of the blade. The straightforward back-and-forth grinding motion is much easier to control, and establishes bevels quickly. You'll note increased sharpness almost immediately.

The back-and-forth technique isn't up to getting a surgical-sharp edge, but even a novice should find it easy to master for achieving a workable cutting edge. I use it to rapidly remove metal from very dull knives, especially if they're made from one of the harder tool steels.

Sharpening a knife, or any cutting instrument, is no more complicated than establishing—then polishing—the edge bevels. Oh sure, it can get more involved when you start considering which bevel angles, alloys, hardness, and blade designs are best suited to a given task. Sharpening experts may hone in any direction, using a variety of movements because, like any expert in a discipline, they can employ options that lesser-skilled honesmen can't make work. Chainsaw sculptors work extensively with the tips of their saw's bar but many a novice lumberjack is sporting serious scars from trying to do the same. If the objective is to have a knife that does what it's supposed to do—which is to cut—then the instructions given here are as complex as you'll need.

Hand Saws

On a recent "survival" series aired on a big-name network, at least a couple of the experts being filmed during a prolonged wilderness outing carried a frame-tensioned bow saw among the limited items they were allowed in this competition.

I have used that type of "buck" or "bow" saw since I was a child, and the two that I currently own are hanging on a nail in the barn, rusting. The best I can say for these saws is that they'll cut a piece of wood *if* they're sharp; the truth of it is that saws like these have been obsolete for at least two decades, since the advent of laser-cut, opposing teeth blades, with trademarked names like Razor Tooth.

Since discovering laser-cut saws in 1993, the saw strapped to my backpack has been an 18-inch Kerambit-type blade (arced like a claw), manufactured by Corona Tools (I mention the brand because the saw is unique). This saw has severed green wind-felled trees with trunks more than a foot in diameter. Its efficiency is surpassed only by a motorized chainsaw, and it maintains its sharpness through years of hard use.

Several sizes of laser-cut saws are available from a number of manufacturers. Traditional carpentry tool makers like Stanley offer cross-cut saws that employ this tooth design, and there are even lock-blade models that fold like a big jackknife, making them convenient enough to be considered a survival necessity.

Every survival kit, be it rural or urban, needs a large, heavy knife that can chop through a door, split the pelvis of a deer, or put an end to a confrontation—like this Mah-Chete, forged of tough 1070 steel.

Fixed-blade laser-cut saws are dangerous to carry, like a sharp machete, and don't come with a sheath. I can tell you from regrettable experience that their blades easily sever flesh. I solved that problem by splitting a section of garden hose, equal to the length of the saw's blade longitudinally, then fitting it over the cutting edge like an envelope. The length of hose is held in place over the blade by a heavy rubber band, cut from a bicycle tire's inner tube, although a wrap of cord tied in place around blade and hose works as well.

Light

When I was a kid (before backpacking was considered to be a sport, just a conveyance for the necessities that made multiple days in the woods more tolerable), the coming of night meant that it was time to make camp. Adventure movies notwithstanding, darkness has historically heralded a cessation of activities: wars were halted, construction stopped, and anything that required vision ceased until morning because humans have poor night vision.

Combat analysts are unanimous in their conviction that night vision equipment was one of the major technological advantages for US soldiers from Vietnam to Iraq. From falling into one of the innumerable holes to defining natural terrain to skewering an eyeball on a tree branch, nightfall by itself can defeat the strongest warrior.

Portable artificial lights didn't become reliable enough to qualify as backcountry gear until the late 1970s, even later than that for me, personally. By the first decade of the new millennium, Light Emitting Diode (LED) flashlights, lanterns, and headlamps had completely changed the game. Sundown was no longer anything but a minor inconvenience.

Part of the trouble with traditional incandescent (bulb) lights is that they're power hogs. Whether they use old-fashioned or latest-generation halogen bulbs, the *milliamperage* (electrical power) needed to heat a wire filament to the point of glowing puts a real drain on batteries. Halogen flashlights are still being manufactured at this time, but their attraction is pretty much limited to law-enforcement and club-like instruments. Incandescent bulbs of all types have a definite life before their superheated filaments fatigue and burn in two, often after just ten hours of use. That's simply not good enough for a serious survivalist.

For uses where light is the primary objective—as opposed to using your light for a (poor) clubbing weapon—the hands-down choice is a solid-state LED. Depending on power output and other variables, manufacturer Cree, Inc., claims a life expectancy of about 100,000 hours—basically, forever. That, by itself, makes LED the choice for a survival light, but unparalleled brightness and very low current draw make LED lights a favorite everyday light with us in the northwoods, where darkness comes as early as 4:30 p.m. in mid-winter, and ambient temperatures below −40 make battery life a must.

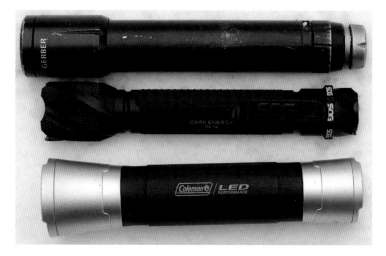

Although many of the changes wrought to our world are factors in needing to be prepared to survive a disaster, some changes have been for the better, like these modern, super-bright LED flashlights.

Flashlights

Flashlights are far from obsolete, even though headlamps are a better choice in many cases. Sometimes you need a bright light that you can hold in one hand and send flash signals to overflying aircrafts, a light that you can stand on its end to light an entire room, or to send illumination into darkened places inaccessible to your head. Or one that you can tape to a firearm for "jacklighting" game at night.

Flashlights have undergone some real improvements over the years. From D-size, powered by dry cells that delivered a couple of hours of service (depending how cold it was) and had to be smacked against a palm frequently to keep them working to today's brilliant LED models, powered by 2 rechargeable AAs, and capable of more than eight hours of continuous, reliable service.

As an aside, I prefer to—and recommend—using only AA-powered appliances for the same reason cowboys carried a pistol and a carbine chambered for the same round. AA batteries aren't inherently better than any other sizes, but they're readily available (as are the tools that use them). Numerous LED flashlights have proven their worth in the past decade, and they just keep improving. For almost ten years, a pair of $16, 2AA Colemans (55 Lumens) have sat on my house's windowsills where they've more than earned their keep through many power outages. For several years a Gerber Omnivore (18 Lumens) rode on my belt, powered by a single AA, AAA, or Cr-123 battery; that flashlight works to this day, but was replaced with a brighter 2 AA Gerber Carnivore (60 Lumens) in 2014. Most recently, that light—which still works well—was succeeded by a SOG Dark Energy 04 (220 Lumens, max, 3 settings) and, based on that light's outstanding performance, a CR-123-powered DE-05 (624 Lumens, max, 3 settings).

Like everything else, the models that I've mentioned by name are likely to have been discontinued by the time this book goes to press. Prices vary widely, but you can get a professional-level AA flashlight bright enough to shine deer, with heirloom quality, for well under $100, and a very good, reliable survival-kit quality model for less than $30. You can pay several hundred dollars—there are lights in that price range—but, having owned a few of these, I can say with assurance that paying that much is more an exercise in social elitism than pragmatism.

Finally, I suggest avoiding lights that employ more than one LED. On the surface it might seem that having several light emitters would be better, but there have been a good number of low-quality, unreliable, and ultimately short-lived flashlights and headlamps that use several low-power LEDs to achieve a brightness that is actually less than better lights employing a single LED.

Headlamps

Although flashlights still have a place that isn't likely to become obsolete, there are many tasks for which a good headlamp is superior. During the winter months, a constant part of our daily routine is feeding sled dogs, and, for almost two decades, the Timberwolves we raised (under

Nightfall has historically given pause to activities ranging from construction to warfare, but today's survivalist has the finest, least expensive lights ever manufactured at his or her disposal.

state-issued permit). Winter days in the far north are very short while lake-effect clouds and almost constant snowfall ensures that you often need a lamp at midday (nightfall comes as early as 4:30 p.m.). For tasks that have ranged from splitting firewood to patching up dogs after a fight (huskies fight among themselves more than pit bulls), a headlamp is a necessary tool when you need both hands.

As with every other device, when possible, we use headlamps powered by AA batteries and, like our flashlights, we've found that models which use only one LED are actually better. Illogically, many—perhaps most—AA and AAA headlamps use three batteries, which is a logistical pain in the butt. For that reason, and because of its rheostat variable control, my go-to headlamp for the past six years has been a SureFire Saint, although its $250 price tag is a bit hard to swallow. Rechargeable batteries take the inconvenience out of having to use an odd number of power cells, and you can get a very suitable headlamp for around $25 these days.

I recommend avoiding power pack–type headlamps (and flashlights), in which a number of batteries—usually three—are inserted, and then the pack inserted into the headlamp body. Reminiscent of a firearm's magazine, this might seem like a convenient feature because you can insert a fresh power pack into a depleted light, but in real life it adds at least two more electrical contact points that can become tarnished, coated with frost, or otherwise break the connection.

Lanterns

When it comes to lighting a room-size area, you need a lantern. Like all our other battery-operated lights, these illuminate from LEDs and they use AA cells—normally Nickel Metal Hydride (NiMH)–type—so that batteries from one unit can be scavenged to power something else.

Unlike headlamps and flashlights, we have several lanterns that use multiple LEDs, and these seem to function well; some of them for more than a decade. Some are fairly modern, with individual detachable palm-lights; some run off separate rechargeable power packs; some look like old-fashioned kerosene-burners; some even look like candles. In all, our own household has accumulated more than a dozen different LED lamps in as many years, ranging from lamps that were included with a larger purchase to units costing up to $60.

Quality generally costs more, but experience has demonstrated that you don't have to spend a small fortune to get a serviceable LED lamp. Chances are you'll need several, so it pays to buy sensibly, and don't go broke buying a lamp that won't give more for your money.

Solar Lights

When they get enough sun-power to work, there's no more sure sign that mankind has the intellectual capacity to save itself than solar light. Photovoltaic cells have existed since the 1970s, but they were heavy, fragile, and less efficient than the still inefficient—but slowly improving—panels of today. Those old solar cells, combined with the incandescent lights and high current draw motors of those earliest days, meant solar had not reached the point where it was useful, except maybe in the unobstructed vacuum of space.

But connect the new flexible, thin-wall high-output panels of today to modern low-demand motors, LEDs, and micro circuitry and you have an energy source worthy of being included in a post-disaster survival kit. In the northwoods the sun is weak and the days short at any time of the year. Attempts to take a house "off the grid" with solar—that is, replace the input of a power pole entirely—have been unsuccessful, resulting in maybe 10 percent of current needed, with a large system in mid-summer. The technology just isn't there yet.

But solar yard lights that operate from two 700mAh rechargeable Nickel-Cadmium batteries are worthwhile. It's very dark at night around my home, with the nearest public street light being 5 miles away—every survival student I've had has remarked on the brightness of stars in the night sky, which illustrates how little artificial light is present to dilute them. Solar yard lights aren't very bright (2.4 Lumens is average), though they have enough charge to stay lit all night for only a few of the longest days of the year and don't charge at all during the winter. But we've used them for six years now, and they've been worth their $20–$30 price tags.

Although solar isn't yet efficient enough to serve as a primary source of electricity, if you want a way to keep AA batteries for a flashlight or radio charged or even keep a radio receiver operating directly from sunlight, then solar power is, indeed, a useful reality. A Brunton Solaris folding solar panel has been part of my "forever" backpack for nigh onto ten years now. Its rated output is 25 Watts, but in the real world you can count on less than half that, even in bright sunlight. Maximum voltage obtained has been 21 volts.

Most chargers today have a built-in voltage regulator, but be aware that it's possible to overcharge. To prove this, I intentionally destroyed an old AM/FM receiver using a small 10-watt solar panel. The panel was putting out between 4 and 12 volts, depending on whether there were clouds obscuring the sun; the receiver was rated to use four AA batteries, or 6 volts. The radio worked for six hours, then never worked again. It is possible to overcharge batteries, too, so if you use a panel that is capable of producing a voltage in excess of the batteries being charged, route it through a charger that has a voltage regulator or, barring that, keep a close eye on the batteries and remove them when their voltage output reaches what it's supposed to be (i.e., 1.5 volts, 6 volts, etc.). Overcharged batteries tend to split, destroying them and, in a few cases, they can explode like hand grenades.

Gas Lanterns

For survival purposes, camping-type butane and propane lanterns (and cook stoves) that operate from canisters of compressed gas are not a good choice. Replacement fuel canisters might not be obtainable, and cold weather can reduce the working life of a canister to mere minutes.

Coleman-type lanterns that run off white gas (Coleman Fuel), which is compressed within the lantern's fuel tank, are more acceptable, but only for household and other stationary settings. They are too bulky to carry and require specific liquid fuel (white gasoline or Coleman fuel) and spare fabric mantles.

Kerosene Lamps

In our home there are three kerosene lamps mounted in holders on the walls, two portable table lamps, and two hurricane lanterns built for outdoor use. Except for the hurricane lanterns, which burn traditional kerosene, they're all fueled with scented lamp oil (liquid paraffin)—not because it burns better but because it smells better.

Like the white-gas lanterns, the wick-type lamps are not especially suitable for a nomadic lifestyle but have proved ideal for shelter-in-place situations. Liquid paraffin is more expensive than kerosene—about $20 a gallon, but we keep two cases (6 gallons) on hand, with a dozen spare wicks, available at hardware and department stores. Keep glass chimneys clean and handle them delicately. Occasionally, a wick burns unevenly (it's important to keep it saturated with fuel) and it must be trimmed—simply cut flat again with scissors to restore brightness.

An added benefit of the oil lanterns, which have served us well in many power outages, is that they produce a significant amount of heat. We have actually had to extinguish all but one of them, even in the midst of a winter storm, because they made our small house too warm.

In most instances, this isn't a concern, but be thoughtful about the oxygen required to sustain a flame. The goal in a shelter-in-place scenario is to seal the building you're in as thoroughly as possible; to keep out dust motes that carry viruses, radiation, or chemical toxins. Exhaust from a burning lantern isn't an immediate concern insofar as toxicity, but it might not be advisable to burn up your breathing air.

Candle Lanterns

In frontier days, light was often most efficiently provided by candle. But a candle lit outside was easily blown out by a slight breeze. Its flame needed to be shielded from air currents without also blocking the light it emitted.

The answer lies in what was known as a "punched-tin" lamp. Essentially a can, usually with a hinged access door in its side (one of the unconventional chores that I've used my folding knife to accomplish), the lamp has an array of closely spaced holes punched into its outside walls. A strong wind couldn't blow into its interior with sufficient force to extinguish the flame, yet the holes permit enough light to escape to keep you from bumping into things. As you can see from the photo, it's easy to fabricate one of these useful lanterns from an aluminum soda can.

Made from a soda-pop can, this punched-tin lantern approximates those dating back hundreds of years, turning a candle into a wind- and rain-resistant all-weather lantern—just be careful not to burn yourself on the hot can.

Buddy Burner

In the rural northwoods, winters are cold and sometimes hard, and more than one resident has learned the hard way about frozen pipes— especially in the record-breaking cold of recent years. Ice is a powerful force, and it can burst an iron pipe, flooding basements and crawlspaces with a frozen mess that cannot be remedied until spring. Even worse, frost lines have penetrated deeper into the ground in recent years than at any time in recorded history, freezing and shattering sewer tiles and causing foul, disease-producing backups into affected residences. There are preventative measures to keep water pipes from freezing, like electrical heat tape, but these require electricity. A very old, time-proven solution was to place a large "Buddy Burner" in the crawlspace or basement.

The most fundamental description of a Buddy Burner is that it's a large candle in a can. It's made by starting with a cleaned metal paint can with a press-down metal lid. Into the can's center is placed a large woven-fabric (asbestos, when it was available) lamp wick, long enough to reach from the can's bottom to its top. A length of fence wire—woven through the wick's length—stiffens and holds it from folding onto itself. Another length of wire pierces the wick crosswise, spanning across the top of the can while holding the wick so that it hangs suspended from the top of the can.

Finally, with the stiffened wick positioned in the desired location, the can is filled with molten paraffin (even old candles, melted for that purpose). The wax is allowed to cool and harden, then the can's lid is replaced and tamped down to seal it. (Do not replace a lid tightly over molten wax—even after just using it—or the lid will pop off explosively.) Clever guys even added a book of matches under the lid for lighting the wick when it was needed.

And when it was needed, on subzero nights—when prudent folks left a kitchen faucet slightly opened, so that trickling water might keep their water pipes from freezing, or on subzero days when they had to go to work—a Buddy Burner or two was lit and placed under the house (in a place where it couldn't cause a fire). The tiny flicker of heat generated by the big canned candle was sufficient to keep pipes from freezing. It was a primitive, but effective, solution that worked for me, personally, for decades.

Just as paint cans are made in different sizes, so can Buddy Burners be made in a variety of sizes to suit different needs. To heat the underside of a house, we used a gallon-size that burned for more than a day. As a camp stove, placed at the bottom of a slit trench that's about 3 inches deeper than the can is tall, a cook pot spanning the trench's top, it works well to heat impromptu meals in the field. Or it can help to light stubborn campfires. A Buddy Burner always lights, it can't get too wet to burn, and it would take a hurricane to blow it out.

Multi-Fuel Stove

I do not exaggerate when I praise multi-fuel stoves as being one of the great survival inventions. I evaluated the best of them for *Consumers Digest* some years back, assigning that magazine's Best Buy Award to the top 3. The least expensive won, incidentally, and is still in service today without a lick of trouble.

The beauty of a multi-fuel stove is that it creates a pressurized, gas-range-style flame that is efficient, and it does so with almost any combustible liquid—from kerosene (with an atomizer accessory) to gasoline to grain alcohol.

Multi-fuel stoves employ a pump-up canister to pressurize and atomize fuel into a fine, clean-burning spray. Unfortunately, most of the detachable-canister stoves I've tested burst into a ball of flames when first ignited. The flame settles down to a pretty burner-like ring of blue flame when excess fuel burns away, but be aware that magazine articles that speak of "vestibule cooking" in a tent are penned by writers who, in my opinion, merit a good beating for dispensing bad advice. Never use a stove inside any portion of any tent that you wouldn't want to set ablaze.

Thus far, for many years, the multi-fuel stove that has served me best has been a Coleman Exponent. This stove is still available (surprisingly) for about $140.

Radio Receivers

For nearly a century before there was the Internet, the world was linked together with radio waves. Suddenly, news from Peking could be heard instantaneously in New York and Paris, and no longer was the world so expansive a place.

Nowhere has the value of radio been made clearer to me, personally, than during my long, frequent trips to wilderness places—most of them alone. It occurred to me out there, sometimes a half day or more from the nearest paved road, that the world could be plunged into thermonuclear war, and I wouldn't even know it.

A radio receiver enabled me to know that there was still a world out there. Beginning with my first-used 9-volt, 5-transistor, AM-only radio way back in 1967. The radio kept me up to date about current world events, it kept me entertained, and it staved off loneliness. Batteries were expensive and short-lived, the electronics sucked power, and reception was limited to one or two stations during the day (pocket FM radios wouldn't come along for a few years).

Since boyhood I've never been without a portable, personal radio receiver—whether at home or deep in the wilderness. Their sizes have decreased, their batteries have improved, range of frequencies received has increased, and working life on a set of batteries has increased dramatically.

AM/FM

Most fundamental of radio receivers are commercial Amplitude Modulation (AM) and Frequency Modulation (FM) types. Makes or models really don't make a lot of difference these days—most of their semiconductor and integrated circuitry is made in the same overseas factories—and virtually all of them are identical when it comes to performance. I have a $5, two-AAA model that I bought new fifteen years ago and, except for its tinny sound—the result of a tiny PM speaker—it receives as well as the $500 Bose in my living room. The important point is that you have a portable receiver both at home and in an evacuation kit.

Again, to make your radio interchangeable with flashlights and other survival components, it should use the same type of battery to power it as every other piece of portable electronic equipment.

Better yet are radios that carry their own on-board power. I tested the first dynamo (crank generator) and solar models back in the early 1990s, and those first offerings just weren't worth owning. Cranks failed quickly, solar panels were so small as to be almost useless, and overall quality was poor.

Since then, I've had numerous other radio receivers with on-board power devices, and quality has continuously improved over the years. Perhaps the most significant feature, insofar as survival purposes are concerned, is an ability to plug into cellular telephones and other devices to recharge them, as well as the radio's own batteries. There are a range of plugs, though, so be sure that your radio generator connects to your current device. I have a (discontinued) Stormbeam from Coleman that I got years ago. Despite having an array of connectors, I never found even one thing that it would plug into.

Shortwave

Band	Megahertz	Kilohertz
11m	25.67-26.10 Mhz	25670-26100 Khz
13m	21.45-21.50 Mhz	21450-21850 Khz
16m	17.55-17.90 Mhz	17550-17900 Khz
19m	15.10-15.60 Mhz	15100-15600 Khz
22m	13.60-13.80 Mhz	13600-13800 Khz
25m	11.65-12.05 Mhz	11650-12050 Khz
31m	9.500-9.900 Mhz	9500- 9900 Khz
41m	7.100-7.300 Mhz	7100- 7300 Khz
49m	5.950-6.200 Mhz	5950- 6200 Khz
60m	4.750-5.060 Mhz	4750- 5060 Khz
75m	3.900-4.000 Mhz	3900- 4000 Khz
90m	3.200-3.400 Mhz	3200- 3400 Khz
120m	2.300-2.490 Mhz	2300- 2490 Khz

No home or long-term survival kit is complete without a portable radio that is capable of receiving these global shortwave bands.

In the summer of 1994, I spent a forced night on the northern side of the Mackinac Bridge after a hair-raising thunderstorm wrought havoc on both of Michigan's shorelines at the intersection of Lakes Michigan and Huron. I drove in circles between I-75 and the village of

St. Ignace, tuning vainly through the FM and AM bands of my truck's stereo to find something on local news that might at least make a reference to why the busiest 5 miles of this interstate highway was closed down.

Nothing. Not even a mention, not on any radio station. Traffic was bumper-to-bumper and there wasn't a vacancy for 50 miles in either direction. Fortunately, we were driving a 4 × 4 that was outfitted as a motor home, complete with sheets and pillowcases.

The next morning, the bridge reopened to traffic. As I passed, the northbound lane's grating was torn up and a small army of workers was laboring frantically amid a constellation of sparks with welders, cutting torches, and grinders. State troopers and bridge patrol officers kept traffic moving along; gawking was more than discouraged.

The forested shoreline on the southern side of the bridge was a section of Mackinaw State Forest that I frequented several times each month, and I spent a lot of time backpacking there. Forty-foot trees in that forest were leaned over like blades of grass, and they stayed that way for years until nature caused them to straighten. I'd seen that a few times before: a tornado had passed through, running down a two-track road—the path of least resistance—until its force was finally diffused by heavy tree cover.

About two months after the incident, I spoke with a state trooper who'd been present the day it happened. I asked him point-blank if a tornado had damaged the bridge. Without looking at me, he stated that no, it had not. I asked him if he'd tell me if one had. He looked me square in the eye and said no, he would not.

The biggest lesson that I took away from this is how quickly and easily news media can be squelched, turned off like a faucet, whenever government officials see fit. If something as important to public safety as a tornado strike on America's longest suspension bridge can be stifled instantly, what else can, and does, get withheld from the public?

For a quarter-century now, I've been "DX-ing" across the short-wave and AM dials, listening to stations that, if the ionosphere cooperates, might skip in from thousands of miles away. Radio Havana in Cuba is a prime example of a foreign commercial station with predictable reception. Radio Havana is Cuba's CNN, and is broadcast on numerous frequencies, on several meter-bands, as well as on the Internet.

The great thing about foreign broadcasts, particularly from those in countries not on friendly terms with the USA, is that their news about what's happening in the US and other countries has a different slant than—and sometimes contradicts entirely—news broadcast by home-grown networks. Unfortunately, the foreign broadcasts are often correct, because no one would listen for long to a news station that tells outright lies. But these broadcasters delight in revealing details that the subject country would rather not disclose. In the event of a major catastrophe, who doesn't believe that the official line, whatever the country, will be "Stay calm, we have everything under control"?

This $10 shortwave receiver, shown here in an EMP-proof Faraday Shield made from a Christmas candy tin, runs for days on two rechargeable AA batteries, and is beyond value in a far-reaching catastrophe.

Coilable Antenna

A problem that we always had with telescoping antennas is that the duress of field use almost inevitably breaks them. The good ol' boy fix was to solder a small alligator clip to a 6-foot length of stranded, insulated copper wire. When the radio was in use, the alligator clip was secured to the broken antenna stub and the wire suspended from a tree branch.

Actual length of the wire used for this antenna isn't critical. There are algebraic formulae, using Greek letters like *Lambda*, that calculate exacting lengths for optimal reception of a given frequency, but 6 or 8 feet of wire is sufficient. Reception strength can be varied just by moving the wire to a different position.

Note that AM radios, or the portion of an AM/FM radio that receives AM frequencies, universally have an on-board "ferric" antenna within their cases. To maximize AM reception on a given station, once it has been tuned-in, the entire radio is rotated. The coilable wire pocket antenna is only for FM and shortwave frequencies that employ a receiver's telescopic antenna, although sometimes signal strength can be maximized on AM stations by wrapping the outside of the entire radio with several turns of wire.

Transceivers

Anyone who's ever endured an extended power outage has caught themselves flipping a light switch. It's a conditioned response—you want a room to be lighted, you flip a wall switch.

The same has happened with cellular telephones. There are kids raising their own kids who have never known what it is to be unable to contact police, fire, medics, or mom and dad whenever they wanted. When I was a kid, if you had a telephone at all it was attached to a wire in your house and you probably shared the line with half a dozen neighbors.

For survival, sometimes it's best to go low-tech. If—when— communications satellites, cellular and repeater towers, and Internet servers get fried by any of a dozen electromotive pulse (EMP) generating phenomena, you'll see people everywhere holding their cell phones against the sky as they search fruitlessly for bars on its display screen. That alone will push the populace toward panic.

AM Citizens Band

In the '60s and '70s, AM Citizens Band, with its original 23 channels on the 11-meter band and a maximum output of 5 watts, were the standard. AM, by its nature, receives a great deal of static which reduced its usable range, and the *Smoky and the Bandit* trucker craze helped to ensure that everyone had a CB in their cars, which made the frequencies so jammed and so short-ranged as to be useless. The Federal Communications Commission (FCC) tried increasing the spectrum of usable frequencies to 40 channels, but only the fact that Channel 9 was a universal emergency channel kept AM CB alive. To make matters worse, outlaw CBers started using illegal "linear amplifiers," which boosted the power of their signal, but succeeded in further jamming the channels with noise. By the 1980s, the band had been virtually abandoned.

Today, there's almost no one on the channels, making AM Citizens Band once again a viable emergency communication alternative. Range is still poor—about 5 miles—but CBs operate from almost any car, boat, or motorcycle's electrical system, and they have the advantage of being able to "skip" a signal thousands of miles if atmospheric conditions are cooperative.

Drawbacks include needing to have antenna tuned to radio, to minimize standing wave ratio and maximize performance. This isn't so much a problem these days, when antennas and radios are pre-set to match at the factory, but it does mean that you might need to do a little studying to get the most from your rig.

Even better, but more complex, are Single Sideband (SSB) transceivers. These are on the verge of "ham" radios and require a little education. But when the hobby was in fashion, I personally logged conversations with several European countries and all of South America.

General Mobile Radio Service

Then there are the GMRS transceivers. These operate between 462 and 467 megahertz, usually in the form of pocket-size walkie-talkies, split into 36 channels, and with an "up to" 38-mile range. In fact, these are line-of-sight transceivers and may deliver a small fraction of that range (except over water).

However, that limited range can be an advantage. There's a reduced chance that your conversations can be overheard, but you and your party can remain in touch for at least a mile or two, which makes the units ideal for perimeter security.

Faraday Shield

A farad is an electrical measure of capacitance, that is, the ability to draw or store electrical energy. The reason a handheld high-capacity shocking device like a stun gun or a Taser can draw electrical energy from a low voltage, low amperage battery and transform it into a single huge discharge, capable of knocking a man unconscious, is because it has big capacitors that store it, increasing pressure (voltage) until it is discharged. Think of a dam holding back a lazy, slow-moving stream, allowing it to build to tremendous pressure behind a retaining wall until it suddenly bursts forth with unstoppable force.

A faraday shield conducts electrical energy away and keeps it from reaching whatever is inside. A familiar instance is a car that gets struck by lightning; its occupants are safe, not because of rubber tires, but because the metal body of a car dissipates ions before they reach occupants.

A traditional form of faraday shield for survival purposes, whose origin dates back to the Cold War–era, is a simple 1-gallon paint can. With its airtight lid tamped in place, it not only makes a tough, portable general-use survival kit when packed with fishing gear, sewing needles and thread, and fire-making tools, but its metal walls are proof against the electromotive force (EMP) generated by a nuclear explosion (or an asteroid impact). Electrical pulses that might easily burn out radio, computer, and other micro circuitry—including car and truck electrical systems.

In the days of vacuum-tube operated radios and straightforward, unrelayed automotive electrical systems, circuits were simply too heavy to be burned out by airborne electrical energy waves. Because of their immunity to EMPs caused by nuclear explosion, even the then state-of-the-art MiG 25 Foxbat—the interceptor jet that scared the United States into creating the F-16 Falcon—used vacuum tubes for many of its avionics systems.

Today's hair-thin micro circuitry needs shielding. Metal walled and roofed pole barns offer some protection, but radio receivers, transceivers, computers and tablets—anything electronic—need to be encased inside a metal container. Paint cans are still among the best faraday shields, but they aren't large enough for every use. They aren't especially watertight (without a layer of duct tape around their perimeters, over can and lid), but Christmas-type candy tins are great faraday shields and shaped to accommodate most receivers, etc. (Their covers must also be sealed to their boxes with duct tape or beeswax to make them watertight.)

Ammunition cans, made of steel, with easily removed, but gasket-sealed, hinged-lid cans may be had in large enough sizes (up to .50 caliber is common, but larger calibers can be had) to accommodate cell phones, tablets, and even laptops. An added advantage with ammo cans is that they can be buried for years as is, or even stashed under a stream bank, and it will take a decade or more for the elements to breach them.

Batteries

Almost everything electronic that qualifies for inclusion in a survival kit runs on batteries. Minimal understanding of types of batteries, their advantages, and their limitation is required.

The most common and most feasible size of batteries, based on our own fourteen years (at the time of this writing) of experience, is AA size, or, if we've had to, AAA size. Small, portable size of the batteries, combined with the low and decreasing current requirements of modern electronic and lighting devices—and ease of recharging—has shown these to be the ideal size for emergency and field uses. We never suffer from dead batteries in anything. It's never dark around here, even though the power goes out with maddening regularity (our home isn't actually "on the grid," but on a single leg extending from the grid), and electrical outages for days at a time are simply inconvenient.

Perhaps the most valuable piece of information, initially, is Milliamp Hours. Abbreviated mAh, milliamp hours is the most common unit of measure for revealing how much power is contained in a battery. The higher this number, the better. Most rechargeable batteries can be recharged about 1,000 times.

Alkaline

The most common batteries sold in hardware and department stores are non-reusable alkalines. They still hold the most electrical energy, and therefore have the longest life. But when they're depleted, they're gone. We've had some luck with recharging alkalines with state-of-the-art pulse chargers, made to refurbish rechargeable batteries, but life is only a few hours at best. And there's always a danger that recharging non-rechargeable batteries could cause them to split or even explode.

Nickel-Cadmium

The first rechargeable type of battery, NiCads deliver poor service. Capacity for AA size is typically 1,000 mAh, maximum, and die-off is practically instantaneous—meaning that a flashlight, for instance, just suddenly stops working. Nickel-Cadmiums are the least expensive rechargeable batteries.

Nickel-Metal Hydride

In terms of price versus performance versus availability and usability, these are the AAs that have won the choice, hands down—especially since they keep improving. Capacity is up to a respectable 2,600 mAh, and most batteries will remain 75 percent charged for a year, or more.

Lithium-Ion

This is currently the benchmark in electrical storage devices, but at this time, there are no rechargeable lithium-ion batteries in AA or AAA sizes. Beware non-rechargeable AA batteries that use the term "lithium" on their packaging—these are, in fact, just disposable alkaline batteries.

CHAPTER THREE

NAVIGATION

Orienteering

One of the most fulfilling aspects of teaching a survival course, for me, was knowing that my students would never again be lost in the woods—or anywhere else, for that matter. Conversely, without a basic knowledge of the fundamentals of orienteering, no one is more than a few yards from being hopelessly lost—even, and perhaps especially, in an unfamiliar city or town.

As I do throughout this book, I'll illustrate that point with what, for me, was a memorable anecdote: I'd been in the woods alone for four days. The nearest village was 14 miles away, but I'd been exploring this place for many years, and I knew it as well as the Ojibwe tribes who'd named it *Skegemog*—Land of Many Mosquitoes. In fact, the mosquito population was minimal, but the place was teeming with wildlife.

The problem with having camped here for so many years is that the numerous campsites I'd established were becoming devoid of firewood. I even burned half-rotted wood, but I was having to go farther and farther to find fuel for my fire (take note).

Now, it was late on a moonless night, my fire had burned down to a few red coals, and I was about 50 yards from camp. Scrounging for a few sticks by the dim light of an old Mini-Mag flashlight, I straightened up, and looked around—and was immediately disgusted with myself. I had no idea in which direction my camp lay. I was as lost in the woods as a proverbial babe.

As has been my habit since childhood, there was a compass on a lanyard around my neck. It just pissed me off that I'd gotten lost so easily—me, a guy who hadn't been lost in the woods since he was in the fourth grade. A quick look at my compass, and I was back on the trail that led to camp, but without either compass or light, I would have been lost at least until dawn.

GPS versus Compass

It was our second day backpacking the Fossil Ridge Wilderness Area of Colorado's Gunnison Basin, and we were still trying to figure out where we were. Barry, who had hired me to track elk for him, insisted that his *Global Positioning System* (GPS) unit and *Universal Transverse Mercator* (UTM) grid map could not be wrong. But my Brunton 8099 prismatic compass and topographical map said that our position was precisely one mile north of his GPS coordinates.

Ordinarily, such a disparity would be impossible, which made the fact that there was one perplexing. We scaled a bald mountain, where, at 12,000 feet, we could look down on most other mountains. Using the compass's sights, I took a bearing from where we stood to two identifiable peaks, then calculated a *back bearing*, 180 degrees opposite.

I transferred those back bearings to my plastic-laminated map using a grease pencil, drawing lines at the calculated angles from each of the identifiable formations. The vector, or intersection, where the lines crossed was where we were.

At that point the picture became clear, and landmarks on both our maps became recognizable. It turned out that Barry's map, printed from software he'd purchased, was exactly one mile off.

That experience proved that the old-fashioned magnetic compass is far from obsolete. It doesn't need batteries, it doesn't wear out, and it can never be in error, providing its user compensates for magnetic declination (the difference between *True North* and the *Magnetic North Pole*). Geographic anomalies that can affect performance (like the magnetized iron veins routinely encountered in Michigan's Huron Mountain range) are usually obvious from erratic movements of the indicator dial or needle. Beyond that, only a sticky indicator or actual breakage can take a compass out of commission.

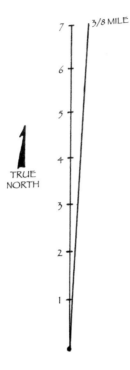

The effect of a 3-degree error over a distance of 5 miles is negligible—don't make orienteering more complicated than it needs to be.

What a compass cannot do is tell you exactly where you are. When I vectored our position in the Rockies, it was from known, distant landmarks in open country. In dense forest where visibility might be limited to only a few yards, even the most sophisticated sighting compass is reduced to merely pointing toward magnetic north. That isn't a problem if you know where you came from and you've kept track of your route, but if you've just survived a plane crash in timber country, or had your kayak blown ashore by a typhoon, you might have only a vague idea of your location.

A GPS receives data from *geostationary satellites* that serve as permanent electronic landmarks. By vectoring microwave signals from these beacons, the GPS can calculate its own location to within a few feet. In real life, heavy forest canopy has been known to block signals, and, to a lesser degree, so can falling snow or rain.

Subzero cold is tough on everything. The dampening fluid inside a liquid-filled compass's indicator capsule, used to decrease needle bounce, won't freeze, but repeated exposure to warm and cold can cause an air bubble to form inside the capsule. Small bubbles have no effect on performance, but air pockets can eventually grow large enough to block the indicator from turning—rotating-bezel types are unaffected by air bubbles.

The most detrimental effect of cold on a GPS is reduced battery life. Even with fresh batteries, a few hours of exposure to subfreezing temps can deplete them. Another problem has been frosting of battery contacts, but this is remedied by rolling batteries back and forth a few times under your thumb. Electronics are tolerant of heat up to about 160 degrees Fahrenheit, but temperatures of minus four or lower can destroy a unit's LCD screen, and may crack circuit boards. The best safeguard is to carry the unit in a pocket, keeping it warm.

Another nice, but potentially hazardous, feature of a GPS is its "plotter" mode. This function allows a person to wander at will, with no thought to landmarks or navigation, while the GPS automatically keeps track of changes in direction and distances traveled. When its user wants to return to the point of origin, he sets the unit to its backtrack mode and follows an arrow displayed on the LCD. This can be a useful feature, presuming the GPS remains operational. The danger is that using the plotter mode induces hikers to pay less attention to landmarks and direction. Should the unit be lost, or otherwise taken out of service, its user is likely to be completely lost.

Orienteers should also be aware that the map grids used to reference GPS and compass readings are entirely different from one another.

The compass references from a geometric scale that divides planet Earth into four equal parts of 180 degrees each, with zero-degrees occurring at the International Date Line in Greenwich, England, for longitude (east-west), and at the equator for latitude (north-south). The large irregular squares formed by intersecting lines of latitude and longitude are sub-divided into "minutes" (one-sixtieth of a degree) and "seconds" (one-sixtieth of a minute).

A GPS uses a system of 60 north-south Grid Zones and 60 east-west Central Meridian lines that begin and end at the same zero points in Greenwich and at the equator. Instead of breaking coordinates down into degrees, minutes, and seconds, the Universal Transverse Mercator grid uses a simpler base-ten system of meters. Depending on how close-up the scale is on your map, determining an exact position can be precise to within forty inches.

Any map is better than no map, but full-color topographical maps scaled to be both GPS- and compass-friendly are available from the United States Geological Survey (www.usgs.gov). These cost $5 per map, plus $4 shipping and handling per order, so it pays to order several at once.

The bottom line is that both GPS and compass are invaluable to a fully outfitted orienteer. A compass virtually guarantees that you will never be lost, but nothing beats a GPS for finding a remote cabin in an untracked winter woods. Maybe the best advice is found on the first page of the instruction manual for Eagle Electronics' Expedition II GPS: "A careful navigator never relies on only one method to obtain position information."

The compasses available to a New Millennium survivalist or prepper were the stuff of science fiction to our first cartographers.

Using a Compass

Human beings don't have an instinctive sense of direction, and anthropologists believe we probably never did. The ferric deposit that acts as a compass in the snouts of most animals is present in our own noses, but we lack the sensory neural connections that would enable us to recognize magnetic north by feel alone.

Because our species has no sense of direction, we need directional indicators to find our way through untracked wilderness. In prehistory, our nomadic ancestors depended on reliable natural indicators, like the sun, moon, and stars, prevailing winds, tall pines whose north-facing branches had been killed by northerly winter winds, and natural landmarks like mountains. Early Egyptian sailors discovered that a lodestone (magnet) buoyed atop water will always align itself with Earth's magnetic north pole. With that constant unfailing point of reference, travelers could always know which direction they were heading, and it was for the first time possible to maintain a straight course across vast areas of land or water that had previously been impassable barriers.

The beauty of a compass has always been its simplicity and near-absolute reliability. All the needle or dial of the most sophisticated compass actually does is point toward magnetic north, but it does that all of the time, without batteries, for so long as there's a north pole. A magnet at the north end of the needle or dial is attracted toward our planet's magnetic north pole when the compass is held flat in the user's palm, parallel to the ground. By turning the compass body or rotating dial (bezel) so that the north-pointing indicator is in agreement with the N on the compass dial, you know east is to the right, west to the left, and south directly to your rear. (Putting the first letters of those four directions together also spells *NEWS*—information from all four directions).

Just knowing where the four directions lie is enough to keep hikers from making the universal mistake of wandering in circles. But if you want to use your compass to get back out of the woods in a place at least close to where you came in, you'll need to take a "bearing" before you start. That means aligning your compass with north as described above, then using the information it provides to determine which direction you'll be taking into—and back out of—the forest.

If you're about to enter thick swamp from a two-track road, you need to know in which direction that road lies once it's out of sight. Landmarks like roads, railroad grades, and rivers are ideal as "back-bearing" targets, because they span large areas and are difficult to miss. If you leave the road by walking eastward into a woods, finding that road again is as simple as walking west. For most outdoorsmen in most situations, that's all the orienteering you'll need to know.

Likewise, most campers, fishermen, and hunters don't need the complexity and expense of precision navigation instruments. Compasses designed to precisely navigate through many miles of untracked wilderness are more than is generally needed to get across a town that has been made unrecognizable by an earthquake. Instead of buying one really expensive compass, you might be further ahead to purchase several less complex (but still quality-made) models.

Beware needle-type liquid-filled compasses that have a bubble of any size inside their capsules. Small bubbles occur over time, and when a bubble grows large enough, it can prevent the indicator from turning freely, or at all. Note that bubbles are usually a problem only for needle-type indicators—not for liquid-filled compasses in which the entire bezel (outer ring) rotates to indicate direction.

A compass I carry always is a simple "pocket" compass, like Silva's Type 7 ($10), worn around my neck on a string and tucked inside my shirt. Simple doesn't mean low quality, because a good pocket compass is as serious an orienteering tool as its more sophisticated counterparts; it just lacks the precision sights and other accessories that most dayhikers won't need.

Natural Compasses

In the 1991 film *The Black Robe*, a circa-1600s Jesuit priest travels with Huron Indians into the Canadian outback to bring unappreciative natives the word of his God. At one point, the priest wanders off to relieve himself, and becomes lost in the forest. Panicked, he wanders aimlessly until a hunting party of his guides passes by, and leads him the hundred yards to camp.

Chuckling at his ineptness, one of the Hurons asks, "Black Robe, did you not look at the trees?" Four hundred years later, my own sister argued vehemently that when she and her husband got lost traveling unfamiliar logging roads in their 4 × 4, he couldn't possibly have regained his bearings by recognizing a water-filled hole in the road.

At any latitude or altitude where cold winter winds kill tree branches, the winds that do the damage will be generally out of the northwest, which means that the heaviest limbs point southeast. This phenomenon is dictated by the rotation of the planet and is true everywhere.

Even without on-board senses that provide a constant, fixed point on which to base navigational calculations (like "lower" animals), no species ever thrived so globally as *Homo sapiens*. Nomadic peoples learned early on that Earth's moon and sun cross the sky from east to west, and humans were navigating over the Earth, using an array of natural compasses to guide them, long before ancient Egyptian sailors invented the compass.

While moon and sun move east to west across Earth's sky, they are directly overhead only at the equator. From anywhere in the northern hemisphere, both are in the southern sky—southeast when they rise, due south at noon/midnight, and southwest when they wane. In Australia or South America, sun and moon cross east to west in the northern sky.

Knowing the course and the horizon azimuth of sun and moon also makes a moot point of the purportedly old woodsman's trick of using your wristwatch and the sun as a compass. This process relies entirely on the same solar and lunar orbits described above. From anywhere north of the equator, a person facing

Most folks know the sun travels across the sky east to west, but the moon also travels east to west.

sun or moon is facing generally south, definitely not north, and if you know whether it's morning or afternoon (early evening or pre-dawn if you're fixing on the moon), then you also have a good indicator of east or west.

In contradiction to one too-common myth, in many a mature northern forest you're actually more likely to find moss growing on the south sides of tree trunks than the north. This is because prevailing winter winds from the northwest, drawn directly from the Arctic Circle by a winter weather pattern known today as the *Polar Vortex* can kill chlorophyll-dependent plants that are directly exposed to its subzero winds. This phenomenon can also be seen on the northwest-facing sides of hills and mountains, which might be entirely devoid of life on one side alone.

Likewise, tall trees—pines and firs, most noticeably—that must endure harsh winter winds are frequently sparse to naked on their northern sides, with all or most of their uppermost branches pointing southward. When these are in the scene, it's possible to maintain a fairly straight direction with no compass, even under a sunless sky. This has been one of my most valuable natural compasses. I have too little imagination to see most constellations, especially the complex forms of animals and people, but stellar landmarks have been a mainstay of humans since before recorded history. Navigation by the stars can be quite precise if you learn to account for seasonal, even daily movements, relative to their apparent location in the skies above us, and if you have the sighting tools to pinpoint those locations. But few people who need to set a course by them will need to be as exact as Columbus tried to be.

Forget about Polaris (the North Star); if you're walking toward the Big Dipper, you're heading north, and that's as accurate as you need to get in all but the longest treks.

For example, most of us can find the Big Dipper. You can learn to count stars on its stellar handle to locate Polaris, the North Star, but this is a lot like the wristwatch trick—if you are facing *Ursa major*, you are facing generally north. Be aware that the Big Dipper turns completely over between the summer solstice, when its handle points toward Earth, and winter, when the handle points upward.

To the south, but visible only in winter, is another of the few astronomical features that I can recognize: the three bright, diagonal stars in the belt of Orion, the Hunter. The figure of Orion himself is beyond my comprehension, but those three bright stars extending from the lower east to the upper west have been a guide for me on many a nighttime snowshoe trail. In summer—an example of how the Earth and stars move in relation to one another from season to season—the belt cannot be seen in the northern hemisphere.

Winds across North America are predominantly from the northeast. Disregard the direction of wind currents near to ground, because these can literally blow from all four directions in the space of a few minutes; instead, look to the clouds, because they will be driven by prevailing air currents, which blow in an easterly direction, because of the rotation of our planet.

These natural navigational icons are reliable and available, which by itself makes them invaluable. They are not the precise orienteering tools provided with a quality prismatic or lensatic sighting compass, or a GPS, but they don't need to be, because the closest recognizable landmark is almost always within 5 miles.

Pace Counter

As important as it is to recognize landmarks, and to know in which direction you're traveling, it might be critical to know how much distance you've traveled. The probability of navigational inaccuracy increases as the length of the trek increases, or if the route incorporates multiple changes in direction.

Not getting lost in the woods is only the beginning of learning to orienteer; finding a remote cabin in thick, untracked forest, where missing it by 50 yards might mean missing it entirely, that's the challenge. You need to know your location, direction of travel, and the distance you've traveled, on any leg of your trek, as precisely as possible.

A pace counter is a time-honored method of doing that. Simple to make, and easy to use, the bead-type pace counter has been helping woodsmen to navigate trackless forest since frontier days. It was invaluable to Long Range Reconnaissance Patrols (LRRPs, or Lurps) in Vietnam, and it's still very much in use by backwoodsmen today, even in this era of GPS. In fact, complete independence from outside technology is precisely why every survival-minded person needs to know the compass/map/pace counter system intimately.

Physically, a pace counter is less complicated than a monkey wrench. Making one requires knowing that there are 1,760 yards in a mile, then stringing 17 beads over a cord whose inside diameter is such that friction holds each bead snugly in place, wherever it's slid.

For every 100 yards, a bead is slid from one end of the cord, where they're grouped together at the beginning, to the opposite end. Two beads equals 200 paces, 5 beads equals 500 paces, and so on. Presuming that one step equals one yard, 100 steps means that 1 bead is slid to the opposite end; 17 beads slid to that end equals 1,700 yards. Add 60 more yards, and you've walked 1 mile. In real life, few people step-off exactly one yard. So, when you're making your own, individualized pace counter, first determine how many of your own steps equals 100 yards. If you have very long legs, that might be only 87 steps; very short legs might require 111 steps.

Pace off 100 yards half a dozen times on a flat, even surface to establish an average. Do not expect tape-measure precision; that isn't possible. Differences in stride length can result from variations in terrain, uphill or downhill grades, snow, sand, and other impediments that may hinder or shorten your normal stride.

When you've trekked one mile—1,700 yards, plus 60—return all seventeen 100-yard beads to their original position, ready to start over again. Then slide one bead in a group of (usually) five beads—separated from the group of seventeen beads by a knot tied in the middle of the cord—to the opposite end. Each bead in this smaller group denotes one mile of walking.

When you've slid all five of the mile-counter beads to the far end, you've hiked 5 miles. There are few places on Earth where you can walk 5 miles without encountering a positively identifiable landmark. But if you happen to be someplace where that is possible, the solution is to add more beads.

Belying this simple tool's usefulness, manufactured pace counters sell for as little as $5 at army surplus stores. But if you have a length of rope or cord (doubled parachute cord is popular) and a handful of beads that fit over it snugly enough to stay where you slide them, you can make your own. The pace counter I use now was made using beads fashioned from half-inch sections of rubber insulation, cut from a length of electrical cord, then threaded onto a 2-foot piece of ordinary clothesline rope. Pace counters have even been made from string and clothing buttons, or steel nuts threaded onto rope—use your imagination.

Likewise, distances: the pace counter shown is calibrated to miles and yards, and meant to be used with a map scaled to miles. If you prefer to work in kilometers, reduce the number of beads in the larger group to 10, then determine how many paces (usually around 60) that you need to walk to cover 100 meters—100 meters times 10 equals 1,000 meters, or 1 kilometer. Each bead in the smaller, opposite group then equals 1 kilometer, instead of 1 mile.

As simple as a pace counter is, it's invaluable for precision cross-country navigation. A compass keeps you traveling in a straight direction, and enables precise course changes, a map gives you a preview of terrain, and a pace counters allows you to keep close track of distances traveled. Put them together, and you have an almost-perfect orienteering system.

With a map. compass, and pace counter, you can find almost anything, navigate anywhere, and these things should be part of every disaster-preparation survival kit.

Map

A huge advantage that we have over humans of even the mid-twentieth century is that no place on Earth is unknown to us. Thanks to centuries of cartographers, modern humans can know where they're going at all times. Every mile of our planet has been discovered and recorded in detail. We can know precisely where we're going—every hill, every river, every road—before we ever get there. There is a wide range of maps with different features, scaled to a spectrum of distances, heights, and depths. Don't get caught up in numbers; even the most sophisticated map is nothing more than an aerial picture of the area. Aside from the scale (miles, kilometers, yards) printed on a bottom border, all you're really interested in is the lay of the land—the location and distances of pertinent landmarks. A gas station map is usually sufficient, if you know what to do with it.

Whatever type of map you have, it might be invaluable to you. Treat it like a valuable instrument. If it isn't laminated, cover it with clear contact paper, ironed on (under a towel) to thoroughly bond it to the paper. A further protection, place the folded map into a Ziploc bag.

Triangulation

We'd been following a mountain road that wasn't on the maps for hours. Terrain was rugged, and the going was slow, and it was late afternoon when we decided that we'd better get our bearings. None of the three of us had ever been here before, and we had only a vague idea of our location.

One of my companions and I climbed atop a granite ridge, where we could look down onto the surrounding countryside. From there, I could see the bay, and a small lake, about a mile inland from it. To its left, I could see a mountain peak whose configuration made it easy to identify on my topographical map.

Using the sights on my prismatic compass, I "shot" a bearing to a point on the bay: 45 degrees. The peak was at 326 degrees.

What I really needed to know was not where those landmarks were, relative to my position, but where I was, relative to their position.

That meant I had to figure 180 degrees—the opposite direction—from where they were. From the mountain peak—326 degrees—I used a grease pencil to draw a line backward, toward myself, at 146 degrees (326 minus 180 equals 146). From the point on the bay—45 degrees—I drew a line at 225 (45 plus 180 equals 225) degrees. We stood at the point where those two lines intersected.

Strictly speaking, this procedure is known as "vectoring," because it doesn't use the three reference points needed for proper triangulation. When you reference from three points, you create a triangle where the lines intersect. Your position is in the center of that triangle. Triangulation is considered more accurate, but vectoring has always been adequate for me.

Simple and easy to use, the newest signal mirrors are so lightweight that they float, while polished, concave reflecting surfaces, and improved sighting apertures deliver unsurpassed brightness when help is needed.

Using a Signal Mirror

Using a handheld signal mirror is simple enough that every child can learn to use one effectively with only minutes of training, and it can be worked with one hand by a person who's severely injured. All of them have a sighting hole through which one can look with one eye while you focus reflected sunlight onto a target. Modern *Lexan* mirrors, like Ultimate Survival Technologies' floating *StarFlash* model have a mesh sighting hole that prevents being blinded.

To start, look through the sighting hole and find the target—airplane or search party, for example—and, keeping the target centered in the sight, swivel the mirror at different angles until a bright spot appears. Place that bright spot onto the point that you're trying to signal, and you can be assured that anyone covered by that spot of light will also see a bright light when they look in your direction.

Next is to positively affirm to anyone who spies reflections from your mirror that they aren't just seeing sunlight glinting off a discarded beer can. The most fundamental of signals is the time-honored survivalists "signal of threes." Three gunshots in the air is an internationally recognized distress call among hunters. Three blasts on a signal whistle, three clacks of rocks being struck together—any sight or sound in repeated sets of threes is a call for help. Three flashes of light, a pause, and then another set of three flashes, repeated over and over are a sure sign to any rescuer that you need assistance.

Even better is the classic SOS signal. Originally designated as Save Our Ship in the days of Marconi's wireless, SOS is also a signal of threes. Three short signals, represented graphically as dots, constitute the letter S. Three longer signals—flashes that are approximately twice as long—are represented by three dashes, and signify the letter O. Three short (...), a two second pause, three long (---), and three short mean SOS to anyone trained in survival or search-and-rescue.

Morse Code

While the letters SOS are fundamental to the most basic survival training, it might one day be important to send actual words. The time-proven system for doing that since the 1840s is Morse Code; only in 1999 did knowing it not become a requirement for US Navy pilots. From the first telegraphs to visual maritime signals to Marconi's lifesaving wireless, Morse Code made transmitting and receiving sophisticated intelligence across vast distances reality a century before voice communications.

A beauty of the Morse system is its versatility. Information is contained in the way a series of signals of short duration—dots—are interspersed with signals of longer duration—dashes. Morse's alphabet works with light, reflections, radio, and telegraph—even with two rocks clacked together.

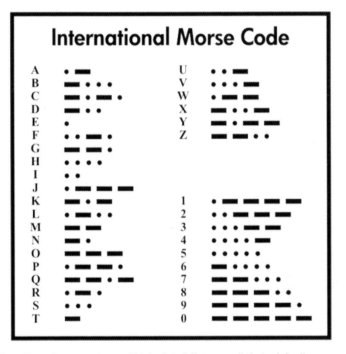

International Morse Code

Even if you just want to tap SOS (a dated distress call that originally was an abbreviation of SAVE OUR SHIP), with two rocks to alert someone far away, you need a system with which to send cogent messages. Morse Code remains as viable an answer to that problem as it ever was.

The FCC has recognized that Morse is no longer a realistic requirement for amateur radio licenses. But even if a rescuer can't decipher the signals he sees, it should be obvious that it's code. You needn't remember it if you have a ready reference. A printed or redrawn copy of the signals shown here is sufficiently lightweight to be laminated, even with overlapping strips of clear boxing tape, and carried unnoticed in multiple locations.

Emergency Ground-to-Air Signals

**International Emergency
Ground-to-Air Signals**

Which Way?	This Way	OK to Land	I'm OK
No	Yes	I Don't Understand	I Need a Compass
I'm Hurt	I Need Medical Assistance	I Can't Proceed	I Need Food and Water

These Emergency Ground-to-Air Signals are recognized internationally by Search-and-Rescue pilots who look for them stamped in the snow, scratched into sand, formed of dead logs—created with whatever might be available.

In his book *Alive*, author Piers Paul Morgan detailed the plight of a Uruguayan rugby team whose plane crashed in the Andes Mountains in 1972. Reduced to cannibalism, the victims were in dire straits. One of the signals they used in vain to attract attention from overflying aircraft was the Cross in the Snow, a stamped-out figure made from two intersected troughs in the snow.

The signal was unsuccessful for the rugby team. It was clearly visible from the air, but not from the angles of jetliners that never passed close enough to see it. It wasn't a proper, internationally recognized distress signal, and it was in a poor location.

These symbols are internationally recognized by every search-and-rescue pilot on Earth. There is no right or wrong way to form them as long as the figures are clearly discernible from a cockpit. Dead graying logs laid out in a mountain meadow, troughs heel-gouged into wet sand at a beach, fires arrayed into shapes at night—any method that will convey a visual image from the ground to an overhead location is the right way.

CHAPTER FOUR

FIRE

Fire

Fire can keep you alive. It's not an exaggeration to state that fire might be *the* thing that keeps you and your loved ones alive. If you can build and maintain a fire, it becomes virtually impossible for you to die from hypothermia, regardless of how inadequately dressed you might be. A metal fuel can, several feet of rubber hose, and a small fire can enable you to distill unpotable water nonstop—which would have allowed all the people who've been compelled to drink putrid water in the aftermath of a disaster to avoid the epidemic of cholera and disease that followed. Cooking kills harmful organisms in food, and it helps to break down proteins, making that food more digestible. A bright fire can be seen from miles away at night, and billowing clouds of smoke will attract attention.

None of those vital uses for fire has the lifesaving urgency of using fire to stave off or remedy hypothermia. An ice fisherman who has just been dragged out of a hole in thin ice doesn't have the lifetime left to warm up the car, or maybe even for an ambulance to arrive. There exists a multitude of serious reasons for needing the emergency warmth of a fire, and you can almost bet that all of them will occur in an environment that is not conducive to making fire—in fact, that seems to be a rule. Troubles are amplified if you're alone, numb fingers curling involuntarily into life-less claws, abdominal muscles cramping as they try to keep vital organs warm, and miserable spasms of uncontrollable shivering that make simple tasks undoable. There is no time to waste with fire-making tools that cannot produce immediate results.

Bark from the White, or Paper, Birch is one of many natural fire-starting tinders available to a survivalist.

Tinder

Tinder is the first, most critical, step in making fire. The most common mistake made by beginners is trying to light a campfire by applying flame to wood that is too massive to be lighted. Every fire begins small, starting with easily flammable tinder materials that burn hot and fast in open air. Burn duration of tinder materials is typically short, but the idea is to use a brief, hot flame to ignite slightly larger dry twigs, then branches, until a hot bed of red coals below provides enough heat to burn the largest pieces of wood.

One of nature's wonders: Nutritious, medicinal, and flammable when dry, reindeer moss is found growing all over the world.

Birch bark, and numerous other natural tinders, burn at the touch of a flame, or even a hot spark.

There is no terrain on which vegetation grows where you can't find tinder for making a fire. Tinders that catch fire with a hot spark or the touch of flame include dried reindeer moss (not really a moss, but a lichen), dead grasses, fine strips of birch bark, or the massed fibers of dead aspen or poplar bark, separated by crumbling the brittle bark from around them. Shed pine needles contain resins that make them burn easily, and even damp ones that won't stay burning can be coaxed by gently blowing the coals to life. The same with tiny dry pine twigs found at the end of dead pine branches; one of my survival class demonstrations is to hold a small bundle of tiny dead pine twigs in one hand, and light them into a flaming mass using only a butane lighter. Even in the dead of winter, grass stems sticking above the snow reveal that there are more freeze-dried, flammable grasses below.

Dried tree sap, or pitch, exuded from woodpecker holes and other injuries in pine, cherry, and some other trees, is always flammable once it has been heated to a liquid state. Sap is long-burning enough to have once been used for torches of pitch-saturated grass. A lump of pitch melted onto small twigs with a match is usually enough to set them afire.

If no suitable natural tinder is available, you can make our own by reducing larger pieces of dry wood to more flammable shavings and splinters. The process is as simple as whittling-off a small mound of shavings from available dry wood with your knife. The smaller and finer the shavings, the more easily they will ignite, but count on needing a dinner plate–size mound of shavings to create a flame of sufficient duration to ignite larger twigs.

Wax-soaked cotton string can be used as a lanyard for a small compass, and pieces removed as needed to start fires.

Cotton string saturated with molten paraffin (canning wax) is possibly the best manufactured fire-starter ever created.

The best and most fail-safe tinder materials are small enough to carry in your own pocket. Simplest, cheapest, and all-around best of manufactured survival tinders is the Fire Wick—essentially nothing more than cotton laundry/packaging string that has been dipped into molten paraffin (canning wax), cooled until stiff, then cut into sections and packaged for carry. Some survivalists get fancy and twist-lock or braid string into thick lengths before dipping to create heavy, long-burning wicks. Some get the same effect from doubling a string several times, and simply tying the combined string into large knots before dipping it in wax. Cotton balls dipped into molten paraffin are also great fire wicks. Wool felt weather-stripping, available in rolls from hardware stores, has been a good alternative; it absorbs more wax and burns longer, but is harder to light. With any of these materials, one end or corner of the tinder should be frayed with a fingernail prior to lighting.

Other homebrewed tinders include cotton balls saturated with petroleum jelly, and carried in a pill bottle (too messy, and they tend to dry out), cardboard or cotton flannel saturated with paraffin, or scraps of singed-brown cotton flannel (char cloth, in frontiersman terms), carried in a watertight tinder box. If you have a gun, the bullet can be levered from a cartridge, and the powder inside used to ignite tinder. In a pinch, a bullet-less cartridge, with powder still inside, can be plugged with a ball of dried grasses, and discharged inside a mass of easily lighted tinder. Although very cool when it works, the muzzle blast sometimes just throws tinder aside without lighting it, and you waste precious ammo with every attempt, so use this method judiciously.

Military fuel bars, like the Trioxane and Hexamine used by American and British armies, are sold, usually inexpensively, in Army-Navy stores and catalogs, and either is a must-have for the all-weather fire-starting kit. Made for cooking with a small folding stove, these fuel bars ignite at the touch of a flame in any weather, and burn hot for several minutes.

Fire-Starting Basics

The first step in starting a campfire is to find a suitable location.

When using a shelter, the fire should always be located directly in front of the entrance, but at a distance that will keep flames or sparks from setting the shelter afire. In windy weather both the fire and shelter should be located on the lee side of a hill or in thickly wooded terrain to help block air currents that can blow hot sparks into the woods and create a wind chill factor in cold weather. As an added precaution, all combustible debris should be scraped or kicked away from the campfire for at least three feet in all directions.

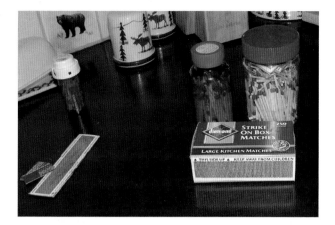

Fire-starting kits can take a lot of forms, many of them watertight.

The next step is to create a fire pit to help contain popping coals, block wind, and to reflect radiated heat back onto the coal bed, making the fire bed hotter. The traditional method of creating a fire pit is to place large stones around its circumference; stones absorb and hold heat from the fire for up to many hours, and a cold survivalist can use heated stones to keep warm through the night by placing one at the foot of a bedroll, or even just hugging a large one against his belly. Be warned never to expose stones taken from a stream bed to open fire; it rarely happens, but I've seen waterlogged stones heat and explode like a grenade. In lieu of stones, excavate the fire pit to a diameter of about eighteen inches by six inches deep, and arrange the excavated soil into a low fire wall surrounding the pit's perimeter.

Starting a Fire

The next step is to lay the fire in preparation for lighting; begin by placing the tinder material—which can be a mixture of different tinders—in the center of the fire pit. A platform of finger-thick dead sticks laid parallel-fashion on the ground, and especially atop snow, gives your fledgling fire a head start, allowing it to develop a hot coal bed before making contact with wet earth. Once a good coal bed has been established, a fire—insulated from below by its own ashes—will just melt away the snow around it until it reaches bare ground, but a platform is essential to efficient fire-making. Lay your tinder in a loose, airy mass in the center of the platform.

Next, lay a teepee of small, dry sticks, none bigger than a pencil, around the circumference of the tinder pile so that they come together and support one another about eight inches above the floor of the fire pit. This cone-shaped pocket of kindling helps to hold the tinder from blowing away, and provides an umbrella for the tinder fire while allowing maximum exposure of each stick to flames. The teepee method of arranging kindling will ensure that a sizeable air gap exists between the tinder pile and the sticks above it, as well as between the kindling sticks themselves.

When the woods are wet, you might use a manufactured tinder (fire-wicks, trioxane, and hexamine) for the initial stage, using it to dry, then ignite waterlogged natural tinders, which in turn burn long and hot enough to dry and ignite the kindling teepee. When the woods are wet, take kindling sticks for the teepee from the trunks of standing trees, some of which will always have dead twigs attached within easy reach. Shielded from rain by foliage and suspended in open air, dead twigs still attached to trunks are always driest, whereas those lying on the ground are likely to remain damp for weeks. Wood from the ground is fine for a campfire that

Decades of experience with spark-type fire-starting tools has shown that bigger is better.

has a self-sustaining bed of coals—in fact, wet, rotting wood thrown on hot coals is good for signals, and as insect repellent (smoke)—but starting a fire requires having the driest kindling you can find.

With platform, tinder, and kindling teepee in place, apply a flame to the tinder, either directly using a match or lighter, or with a lighted fire wick or other combustible material. A good flint-and-steel, like the *Strike Force*, permits the grip and pressure needed to strike sparks hot enough to ignite even damp tinders. Add more tinder to the base of the teepee until the teepee sticks begin to flame hotly, then carefully add more sticks,

one at a time, and so as not to smother the still-weak flames. When a solid bed of red coals has formed atop the platform, begin laying progressively larger kindling sticks lengthwise and parallel to one another atop the coals. Gently blow into the coals until they glow hotly, causing the fresh sticks to smoke, and the flame. Continue adding more wood until the parallel furnace pile is as large as you need it to be.

A Fire Wick burns completely, even when wet or atop snow.

Getting Firewood

Where you can start a fire, there will probably be fuel to sustain it, but available large-diameter, long-burning logs will not be in convenient lengths. Do not waste energy trying to break large wood to fire-size lengths. The simplest method is to simply lay the ends of two or

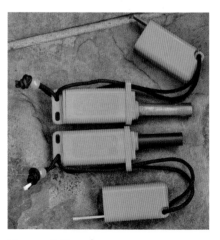

The new Strike Force fire starter has been changed over the years, but trials show that new versions work equally well.

more large trunks onto the coal bed from opposite sides, parallel to one another. As the ends are consumed, feed each length farther into the fire. Alternatively, you can burn lengths in half, but if the length is elevated at either end, be prepared for the fire to burn down under and away from the log. You might have to keep adding wood from below before large ones burn in half.

Forests are constantly shedding dead branches, and there should be an abundance of smaller branches on the ground, along with a few wind-sheared tree tops, and an occasional whole dead tree. Drag lengths to your fire butt-end first, so the natural upward angle of still-attached branches helps to keep them from snagging against other trees. On deep hardpack snow, all firewood must come from standing trees, and sometimes standing dead trees will have rotted enough to be pushed over and dragged back to your fire.

Be sure to lay in a good supply of wood before making camp each night, because, even if you have a flashlight, there is a potential for injury in untracked woods. In some places, you could walk off a cliff, or turn an ankle, or suffer a twig to the eyeball.

The Heating Fire

Fire generates heat, and how a fire is arranged determines how much. Many cold nights have proved that once a hot bed of coals is created, laying firewood lengths side-by-side atop them is most efficient. Seen end-on, the stacked wood resembles a pyramid, and it can be built higher and hotter by adding more wood of almost any length or diameter to the pile. This type of heating fire throws its heat to either long side. That heat can be used even more efficiently by placing yourself between the fire and any solid reflecting surface at least 3 feet. This *reflector* can even be made of snow.

The Coal Bed

A coal bed was once used by mountain men to help keep warm during frigid winter nights, when a five-point wool blanket was a standard bedroll. A coal bed prevents a sleeper from getting cold by providing a constant, slowly diminishing, source of heat from below. A coal bed can keep a person warm throughout the night, even with a light bedroll in— −25 degrees Fahrenheit, and I can attest to that personally.

The first step is to build a long, hot fire that measures approximately 4 feet wide by 7 feet long using a small shovel or entrenching tool, or even a slab of wood (a shallow grave, jokingly). The fire should be fueled until a 2- to 3-inch bed of red coals forms. The glowing bed of coals is then covered with loose dirt that you removed from the hole, then tamped down. An alternate method is to excavate a shallow, body-length depression and then shovel hot coals into it, again, covering them with the dirt taken from the excavation.

The dirt-covered coal bed can be used without further work, but I've learned that the normal rolling and shifting of position that occurs during sleep can brush away protective earth and bring the sleeper to a rude, painful awakening. As protection against this, I lay a thin layer of pine boughs or leafy branches over the dirt, and cover them with a poncho or ground sheet.

Cooking Fire

Cooking over an open fire makes a fool out of most skilled gourmet cooks. The most common mistake is trying to cook over a flaming campfire; a campfire generates greater heat than a kitchen range, and food cooked in flames tends to burn on the outside before it cooks on the inside.

A fire made using the "furnace pile" configuration of parallel logs provides at least one flat, heated spot on which to set a cooking vessel. Flames forced through gaps between burning logs make ideal range burners. Larger logs do not burn away below a cooking vessel, allowing it to spill, and focused heat blasting up from between logs is easier to cook over. Bear in mind that you can't regulate heat, so you regulate exposure—if food is cooking too fast, move it farther from the heat.

A spit is a traditional way to cook small animals; it doesn't require any cooking vessels, and is the easiest way to cook game in a survival situation. A spit begins with two forked sticks driven vertically into the ground on either side of a fire pit. The straight, bottom end of each stick should be pushed at least six inches into the soil, and both should be stable enough not to fall over under the weight of the loaded spit. The crotch of these support sticks should be approximately two feet above the floor of the fire pit. The sticks should be made from green wood, although dry wood can be used if the sticks are placed far enough from the fire to keep them from catching fire.

The spit itself should be constructed of green wood at least an inch in diameter and long enough to extend beyond the crotch of either support stick. The spit is sharpened on one end and threaded through the rib cage, and through the pelvis, for small mammals. Small birds or fish are simply speared through the ribs and slid over the spit. Larger fish are spitted by piercing them at an angle near the tail, bending the body into a U and piercing again near the head. I recommend avoiding pine woods for a spit, as these can taint food with a taste of turpentine.

Suspend a spitted animal or fish over a low fire by setting the end of the spit into the crotch of the support stick at either end and sliding the meat to the center of the spit. The fire beneath it should be kept low, and the meat turned frequently. Cook all wild meat or fish completely, and never eat raw wild game or fish, because most species can carry parasites.

Wilderness cooking is just one of the activities in which the leather work gloves are a useful tool. Leather gloves offer protection when working around burning wood. They aren't impervious to fire, but they enable quick handling of burning wood or hot cookware, as well as protecting against cuts and slivers.

Ashes

When boiling wild plants to eat, add a tablespoon of wood ashes to the water. Adding wood ashes to soups is a tradition among Indians—an Odawa friend told me that his grandmother used to sneak a spoonful of wood ashes from the fireplace into cookpots when his mother wasn't looking. This was long thought to be a ceremonial habit among Native Americans, but in 1996, modern science learned that caustic elements in wood ashes break down tough plant cellulose, allowing the human digestive system to convert indigestible proteins into usable amino acids. An ability to enhance the digestibility of tough plants (and meat) broadens your food choices, and helps to get the most from plants you eat.

In times past, no one put out a fire when they left their cabin or camp; they banked it.

Banking a Fire

Aboriginal humans have never extinguished their camp fires unless they were leaving the place for a long time. In real life, putting out the fire to go hunting for a day was impractical, and maybe unwise, because it would be needed that evening, and conditions might not be so agreeable for making fire by then. The trick was to "bank" the fire so that it neither burned nor died out, but remained at a smoldering idle that could be quickly rebuilt into a warm blaze. This uncomplicated, but seldom-described technique is basically little more than half-smothering a bed of hot coals with one or more large-diameter logs placed side-by-side on top of them. Good banking logs include wet, rotting trunks that are too big and damp to catch fire, but can slowly dry and smolder just enough to keep the coals below hot. Just roll the logs over to expose hot coals that can be used to ignite tinder by gently blowing them to flaming hotness—when restarting a fire from coals, remember that dead coals placed atop red coals will reheat to red-hotness from contact. Left for too long, the banking logs will smolder away from the coal bed, until the gap between them is too great, and the coals starve.

A banked fire can smolder for more than a day, then quickly be brought back to life.

Making a fire atop snow or wet ground is an essential skill for every urban or backcountry survivalist.

The Signal Fire

In a conversation with Bob Garner, who once hosted the *Michigan Out-of-Doors* television program, he told me that his idea of wilderness survival was to "build a great big goddam fire and wait for someone to come and get me."

A signal fire differs from a cooking or heating fire in its large size and intentional high visibility. It has to be large and bright to attract as much attention as possible from as many miles away as possible. The heat and sparks generated by such a big fire precludes it from being located anywhere near a shelter or other flammables. Bluffs, open beaches, and other clear, preferably high places are among the most visible choices for siting a signal fire.

To be as effective as possible, a signal fire must be as large as it can safely be. It will consume a great deal of wood quickly. For that reason, the tall teepee-shaped pyre is probably best pre-assembled and left ready to be lighted from a smaller fire nearby. Construction of the ready-made signal fire begins with a hot-burning tinder, such as dried grass, topped by a large teepee of dried twigs and sticks of a fast-burning softwood. Next comes a larger teepee of heavier branches about six feet in length. The two teepees will help keep the tinder dry by forming a roof over it. When the survivalist spots a plane or some other potential rescuer, he lights the tinder, which lights the smaller teepee of sticks. The flames from the smaller teepee will in turn ignite the larger teepee, sending a brilliant pyre of flame into the night to a height of ten feet or more.

Assuming that both tinder and wood are dry, the signal fire will flame up very quickly, usually within minutes. But be warned: the larger teepee will consume itself from the bottom up and can be expected to burn for no more than fifteen minutes before collapsing to one side. For this reason the signal fire must be located in a place where there's no danger of causing a forest fire when it falls over.

During the hours of darkness a signal fire can be seen for miles, but in daylight the flames fade to near obscurity. Watchers who man fire towers know that flames from even the hottest forest fire are difficult to see in full daylight, but a plume of smoke against the sky is highly visible. Armed with this knowledge, one can continue to signal during the day by building a large, hot fire and then partially smothering it with a layer of damp, rotting wood or wet leaves. The coals will have enough heat to burn the damp material but not enough to ignite it, and the fire will smoke heavily.

The Safe Campfire

A fire warms the body and soul, lights the darkness, makes hot meals possible, repels biting insects and every species of animal, dries wet clothing, and provides an effective means of signaling for help in an emergency. The hissing blue flame of a propane or liquid-fuel cookstove just doesn't have the same hypnotic effect that a crackling wood fire has, and old-timers can appreciate that a stove outfit weighs a heck of a lot more than a fire-starting kit.

Problem is, campfires have become politically incorrect because a few campers have, for whatever reason, improperly managed their fires. Used correctly, a campfire does no harm, and can become an island of lush new growth in a few months. Used carelessly, though, a fire can burn uncontrollably through thousands of acres, so practicing this art has become problematic in many places.

Unavailable to previous generations, a multi-fuel stove, capable of burning everything from gasoline to lamp oil, is essential to every post-disaster survival kit.

The first rule of campfire-tending is, always dig a fire pit. Unless you're camped on solid rock or beach sand, never simply build a fire atop the ground, but always lay it in an excavated hole about two feet in diameter by roughly eight inches deep. If you can accept an extra three pounds, an e-tool (folding shovel) makes digging a fire pit easy. My own SP-8 survival machete (made in the USA by Ontario Knife) works nearly as well, and in a pinch, you can even use your belt knife. Be prepared to resharpen any edged tool you employ for chopping through roots, sand, and dirt.

One caveat about the fire pit is that it must always be excavated in dirt (i.e., non-flammable soil). In a few places, like Northern Michigan's cedar swamps in summer, dry peat-like sphagnum moss can extend several feet below ground level. History has already shown that a fire in such terrain can smolder below ground, traveling slowly for perhaps a mile before springing to life as an inferno. Soil excavated from the fire pit is best formed into a low wall around the pit's perimeter, where it provides extra containment. Leave about a quarter of the wall open to facilitate cooking and fire tending, and to help maximize the amount of heat radiated.

In cold weather, I wrap a fire-heated stone inside a towel and then shove it to the foot of my sleeping bag, where it keeps my toes warm all night. Never place any rock taken from water in or near a fire; stone is porous, and when it remains submerged for an extended period, it absorbs water. Exposing a waterlogged rock to fire causes moisture inside it to expand rapidly in the form of steam, sometimes building sufficient pressure to explode the stone into sharp, hurtling fragments. I made this mistake once as a boy, and although no one was injured, the incident made a believer out of me.

After excavating and walling the perimeter of the fire pit, clear a firebreak at least four feet wide all around it by scraping any flammable material into the fire pit. This ensures that popping embers find nothing to ignite.

An old Indian proverb claims that one could always identify a white man's camp because his fire was too big. A large fire is too hot for cooking, which is best done on a bed of coals, and the bigger the fire, the more airborne embers it generates. And it's also easier to spot, should you want to remain unobtrusive.

Never site your fire under tree branches, always be sure it has a clear chimney to the sky. Aside from the obvious fire hazard, subjecting live overhead branches to smoke and heat does nothing to promote their health. Likewise, site your fire at least six feet from trees and saplings that might be ignited by heat from the sides.

Banking a Fire

In frontier times, it was actually a whipping offense for boys to let the fire in a cabin's hearth die out. Starting a new fire was often difficult, and doing so used up valuable, hard-to-replace resources. Speaking personally, it's just dumb to restart my campfire whenever I leave to go fishing, squirrel hunting, or any other short period.

Banking a fire keeps it safe, unable to catch anything else afire, but smoldering, ready to be coaxed back to flames in just a couple of minutes.

CHAPTER FIVE

SURVIVAL STASH

Caching Gear

At some point, you're going to arrive at a conclusion that maybe you just might want a cache or two of necessities hidden in an easily accessible location that nobody else knows about. The most fundamental reason behind establishing a string of caches is that there's no incriminating (remember, the patriots of the Revolutionary War were, in fact, criminals in the eyes of the ruling government) or theft-worthy goods on your person, at your house, or otherwise in evidence. A string of cache sites across the land can serve as resupply posts, keeping you healthy and strong until you reach a more defensible location.

Barrels

What you put your cache into is important. Containers that I've have good luck with include food-grade 30- to 60-gallon high-density poly-ethylene (HDPE) open-top drums. These barrels have proved themselves to be bear-proof many times (I did have a black bear unlatch a metal locking ring once, when I'd failed to secure it with a pin); a barrel I'd used at my cabin has deep claw marks in it, but no holes. Open-head barrels

Fifteen-gallon open-head barrels with a locking ring—available online for about $60—are ideal for airtight storage.

Sixty-gallon screw-top polyethylene barrels are large enough to provide weatherproof protection to long guns, with room to spare for the rest of a post-disaster survival stash.

are airtight and ideal for storage of anything that will fit inside them. They can be buried under dirt or even totally or partially submerged in mud or water. One barrel has been in place for more than thirty years, camouflaged to look like a dead stump.

Dehydrated foods are sometimes sold in resealable, multiple-meal containers, but these foil-lined cardboard "cans" are not impervious to prolonged exposure to water, and should be placed inside larger, more weatherproof tote boxes or barrels.

Totes

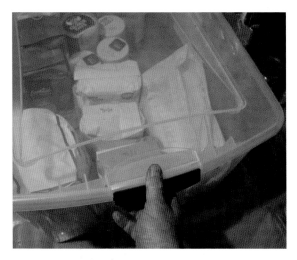

Although most are not hermetically sealed, plastic tote boxes, sold at most department stores, are good choices for assembling survival kits into all-in-one, transportable containers.

Plastic tote boxes with snap-down lids have actually surpassed expectations as cache containers. There are numerous makes and models in different capacities and price ranges, but most have overlapping lids that, if not water-tight, prevent water from gaining access there. Two of those we've personally evaluated have kept packaged food, binoculars, and a host of other gear (packaged in Ziploc) from moisture or other environmental damage. One tote was buried under six inches of soil, the other hidden under a pile of brush. Both endured a full twelve months, with winters of 200+ inches of snow.

Treasures in the Trash

My wife thinks I'm a little off plumb for carefully washing used Ziploc bags and reusing them. She has an aversion to using the recycled bags, which works out well for me, because I always need them in my backpack. She also thinks I'm weird for washing and saving clear plastic peanut butter and similar jars. I told her I need those to store my washed Ziplocs.

Now, I'm not a hoarder—I don't think I am, anyway—because I use the containers I scavenge—and I *do* consign many of them to the recycling bin. Having come from a time when backpacking was not an end in itself, but a means of remaining longer in the woods, when all tents leaked, and securing the old 9-volt AM receiver in a frameless rucksack meant wrapping it inside a plastic bread bag, I can't help but be awed at the waste my species leaves in its wake.

If a homeless man sleeping in an urban dumpster were to be somehow transported back in time three hundred years, he could be rich beyond his wildest dreams. No homesteader had ever seen a lightweight, insect-proof, see-through, dried-goods storage container to equal a screw-top peanut butter jar. Two-liter soda bottles that kept gunpowder safe and dry in any weather would be beyond value, and no canteen of the time could compare to them for water tightness and light weight. Everything from discarded spray bottles to braided nylon shoelaces, even garbage bags, would have been elevated from trash to treasure at any point in time before the mid-twentieth century. Travel back more than three hundred years, and you might be worshipped or burned at the stake, depending on locale.

Most households already salvage some items of manufactured trash, whether it's storing toothpicks in an old pill bottle, keeping screws in a mayonnaise jar, or using a cut-open Clorox jug to hold a toilet brush. In my film photography days, when airtight plastic film bottles could be had for free by the bagsful from most developing outlets, these became all-in-one fishing kits, carrying hooks, line, and sinkers securely and safely, while a strip of colored vinyl tape around the perimeter enabled an empty bottle itself to serve as a fishing float. The wrists—the part that never wears out—of old rubber gloves can be cut into hourglass shapes, and stretched over unprotected riflescope lenses like the Bikini scope covers sold at sporting goods stores.

Many of the best environment-proof containers are free.

Empty plastic coffee cans are pressed into service as multi-serving dog-kibble containers, and as easily gripped buckets for rock salt during icy winters. Screw-top polyethylene salsa bottles are great, easy-to-pour rice canisters. Flour, which is still packaged in leaky, easily damaged paper bags that are an open door to weevils, we repack more securely in large plastic tote boxes. Dried beans sold in plastic sacks, and pasta that comes in cardboard boxes that invite decomposing moisture, are stored in my great collection of peanut butter and other plastic jars. This strategy not only protects easily perishable foods (pasta) from moldering, it separates portions into stand-alone units that are less likely to all be destroyed by a single tragedy. Macaroni-and-cheese, repackaged in a plastic screw-top jar, has remained edible, after frequent exposure to elements of all types, for more than two years.

Many dehydrated food distributors are now packaging the meals they sell into larger bucket-style containers that are packed for a predetermined number of people for a given duration, helping to make preparing for a disaster as easy as it has ever been.

A manual-pump, shallow-water well ensures that we have unlimited clean water on hand for drinking, cooking, and flushing the commode, but our basement also holds forty gallons of tapwater, stored in plastic jugs whose volumes range from one gallon to six gallons. Some of these containers have stored water, with no degradation to potability, for more than sixteen years. One-gallon juice and tea jugs with carry handles are ideal, sized to be handled easily by a child, easy to transport as a canteen, and reusable for years to come.

Every post-disaster survival outfit must contain at least 2 gallons of water per person, per day.

Wire bread-bag ties, bundled and wrapped together find innumerable uses. Reused Ziploc bags protect my shortwave receiver from the elements, and keep its spare batteries handy. Twist-top Dramamine-tablet cylinders are perfect for holding acetaminophen or other pills in a first-aid kit. The number of applications a person can find for items that normally go into a garbage dump are limited only by ingenuity.

CHAPTER SIX

SHELTER IN A STORM

Shelters

Depending on conditions, shelter might well be the most important thing in your life. A cold autumn rain can kill you in a matter of hours, and, even if it doesn't, a dose of hypothermia can break down your immune system until you contract a virus.

The Versatile Debris Shelter

Nothing is more fundamental to human survival than shelter from the elements; among mammals, only our species is in peril from simple naked exposure to the out-of-doors. At 40 degrees Fahrenheit, with a wind of 25 miles per hour, the cooling effect is the same as it would be at an ambient temperature of only 10 degrees. Throw in a soaking rain that can lower felt temps by 20 degrees in a windless environment, and the result can kill an underdressed human. Lower the temperature of the strongest man's internal organs by just 5 degrees, and he will be incapacitated, probably unconscious. Any air temperature below the normal 98.6-degree human body temperature is robbing warmth from uncovered skin, and the rate of heat loss, without wind or rain, can be life threatening in temperatures as warm as 50 degrees Fahrenheit.

A debris shelter is easy to manufacture, from natural or man-made materials, in any environment.

The debris shelter is a usually compact long- or short-term emergency den that is constructed from whatever the surrounding terrain provides, not necessarily just natural materials. The name alludes to a specific type of shelter, but no two debris shelters are exactly alike, and

This debris shelter was constructed thirty-five years ago.

Regardless of season or environment, there are virtually no locations where a debris shelter cannot be constructed to get you and yours out of the weather.

A debris shelter is the only type emergency shelter that you need to master.

construction materials can vary broadly, from high-desert sagebrush to alpine evergreens, and even construction refuse found in a dumpster. The beauty of a debris shelter is that, once you have a grasp of its basics, it can be constructed from virtually any terrain, from forests to the roof of a high-rise—so a creative eye is beneficial when scouting for building materials.

The most important component for all debris shelters is a main support, a stout pole 8 to 10 feet long, 3 or more inches in diameter at the base. Suitable candidates can often be found standing upright, but dead, because some trees do not live to maturity. Ideal choices will stand more than a dozen feet tall, dry enough to snap off when you push hard against them, but solid and unrotted throughout. Bridge the thinnest end of the pole across a solid object, and heel-stomp or chop it to length; a suitably long main support should be at least 2 inches in diameter at its narrow end.

Elevate the thick end of the main support by wedging it into the limb crotch of a standing tree, into a rock crack, or onto an X-frame of two lashed-together and crossed saplings—whatever solid support will hold it at least 3 feet above the ground. It is important that the narrow end of the pole be the one against the ground, because if it should give under weight of snow, for example, only a few inches at the low end are likely to break, and the entire shelter will not come crashing down.

At this point, install the sleeping pallet on the ground directly below and parallel to the main support. This critical part of any emergency shelter serves to keep a sleeper's body from making direct contact with the Earth, which will absorb body heat faster than it can be generated, even in summer. In woodlands, the usual configuration is a platform formed by placing relatively straight, body-length, dead saplings and limbs on the ground, alongside one another, until a rough bed, about 2 feet wide, takes shape. Minimal diameter of each pallet member should be two inches to ensure adequate insulation.

The shelter's triangular walls are constructed by leaning lengths of branches at an angle between main support and ground from either side. The amount of floor space is determined by how far apart the wall supports are set; smaller interior space retains body heat better. Place a few framing sticks against the main support to set the shelter's internal

A quickly constructed Dugout Shelter.

dimensions, then add onto that skeleton with more layers of dead sticks. Set the placement and width of the triangle-shaped door at the high end on the shelter's leeward side, faced away from prevailing winds (some prefer to set it at the open, highest, end, but this forces feet-first entry). Although held in place only by friction and weight, every wall stick added increases overall strength. Note that shorter sticks can be used at the lower foot end of the shelter, and it doesn't matter if a wall stick extends beyond the main support—in fact, having wall sticks cross in an X above the main support provides a place to hang wet clothing and frequently-needed gear. Add branches to the wall, including the head-end, until only the inverted-v doorway is left uncovered, and gaps of less than two inches exist between the sticks.

Next, seal the frame to keep air inside the shelter as motionless as possible, impervious to howling winds outside, and able to shrug off rainstorms of less than biblical proportions. In many places, bracken ferns are an ideal roof covering until winter snows bury them, but so are layers of wet, compressed leaves peeled from the forest floor, or clumps of sphagnum moss pulled from the ground in a cedar swamp. The objective is to seal the shelter frame sufficiently to block out daylight—and rain—and almost any material that will cover an area of the frame is suitable.

Shingle the roof, beginning at the bottom with a row of overlapping cover material, with each ascending row overlapping the one below, to ensure that rain runs off. Whether roofing material is made from slabs of compressed leaves, sphagnum moss, sod, birch bark, or slabs broken from rotting stumps, it's critical that layers overlap from the top down—like fish scales or bird feathers.

Alternatively, a quicker, slightly more skeletal, frame can be erected, and simply draped with a tarp, or a plastic painter's drop cloth. In winter, the frame can be sealed with packed snow to form a solid shell that retains body heat more efficiently than a double-wall tent. Whatever roofing material you use, add another layer of spaced-apart poles over it to hold everything in place, should a wind come up.

When no daylight penetrates the roof, add a thick layer of dry foliage—dead leaves, ferns, grass—to the sleeping pallet inside, to soften protuberances, and add insulation. Dry foliage can also serve as a blanket, trapping radiated body heat with surprising effectiveness. In a pinch, green foliage will suffice better than no padding, but the moisture in green vegetation means that it is constantly cooling as it dries, and some—like pine boughs—exude glue-like sap for days after being cut. The goal is to create an effective shield between your body and the cooling effects of earth and air. Whatever material you use to accomplish that, a good rule of thumb is to use more than you think you'll need.

As mentioned, doorway placement should always be away from prevailing winds—preferably, the shelter site will itself be isolated from wind. The doorway can be closed to minimize heat-stealing air flow by pulling a layer of dead branches over it from the inside, with a ground sheet, with slabs of wood pulled from the outer shells of rotting stumps, or with sheets of birch bark stripped from fallen trees.

Or you might opt to leave the doorway uncovered, with a small fire outside, about five feet in front of the opening, far enough to avoid burning the combustible (never forget that) shelter, but close enough to radiate warmth to its interior. A reflector wall of dead wood, snow, or anything else that can be stacked densely to a height of at least two feet, helps to bounce radiated heat back toward the shelter opening, and blocks ground winds.

In most environments, a single-occupant debris hut can be built solo, and with no tools, in well under three hours. Despite its ease of construction some debris shelters have withstood heavy winter snows for more than ten years; the design is functional anywhere it can be built, and a few have literally served as home to adventurers for months at a time. Subzero wind chills and driven precipitation have no effect inside its walls, and solid construction promotes a greater sense of security than collapsible fabric shelters. If you had to, you could live in—and build onto—this shelter for years.

Dugout

As every Vietnam veteran can attest, the dugout, or bunker, is an ideal long-term shelter. I've constructed a few of these, and they've remained inhabitable for 30 years.

A dugout begins as a 3-sided hole excavated into a hill—2 side walls, a back wall, and a dirt floor. The open top of the hole is roofed over with logs (4 × 4 timbers in Vietnam), then covered with leaves, humus, and dirt. During the war, front walls, with doors in them, were comprised of stacked sandbags, but my front walls were made from small logs leaned, parallel-fashion, against the front roof, then covered with dirt. A hole excavated into the back wall, and upward to the sky, forms a very good fireplace, making this shelter an ideal long-term, all-season shelter in most terrain. The drawback is that construction requires a bit of hard labor.

Another advantage of the dugout is that you can excavate a square-like hole in the back wall, its flat bottom a few inches below the shelter floor. Punch a rough hole up through the top of the hole in the wall, to the surface, to form a chimney. Laying a small fire in this hole turns it into a small fireplace for heating the interior or cooking.

Snow Dugout

In January of 1984, I was written off by the Michigan State Police—the local search-and-rescue authority in Traverse City—while I was

A wintertime variation on the debris shelter, packing the frame into a solid wall of frozen snow is much easier than building any of the more conventional winter survival shelters, like an igloo or quinzee.

backpacking alone in Fife Lake State Forest. A blizzard blew in, with -30 wind chills, and I went to ground to wait it out—back roads were impassable, so there was no point in snowshoeing to the nearest road, anyway.

In truth, I was in no danger; I had my backpack, and in it, the ability to survive anything short of a giant asteroid strike. But my panicked girlfriend called the police, who informed her that they'd go looking for me after the storm ended. More than anything, it was that experience that prompted me to start a survival school—because if I had been in trouble out there, I'd have probably died.

The snow dugout is essentially the same as the earth dugout, described above, except that, in this case, the hole that is roofed over is melted down into the snow by a hot fire (this presumes a hardpack snow layer that covers the ground to a depth of 4 feet, or more). When a large enough hole has been melted, move the fire to one side, lay down a sleeping pallet of dead wood—to insulate your body from the cold Earth—and roof over that half of the hole with logs and snow. The snow walls act as efficient reflectors, throwing heat from your fire back at you from all directions.

Tents and Bivvys

No emergency evacuation outfit is complete without a quickly erected portable shelter.

You'll hear otherwise, but a tent worth buying does not leak, regardless of weather. There's no denying that they used to—and some still

A good tent does not leak, regardless of weather.

do—but bad rain or snow has never kept me from spending many thousands (that is not an exaggeration) of nights sleeping in the deep woods. It is true, however, that for most of my youth, tents were simply not good enough for backpacking, and I got pretty adept at just building my own shelter whenever I stopped for the night.

For the past twenty years, however, there have been a good many tents in my backpacks and kayaks, and while I was building a log cabin homestead, for a book titled *The Log Cabin*, I lived in one tent for six months, while another served as my supply closet. Neither of those tents leaked—in one of the wettest years I've ever seen—and they're both still in service today.

You don't know what form a major disaster might take, but you do know that shelter from it will be one of your basic needs.

I won't recommend a specific brand of tent here. For one thing, there are often several brands under one blanket corporation (Chevys and Buicks are both made by General Motors), and competition in the outdoors arena guarantees that any tent—like most other products—that I recommend by name will have been discontinued and supplanted by the time this book goes to press.

Instead, I'll focus on what you need in a tent worthy of the name, regardless of model or make. Nearly all tents are stitched together from woven fabric. Terry Pogue, of *Slumberjack*, once told me, "Every spot you pierce with a needle is a potential leak." For that reason, all seams need to be taped, that is, spanned with another piece of waterproof material, bonded across them.

A lightweight, weatherproof bivvy shelter is inexpensive enough to make one part of every survival pack.

No loose threads, particularly around zippers, because threads will catch in zipper teeth, causing zippers to bind, and—worse—pulling apart stitches. Do not attempt to pull free loose threads; instead, burn them off—cauterize them, actually—taking care not to burn or singe the tent fabric. Two or three loose threads are usual; more than that, and quality control at the factory is suspect.

Seams need to be tacked down tight, with no loose or raw edges. Zippers need to slide easily, with as little binding or snagging as possible. Interior surfaces should be clearly and completely coated with polyurethane (abbreviated as PU).

More than ever before, a fabric house can be transported in a backpack, as part of a complete survival system.

Poles should be high-quality aluminum-alloy (the Easton brand name on them is good enough for me). Fiberglass poles are heavier, and they tend to splinter over time. The way poles are designed to be inserted into fabric doesn't really matter, so long as a tent itself is quality-made.

CHAPTER SEVEN

SUSTENANCE

Food

Many survival authorities downplay the importance of keeping well-fed in a survival scenario, because, theoretically, it takes about three months for a healthy human being to die from starvation. This bit of mal-advice disregards the problem of hypoglycemia; when a typical modern human being says "I'm starving," what he really means is that he missed dinner. A typical modern human—especially in North America—has never known what it's like to forcibly endure hunger for days at a time. As one example of the proof of that assertion, visit any Wal-Mart in the country.

Depletion of available blood sugars demands that one's body switch over to burning body fats to keep it going. This is known as "hitting the wall" by marathon runners, but for most people, it's called hypoglycemia. Symptoms of this condition can range from dizziness and nausea, to outright loss of consciousness. I can't count how many survival students and, especially, snowshoeing companions that I've seen go to their knees—even fall into a fire one cold and rainy day. The cure is as simple as restoring the energy to their blood with quickly assimilated foods, then keeping it there with slower-burning foods, like rice, oatmeal, cheese.

So, you see, it isn't about whether you're tough, or even whether you're heartless enough to watch loved ones slowly starve. It's about staying strong in an environment that does not favor the weak. Low blood sugar means a compromised immune system, and that means susceptibility to diseases, infection, and other ailments that a well-fed body might shrug off.

The recommended minimum daily calorie requirement is 2,000. But that determination is based on a normal man in a normal environment. A snowshoer, for example, can burn in excess of 1,000 calories an hour. The United States Department of Homeland Security suggests having three days' worth of food, and other necessities, for every person in a household. But storing only 6,000 calories of food per person isn't nearly enough, in this author's opinion: Is it really that great a hardship to dedicate a closet to store a month's supply of food, at 3,000 calories a day?

The Human Diet

Talk about the proverbial muddied water. There are so many fad diets, so many "super" foods, and so many dietetic secrets to losing weight, living forever, and achieving the libido of a bunny rabbit, that any sensible person would just throw up his hands and eat fast food for the remainder of his life.

In truth, Mother Nature has a whole lot to teach anyone who'll pay attention. A carnivore is endowed with the canine teeth for rending flesh. Homo sapiens has small canines, like chimpanzees, which do eat flesh, but not primarily. Homo sapiens also possess grinding molars, for masticating tough plant tissues. A naturalist might say that humans are therefore evolved by natural selection to eat a modicum of meat with their vegetables.

Americans, especially, eat too much fat in their normal, civilized diets. Fat tastes good to us, like sugar, and an abundance of either, or both, in processed food increases the desire for, and sales of, such foods. It is the objective of capitalist producers to increase revenues, and that means producing goods that consumers want to buy. Our taste buds see energy-rich foods as desirable, even to the point of eating too much of it.

It doesn't help that food manufacturers add fats to everything, in a world where lives have become less labor-intensive than they've ever been.

But the opposite of eating too much fat is malnutrition, and that, according to the journals kept during the Lewis and Clark expedition (1804–06), can be outright debilitating. Symptoms range from general weakness and malaise, to chronic dysentery, and a compromised immune system that can make normal mild injuries and ailments severe enough to be life-threatening. The Lewis and Clark party curbed their symptoms by drinking their supply of tallow (animal fat) candles, melted down for them after the Shoshone girl, Sacajawea, recognized their deficiency. At first, the men were repulsed at the idea of drinking melted rancid fat, but once they began to give their bodies what they were craving, they drank up their entire candle supply.

Keeping one's body healthy is a fundamental of survival that cannot be overstressed. Fad diets have no place in an environment that might demand a supreme effort.

Storing Food

The following information is invaluable, because it could only be determined through the passage of years. It isn't theory or conjecture, it's verified empirical data. Nor is it a study that was performed, then finished—there's a three-year supply of foods in my basement right this second, as there has been for as many decades. The stash is rotated, oldest to the front, with every replenishment (where we live—an hour's drive from the nearest supermarket in summer—ours is a working larder, used to restock cupboards, in lieu of a half-day shopping trip).

Beans

I have stored dried beans—pinto, navy, kidney, and black for more than fifteen years. A month ago, from the time of this writing, I made ham-and-bean soup from a variety of beans whose ages ranged from twelve to fifteen years. The beans have not been hermetically sealed, but packed in their original bags inside cleaned 1-gallon plastic ice cream buckets, with snap-down lids. The buckets were then stacked into polyethylene tote boxes (available from most department and hardware stores), and the units stored in a cool (45–50 degrees Fahrenheit), dry place—as recommended by the USDA.

Beans are one of the best choices as a survival food, not just for their longevity, but because they're higher in proteins than red meat. A 2-pound bag of pinto beans yields about 24 servings of 1/2 cup (after cooking). One and a half cups of cooked beans satisfies the minimum daily requirement of 2,000 calories.

Most cooks recommend soaking dried beans in water overnight before boiling them. However, there seems to be no difference in the end product if dried beans are boiled until tender, except for a longer cooking time. Experience has also shown that dried beans can be cooked quickly, in about 90 minutes, in a pressure cooker.

Rice

Our personal experience with storing rice has only been 4 years, but it seems probable that as long as the cool, dry place rule is followed, this strain of grass seed will probably remain edible for a much longer time. The United States is a major producer of rice in four regions, on the east and west coasts, and two along the southern coast, each specializing in a different type of rice. The widely spaced growing regions also speaks of the importance that Washington, DC, places on the nation's ability to produce rice, should one region become contaminated, or otherwise unusable.

Rice has been a staple in my own wilderness kit for more than forty years. Like beans and barley, it's one of the original dehydrated foods, and is as lightweight as any of the more modern freeze-dried, packaged foods. Rice, raisins, and sugar, maybe a little cinnamon, was a traditional backwoods breakfast around many a campfire when I was a kid.

Another beauty of rice is that it is not only good to eat by itself, but it goes with almost every type of food. Mixed with wild berries, apples, or any fruit, it becomes a dessert. Blend it with meat, fish, or poultry, add a few wild or domestic vegetables, and you have a hearty, stick-to-your-ribs dinner. The Vietnamese lived mainly on rice, and they drove the mightiest army on Earth out of their country.

Blueberries are one of many edible fruits that grow wild throughout the year.

Wild raspberries.

Wild strawberries.

Wintergreen berries are not only tasty, but they help to settle an upset stomach, and the minty leaves can be chewed to freshen breath.

Pasta

This concoction of dried wheat is less amenable to long-term storage, but it has remained edible, even in a backpack, for up to three years. The trick is to absolutely protect it from moisture, because pasta can become mold-covered within a week. Yet, macaroni and spaghetti are sold packed in cardboard boxes that offer less protection than tissue paper. If sizes permit, boxes of macaroni-and-cheese can be prepackaged, box and all, in a resealable Ziploc plastic bag, with a silica pack thrown in for good measure. (I save all of the silica packets that come in any other type of packaging.)

Allowing circulation of air is great if you can guarantee a cool, dry place, but if the least humidity gets to stored pasta, it'll mold within days. To be safe, I like to repackage pasta into a hermetically sealed container, then pack those into larger plastic tote bins.

Salt

Often overlooked as a part of the survivalist's food cache, iodized salt is essential to good health.

This critical component of survival foods is often overlooked, because, like fat, today's human being gets far too much of it in his or her diet. But necessary it is, as evidenced by the real value that was placed on it in ancient times, when salt was actually a form of currency.

Actual needs vary with perspiration, exertion, and climate, but sodium deficiency manifests itself as cognitive difficulty (fuzzy thinking), blurred vision, cardiac arrhythmia, and a number of other ailments that often reveal themselves at the onset as an insatiable craving for salt.

At least as important is iodine, which is critical for thyroid health, especially for pregnant or nursing women, and children. Iodine is fairly abundant in seafood, less so in dairy products, and more or less in vegetables and grains. About 70 percent of American households use iodized salt to meet the 150 microgram (mcg) daily requirement for an average adult—pregnant women need about 50 percent more, nursing mothers about 100 percent more.

Bottom line: Definitely include salt in your survival food stores. Salt intake does not, by itself, cause hypertension—that's why few doctors restrict salt intake of patients with high blood pressure these days. It does cause a body to retain fluids, which can raise blood pressure; if you suffer from diagnosed hypertension, it might be a good idea to have a sphygmomanometer (blood pressure cuff) on hand—disaster scenario, or not. Several long-lived, battery-operated digital models are available inexpensively from most pharmacies.

Canned Foods

Although they could not have known of the wealth of nutritional and other information that has since become common knowledge, the generation of Americans who lived through the Great Depression and WWII were probably the most capable survivors in modern history. Those were hard times, when money, jobs, and manufactured goods were all in short supply, and most folks built it rather than bought it whenever possible. Fortunately, most Americans were farmers then, and almost everyone knew how to hunt, catch, or grow edibles, then can, dry, or smoke them for long-term storage.

Even today there are rural places where grandmas routinely fetch jars of freshly canned fruits and vegetables, fish, even meats from their root cellars. These people are no more paranoid than survivors of the Great Depression. They don't anticipate that society will unravel, nor do most live in any particular expectation of apocalyptic events; they're just people who've learned that it's smart to have a few meals on hand, should the road to town get buried under snow, washed out by floods, or blocked by fallen trees. They understand—often from hard experience—how unstable the luxuries we tend to take for granted really are, and they know the value of being prepared when you can't just go shopping for more of anything.

Canned foods are ideal for home-survival pantries. At this time they are cheap, compact, durable, and military tests claim a storage life of at least a quarter century, if cans are undamaged and properly stored in a cool, dry place. On Lake Superior, Whitefish Point, it's a way of life for year-round residents to lay in cases of canned foods each autumn in preparation for winters that typically exceed twenty feet of snowfall, and blizzards that sometimes prompt county snowplows to be withdrawn until skies clear. Knowing that, many local supermarkets (our nearest is forty-five miles away) run autumn case sales, in which usually 24-can cases are offered at discounted prices.

Or you might opt to just add an extra can or two to your cart each time you go shopping. However it's done, the Federal Emergency Management Agency recommends having at least three days of supplies on hand for each person in a household.

A word to the wise: Everything carries an expiration date printed or stamped on it somewhere. You can pretty much disregard those dates when it comes to standard sealed steel cans—like most of those found in a supermarket. Tests by the US Army, as well as other canning companies, have shown that a can of food—any canned food—can be counted on to remain unspoiled and edible for more than 25 years. *That is not true when a can wears a pull-ring and a tear-off top.* Our experiments with

While conventional canned foods have a shelf life of up to twenty-five years, pull-tab cans have gone bad after four years.

top-of-the line Campbell's brand condensed soups show a shelf life of just four years, before the entire case had to be thrown away.

Storing Canned Goods

Stored in a cool, dry place, as directed on their labels, today's rust-resistant, steel cans are lined with a polyethylene plastic, and more hermetically sealed than ever. For the sake of convenience, and as an added layer of protection, canned foods may be organized inside sealed plastic bags. Isolating cans this way helps to protect paper labels that are notorious for coming off during long-term storage, and especially from floodwaters that are almost guaranteed to remove them, making it impossible to tell sweet peas from peaches.

Confusion can be averted by labeling containers with permanent marker B for green beans, AS for applesauce, and so on. Some of the best storage containers are plastic tote boxes with snap-down covers, available at most department stores; these are available in different colors, allowing contents to be identified at a glance; they stack well, transport easily, and some can contain more than a hundred cans.

Hazards in Canned Foods

A danger you need to be aware of when stockpiling canned goods is spoilage that might occur when the seal of a can is breached, exposing its contents to the outside and creating poisons that might not be detectable by smell or taste. One of the deadliest is a toxic protein created by the growth of Clostridium botulinum spores. Others are decay- borne bacteria like listeria and salmonella. Most organisms are killed by boiling at 100 degrees Celsius (212 degrees Fahrenheit), but the "exotoxin" that persists after botulism spores have been killed by heat can only be rendered harmless by a temperature of at least 350 degrees Fahrenheit.

When opening a can or jar of food for the first time, the interior should be a vacuum, and it should make a small sucking sound when its seal is broken. Someone once referred to this sound as a "kiss of freshness." Be wary of cans with dents, especially around their crimp-sealed rims. Tomato products that have gone bad are usually easy to spot because their contents decay quickly and create internal gas pressure where there should be a vacuum. Tainted tomato products typically flow out of a container when its lid is perforated. Never consume the contents of any jar or can that exhibits signs of internal pressure; jar lids should be concave (sucked inward) at their centers, never popped upward. Metal cans should never be bloated, with walls or ends bulging outward.

Home Canning

Credit for discovering the secret of canning fresh-cooked foods to keep them edible for long periods is often given to French troops fighting during the Crimean War in the 1850s. Forced to march long distances across the Russian frontier with inadequate supply lines, French soldiers hurriedly dipped boiling soup from a camp cauldron into wine bottles. To their surprise, soup in the corked bottles remained unspoiled for weeks under hot sun, and the science of canning food was born. Soon every rural family was bottling boiling-hot garden produce, meats, and fish in glass canning jars sealed with wax and screw-down lids as fare to see them through future lean times.

As canning evolved, it included pressure cookers that enabled food in open jars to be super-heated beyond the 212-degree Fahrenheit boiling point before they were sealed. When refrigeration wasn't possible and there was several days' worth of canning to be done, it was important to achieve such elevated temperatures to guard against botulism. Nearly all organisms will have been killed by the time prepared foods reach 180 degrees F., but that temperature is not visible, while a rolling boil at 212 degrees is obvious to anyone who looks inside a boiling pot.

My own experiments using fresh-cooked chili and soups have borne out what French troops learned so long ago. Even without a pressure cooker, boiling-hot foods ladled into jars that are then hermetically sealed have remained edible after three months (probably longer) of storage on an open-air shelf at room temperature. The key, as with any canned goods, is to achieve a vacuum-seal that sucks in the center of the jar's lid after cooling.

Added advantages of having a cellar, or even a closet, stocked with at least a week of canned victuals (estimated at 2,000 calories per person per day) is that sealed containers are impervious to outside contaminants. Chemical and biological agents are sealed out, as are harmful physical elements, like the abrasive ground-glass of volcanic ash, and containers can be washed clean before opening, with no harm to contents. Some claim cans even resist radioactive contamination.

The Office of Homeland Security has stated that every American can expect to face at least one major disaster in his or her lifetime. We have been warned.

MREs

Brownell's Gun Parts asked me to write several reviews for its "magalog." One request was to take a look at Voodoo brand MREs (Meals, Ready to Eat). I had my doubts, because previous forays into the land of manufactured meals have not convinced me to give up my old stand-by survival foods, like rice, beans, oatmeal, and pre-blended baking mixes. Military MREs literally tasted olive-drab; as one soldier put it back in the '80s, "The best tasting part is the toilet paper."

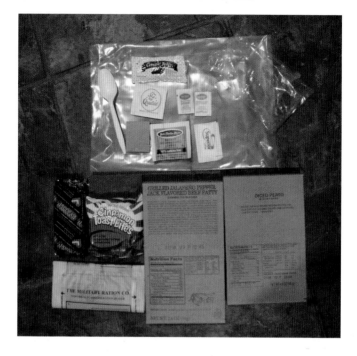

Times have changed, and MREs have vastly improved with them. The several meals that I've tried have not only been palatable, but indistinguishable from their canned supermarket counterparts.

There are currently numerous brands and types of MRE available. The USMC-issue meals reportedly provide about 1250 calories per meal (13% protein, 36% fat, 51% carbohydrates). Hermetically sealed heavy plastic envelopes are said to withstand drops from up to 98 feet. Shelf life is usually 10 years when properly stored.

There exist approximately 24 meal variations—although, that is always subject to change. Typical contents are listed below. The downside to this otherwise excellent choice in survival foods is that MREs are the most expensive of all of them, with prices per envelope running from $3 to more than $10 per meal, depending on manufacturer and retailer.

MRE Typical Contents

Entree (main course), typically Spaghetti or Beef Stew.

Side dish, like rice, corn, fruit, or potatoes.

Cracker or Bread.

Spread—peanut butter, jelly, or cheese.

Dessert—cookies or cake.

Candy—M&Ms, Skittles, and Tootsie Rolls.

Beverages—fruit drink mixes, cocoa, dairy shakes, coffee, tea.

Hot sauce or seasoning (not available in all meals).

Flameless chemical ration heater.

Accessory Pack—spoon, matches, coffee, creamer, sugar, salt, chewing gum, toilet paper.

Freeze-Dried

For grab-and-go situations, consider the freeze-dried offerings from companies like Mountain House and Wise Foods. Just add water (heating is optional with many recipes) to reconstitute a wide variety of dishes that are sometimes hard to differentiate from fresh-cooked.

Freeze-dried foods are packed into featherweight Mylar/foil, vacuum-sealed, tear-open pouches of 2 or 4 servings each. As Wise Food's Blaine Furner noted, smaller individual pouches help safeguard against loss and spoilage. Purchased individually, single-entree pouches of anything from spaghetti and meatballs to beef stew cost around $6 to $8, depending on contents, and some come with their own chemical-type, water-activated heater.

Shelf life of freeze-dried fare is almost moot. To quote Mountain House's R&D manager, Norm Jager, "We're not just guessing that our products will last over thirty years, we know it."

Available individually, in sampler boxes, or stackable polyethylene buckets that can feed one person for one to two months, meals from either company are less expensive than fast foods (and more nutritious). Prices vary with size and assortment, but average about $75 for

Mountain House's 29-serving Just-In-Case Classic Assortment Bucket or Wise Food's 60-serving Grab-And-Go Bucket.

Foraged Vegetables

While I've never been too long away from the northern forests where I grew up, I did bounce around a lot as a young man. One summer I spent working for a steel-drum refurbishing company in Grand Rapids, Michigan, and even then, in the early 1980s, the city was a vastly different world than the one I'd known up north. It probably made a difference that my rented room was on the city's south side, where drug peddlers and the homeless mingled with three-piece suits on the edge of high rises and prosperity.

One feature that was burned into my memory was the sight of famished street people lined up each day at noon and supper time in front of an obscure door that was marked only by a small neon crucifix, waiting to get a hot dog or sandwich. Whatever else those people might have been, they were hungry and they were fellow Americans. Most disturbing to me, these malnourished citizens whose very lives depended on handouts and charity were going hungry in the midst of a crop of wild vegetables sufficient to feed them all.

Wild plants are generally the most dependable food source. The majority of nutrients necessary to sustain human life can be obtained from plants alone, but as the Indians and mountain men of old were aware, meat is important in a balanced diet in a high-demand environment. Most plants are edible in terms of toxicity, but some of those that are considered edible are neither palatable nor digestible. And some of those that are very nutritious and digestible also taste terrible. This section will cover only those plants that are easily recognized, widespread, nutritious, and tolerable to the human taste buds. Plants that have a short growing season, are limited to specific areas, or require boiling in several changes of water to remove their toxins won't be mentioned here. Mushrooms will be entirely ignored because they contribute little in the way of nutrition and are sometimes difficult to recognize, and certain species are lethal if eaten. The wild vegetables covered in this book represent only a small fraction of all edible wild plants. For those who want to include a more comprehensive catalog of wild plants in their survival kit, I recommend the Reader's Digest book *North American Wildlife and Edible Wild Plants*, by Oliver Perry Medsger.

Queen Anne's Lace (Daucus carota)

Queen Anne's Lace is the most common member of the wild carrot family. Its tall stems, with their frilly white umbels (many-lobed flowerheads), can be seen in open fields, pastures, and abandoned lots from May through October. The vertical leaves are frilly, and a bit scraggly, and the center of the umbel is usually dotted with a single, dark-colored flower. There is some danger of confusing this plant with the similar, very toxic poison hemlock (*Conium maculatum*), but positive identification can be made by smelling the root: Queen Anne's lace and its relatives have a strong odor of carrots, hemlock does not.

Queen Anne's Lace is best eaten in early spring, when the roots are tender; roots become progressively tougher and more woodier as the warm months progress toward autumn, and are especially tough after the plant has flowered.

Green foliage becomes less tender with maturity, also, but may be eaten at any stage of life. Too much of it almost inevitably causes gas and

The root of a springtime Queen Anne's Lace plant is very much a wild carrot.

an upset stomach, but both roots and foliage contribute flavor to the taste of often mundane wild vegetable dishes.

Common Plantain

Most obvious and plentiful of wild edibles is a weed known as Common Plantain (*Plantago major*), that grows from almost every patch of dirt, and even from cracks in concrete. This bane of suburbanites across the continent was brought to America from the Old World to serve as a fast-growing vegetable half a millennium ago, and it has since established itself virtually everywhere. Able to thrive in the poorest soil, and in almost any climate, plantain is also one of the fastest-growing ground plants; a mature plant that is cut off at the roots will begin to replace itself with a whorl of new leaves in about forty-eight hours.

Nutritionally, plantain is equally amazing. Closely related to spinach, plantain leaves are even richer in vitamins A, C, and iron. When the plant

Called "whitefoot" by Indian tribes, after the European settlers who had purposely brought it to the New World as a food plant, plantain has become one of the most common weeds in America.

matures, stalk-like seed pods that rise from its center are loaded with B vitamins. Taken as a whole, plantain is an almost complete multivitamin, including simple plant sugars (glucose and sucrose), proteins, and fiber. Some authorities have suggested that eating seed pods will also bolster the body's natural defenses against biting flies and mosquitos.

Plantains may be eaten uncooked, but adult leaves tend to be a little stringy, and seed pods are a bit tough. Preparation is as simple as boiling washed plants until tender, then serving the leaves as you would spinach, or the seed pods as you might green beans or asparagus. A little apple vinegar helps to liven the taste of cooked leaves, and I personally like them served hot with butter, salt, and pepper. Seed pods are good in stews and soups, stir-fried, or with melted cheese over them.

The value of plantain is not limited to its culinary uses. An old and proven medicinal use of the crushed leaves is as a poultice bandaged directly onto bee and scorpion stings, spider and centipede bites, and infected lacerations. Modern medicine has been somewhat reluctant to identify just how a poultice of plantain leaves draws out venom and infection, but the plant has been a useful home-brewed first-aid remedy for many generations. People who take dietary fiber supplements might not recognize plantain by its common name, but know its seeds by the brand name Metamucil.

Maybe best of all, common plantain is not only hardy enough to sprout up from cracks in asphalt and concrete, even gravel roadsides, it can tolerate a wide variety of climates. Plantains can be found in open places from Alaska through Mexico, from swamps to semi-arid deserts. All of these qualities taken together make common plantain one of the first wild plants a survivor should learn to recognize and use.

Burdock (*Arctium minus*)

Burdock is a familiar biennial plant; only Alaska and the extreme northern territories of Canada are beyond the range of this hardy weed. A thornless relative of the thistle, burdock grows to a height of five feet and is common to fields, abandoned lots, open woods, and streambanks throughout its range. Immature first-year plants resemble a fuzzy-leafed rhubarb plant, and the purple-tufted burrs of the mature growth can be seen rising above the surrounding grasses in open fields. The leaves, stems, and root of the burdock plant are all edible, but only the large, deeply buried root is actually palatable.

Burdock is widespread around the globe. In China, it is cultivated as a vegetable, and exported to America for those who believe that the plant possesses some sort of curative power. In fact, any medicinal properties that might be contained in burdock is conjecture. A very mild antibacterial property has been proved, but nothing else, so far.

Some old-timers say that the fleshy stems can be peeled and boiled or eaten raw, but my experience is that, even with the bitter rind removed, the taste is sufficient to cause an involuntary grimace. The young leaves

Looking much like a fuzzy rhubarb plant, burdock is common from America to Asia, and its long taproot is both digestible and palatable.

are also said to be good as a potherb, but these too are bitter. Many people argue with me that their mothers used to create a palatable dish from stems and leaves—no portion of the plant is toxic or indigestible—so I concede that there must be a way to make them agreeable.

Burdock roots, however, are very palatable, eaten raw or cooked. In stews and other boiled dishes, they make a fine substitute for potatoes. Be advised, though, that the thick, whitish root extends for several feet underground, and may be impossible to excavate completely. That's okay, though, because it appears that broken-off roots will regenerate into new plants.

Watercress (*Nasturtium officinale*)

Watercress is the survivalist's best, and sometimes only, source of fresh greens in the winter. It grows in running fresh water almost everywhere in the world, and when snow covers the ground it will be the only leafy green plant found in streams, rivers, and springs. In summer it can be found growing in thick green carpets that sometimes choke smaller streams. The small clusters of tiny four-petaled flowers bloom from March to November, rising vertically from the surface of the water on slender stalks and ranging in color from white to light pink.

Watercress has long been sold commercially as a low-calorie, vitamin-rich vegetable. Eaten raw, it has a tangy, pungent taste faintly reminiscent of horseradish, but since its vine-like growth form is a favored browsing place for parasite-carrying freshwater snails, I recommend that it be boiled before eating, or at least washed very thoroughly.

Vine-like growth forms up to 10 feet long. Small, white four-petal flowers from March to November. Leaves are dark, shiny green, and divided into many leaflets. May be found in nearly any fresh water and stream at all times of the year, sometimes growing so densely as to resemble a solid mass. Often creep up on streambanks during the summer months. Should be thoroughly washed before eating.

Violets (*Family Viola*)

Violets are an abundant, nutritious, and very palatable wild vegetable that should never be overlooked in warm weather. There are more than sixty species growing in North America; some have violet flowers, some white, some yellow, and at least one species is pink. Regardless of the color of the flower, all species are edible, although the downy yellow violet may cause a mild case of diarrhea if eaten raw.

Violets, identifiable by their heart-shaped leaves and unique 5-petaled flowers, grow everywhere there is rich, damp soil—although not all flowers are violet.

Most common of the more than 60 species of violet in North America. White flowers with 5 petals. Toothed leaves. Entire plant is edible and tasty, raw or cooked as a potherb. Flowers taste sweet. May grow up to 18 inches tall.

The most common species of violet in the forests of the United States and Canada are the common blue violet (*Viola sororia*), arrow leaf Violet (*Viola sagittata*), white violet (*Viola macloskeyi*), Canada violet (*Viola Canadensis*), and downy yellow violet (*Viola pubescens*). The leaves are generally heart shaped but in a few cases resemble the scraggly multi-lobed leaves of the toxic buttercup. For this reason I recommend avoiding any violet that doesn't have heart-shaped leaves, especially if no flower is present. All violets in bloom will have five petals, and the two top petals will almost always stand vertically together above the other three. The bottom-most petal will point downward and will be marked by a number of ray-like lines spreading from the center of the flower in all directions. Flowers stand above the plant on their own stems, and each of the leaf stems support only one leaf. Plant sizes vary with species but typically range from two to twelve inches tall. Most violets can be found growing almost anywhere, but all of them prefer moist or even wet soil. The white violet especially prefers swamps and marshes. The entire violet plant may be eaten raw or boiled as a potherb, and the flowers are a good source of raw sugar. The uncooked leaves and stems have a mild, pleasant taste that's hard to distinguish from raw lettuce.

Reindeer Moss (*Clandina rangiferina*)

Reindeer moss is an easily recognizable member of the lichen family common to every continent on Earth. One of many species of lichen (hybrid plants that are half algae, half fungus) found throughout the world, most are not only edible (after boiling) but contain nearly all of the nutrition required to keep a human healthy. Many a stranded explorer has survived a prolonged stay in the wilderness by eating these lowly plants; the most famous case was in the winter of 1943, when Norwegian commandos dropped into Nazi-held territory were forced to subsist on a diet of mostly reindeer moss until spring, when they completed their mission. Nazis had all but given the commandos up as dead, but they were healthy enough to complete their mission by blowing up Germany's chance of beating the Allies to the atom bomb.

Reindeer moss.

Grows from 2 to 4 inches tall. Color ranges from gray to green to blue. Dry and crunchy when dehydrated. Contains stimulant, antibiotic, protein, sugar, and a laxative when eaten raw. Usually grows in thick clusters or "carpets."

Reindeer moss is easy to recognize. It prefers sandy, open meadows and fields where it grows in carpet-like masses of dull blue, green or gray that may extend for several yards in all directions. Individual plants will range from two to four inches high. During dry weather these carpets will be brittle and crunchy underfoot, changing quickly to a spongy mass in the lightest rain. Reindeer moss and other lichens should always be cooked before eating because many of them contain a potent laxative that is destroyed by boiling or baking. Other ingredients that are not destroyed by cooking include a high sugar content, most vitamins, most minerals, and a broad-spectrum antibiotic similar to penicillin. Canadian "sourdoughs" are reported to make a stimulating tea by boiling a strong concentration of crushed reindeer moss in water. I've tried this tea and the lightheaded feeling it gave me was anything but stimulating. Reindeer moss can be prepared as a food by boiling it for ten minutes, and eating it right out of the cook pot, but the most common method of preparation is to boil it, mash it into a paste, then bake it into cakes on a hot rock. Eskimo hunters once ate reindeer moss as is from the first stomach of freshly killed caribou. This dish is known as "Eskimo salad" and although I haven't tried it, I'm sure it isn't an improvement on the taste of baked lichen cakes.

Broadleaf Cattail

No survivalist need ever go hungry where cattails grow. The common cattail (*Typha latifolia*) is a source of wild food at water's edge every month of the year. The tall, reed-like growth form, with vertical green leaves that resemble giant blades of grass, is familiar to most people. The plants can be found growing in ditches, marshes, along streambanks, and almost anywhere else fresh water is found. The edible parts of the cattail plant are the root, the core of the young shoots, the immature green seed head, and thick yellow pollen shaken from the spike atop the mature brown seed head. Young shoots begin to sprout in early spring, sometimes pushing their way upward through unmelted snow. These can be snapped off just below the surface of the ground and the white core eaten raw after

Cattail root in spring, when it is most edible.

the stringy green leaves have been stripped away, or they can be boiled briefly to make a dish known as "Russian asparagus." The raw shoots are crispy and pleasant to eat, with a flavor that I can only describe as a cross between celery and water chestnuts.

Rootstocks of the cattail can be eaten raw or boiled any time of the year. Some have likened them to potatoes, but the similarity is limited to the fact that both of them contain starch. Cattail roots have a tough outer "bark" and a fibrous, woody texture that bears little resemblance to the soft, fleshy potato. They are nutritious and generally palatable after boiling, although some may find the high starch content objectionable. Probably the best way to prepare them as a survival food is to use the same method as the Indians of old: Simply roast or boil the roots for a half hour, then chew them, swallowing what seems edible, and spitting out the woody parts. Green, boiled seedheads were also eaten by the American Indians, who roasted or boiled them and then ate the cooked fruits like corn-on-the-cob. The flesh is reportedly nutritious and digestible, but the taste and texture are only tolerable.

From May to July the male cattail plants produce large pollen-bearing spikes that sit atop the mature seedhead. Large amounts of it can be gathered in a relatively short time by using a stick to knock the powder into a bush hat or similar container. When enough of the powder has been collected it can be mixed with a little water, stirred into a thick batter, and made into "pollen cookies" by spreading the mixture thinly over a hot rock or mess tin. A couple of turtle or bird eggs will enhance both the taste and texture.

Grows 2 to 10 feet tall. In bloom from May to July. Has starchy edible root. Tender young shoots may be prepared by boiling or steaming like asparagus. Basal portion of stem may be eaten raw. Found in marshes, ditches, and along lakeshores and riverbanks. Leaves inedible, but may be woven into mats, blankets, and other items.

Homemade Wild Blueberry Roll-Ups

It was mid-January, and it was the first many trips afield with biologists from the Little Traverse Bands of Odawa Indians. We were gathering data about a small pack of gray wolves that had recently migrated into the region.

Blueberries are only one of many fruits, vegetables, and meats that can be dried and stored in that state, with no refrigeration, for years.

I'd already had a solid year of staying a week at a time out there, almost every week, and these excursions were old hat to me. But this was my Odawa friends' first trip out wearing snowshoes; we'd started just after sunup, and now, as we neared the parked Natural Resources Commission truck, with 10 miles under our shoes—most of it breaking trail—one of them announced that he was starving. With all the activity of that day, food had never once crossed my mind—I rarely ate any meal except supper when I was alone. Now, I saw effects of hypoglycemia creeping up on my companions. I'd seen it before, and it had never been a positive experience.

I dug into the daypack I was carrying, and withdrew a nutritious, tasty snack that should have struck a note of familiarity in my friends' genealogy. As I held out the opened Tupperware dish, I hid a laugh; one of my companions was gobbling them so enthusiastically that he bit his own fingers. The snacks that my friends were scarfing down were, in fact, a homemade version of the popular Fruit Roll-Ups, marketed to children—probably more to parents—as a healthy alternative to candy.

Roll-ups are easy to make, and durable and lightweight enough for backpacking. This recipe concerns itself with making them from blueberries, but they can be made from almost any fruits or vegetables. A bonus is that, whatever they're made from, they have a shelf life of at least several months in open air.

The concept is ancient; every society has dried meat and produce to decrease trail weight, and to extend storage life to last from harvest to harvest. Before refrigeration, dehydrating fruits and vegetables was essential, and fresh produce was a rarity, available only in season. The ability to buy recently ripened fruits and vegetables is a recent phenomenon that we've come to take for granted.

Preparing the Berries: First, you need to render the fruits into a form that dries most easily into a thin tough sheet. This step is the favorite of Neanderthal types, because it gives us an excuse to get down and physical with our food.

Start with 3 quarts of blueberries. Volume is dependent on the size of individual berries; domestic blueberries are much larger (and less tasty) than their wild cousins. The objective is to take a bowlful of blueberries, and do your level best to destroy them, to mangle them, reduce fruits to a homogenous pulp. A food processor or blender may be used, but just squishing the mass between your fingers suffices.

Super-fine consistency isn't necessary; a little pulp gives the finished product personality. When berries are sufficiently blended, mix in a cup of granulated sugar (optional) to add a few more calories on the trail. I also like to add 2 tablespoonfuls of lemon juice, for increased tartness.

This next step is purely preferential: I like to simmer the mass of crushed berries in a saucepan, boiling it for about 10 minutes, stirring every few seconds. I add a quarter cup of cornstarch, dissolved into about the same amount of water, to further enhance the finished product's Gummy Bear consistency.

Dehydrating: To render pulped fruits into a dried sheet, you can use a commercially made dehydrator, sold at department stores for around $40. Or, if you live where the weather is hot enough, you can get the job done the same way our forebears have done for millennia, by just spreading them thinly on a sun-hot surface.

I generally use a convection oven. Spread the fruit, evenly, about one-quarter of an inch deep, onto a very lightly oiled cookie sheet. Place it on your oven's center rack.

Ovens vary, but I find that 185 to 195 degrees Fahrenheit is usually ideal. You aren't cooking the fruit (it has already been cooked and pasteurized if you simmered it in a saucepan, anyway); your aim is to just drive moisture from it. The thin sheet can burn easily if dehydrated too fast, at too high a heat. Too little heat is always preferable to too much.

Check periodically, but expect that it will take 4 to 5 hours for the sheet to become tacky enough to be peeled up at its edges. If the bottom is still wet, drying can be hastened by freeing the fruit carefully with a spatula, then turning it over on the cookie sheet, and placing it back into the oven.

The sheet should come free of the cookie sheet easily enough, but don't fret if you tear it. I like to sprinkle it with a little more sugar, confectioners or granulated, and then use scissors to cut it into strips. A light sprinkling of sugar gives what I think is the ideal tackiness, and on the trail, especially if you're snowshoeing or backpacking, it's hard to get too many calories.

Storage: The most important feature of dried foods is that they keep for long periods of time, without refrigeration. Moisture is the enemy, allowing bacteria that causes decomposition to gain a foothold. Open air is an

ally. I've stored dehydrated blueberry strips up to three months in a cloth sack, exposed to air. Move the strips around every day, to ensure that air circulates evenly, and, if you want to roll them, don't do it until you're ready to hit the trail. Eventually—depending on factors like humidity and temperature, primarily—strips will become drier, tougher, and more jerky-like.

Edibility of dried fruits has been reported after years of storage. Personally, mine have always been consumed before half a year passes.

CHAPTER EIGHT

FISHING

If you're near a permanent source of water, you can eat. That's a truism almost everywhere on the planet, because an aquatic environment is an ecosystem in itself, with numerous species of fish, crustaceans, and mollusks, nearly all of them edible, even though some are more palatable than others. The trick is to catch them.

Handlining

The classic image of a backwoods hillbilly is a bearded, barefoot man, wearing patched overalls with one broken shoulder strap, lying under a shade tree, fast asleep, with a fishing line tied around one toe, so that he could feel it when a fish took his bait.

An awful lot of sometimes large fish have come to the dinner table through this method, and it should not be discounted as an essential survival technique. Everything you need fits into, and can be carried safely, in a plastic pill bottle, snapped down into a jacket pocket.

Making a Fishing Pole

Pole fishing has been practiced for a very long time, long before the invention of reels, monofilament line, and fiberglass rods. The advantages of a pole are that it allows an angler to reach out from a bank, without exposing himself or casting a shadow onto wary fish below. A pole enhances the feel of when a fish takes the bait, allowing you to set the hook quicker and more surely, because it extends the distance that you can pull. A pole also acts like a spring, bending as a hooked fish pulls against it, but not allowing it the solid yank that it needs to break your fishing line, tiring it like loose sand tires a runner. Lastly, a pole's butt end can be sunk into the ground, so that it stands upright, and twitches visibly when a fish bites.

Most simple, expedient, and maybe even most valuable, because it can be made virtually anywhere in minutes, is the sapling-type. Find a long, relatively straight sapling, found growing along the banks of every river or body of water where fish live. The pole need not be large in diameter, about three-quarters of an inch in diameter at the base, tapering to about a quarter-inch at the opposite end. A pole this size will hold up against fish up to 8 inches long, making it ideal for pan fishing. For bigger fish, you can increase the diameter and, therefore, strength of the pole.

There are numerous methods to cut a pole. Easiest, because it requires fewest tools, is to cut diagonally downward into the sapling near the ground with a sharp knife. If the sapling is too tough, or the knife too dull, to cut completely through, make an identical cut from the opposite side. Continue making diagonal cuts all the way around, until the sapling comes free, tapered at its end something like a sharpened pencil.

The opposite end is just cut off—try not to splinter it. Being thin enough, I just lay that end against a solid surface, like a fallen log, and press hard, straight down, with the cutting edge of my knife until it shears off cleanly.

Tie a length of fishing line around the narrow end of the pole, about an inch inward, using a slipknot noose, anchored with one or two— preferred—timber-hitch "choker" knots (refer to the Knots section of this book on page 329). Less than 10 feet of line is usually enough, but you might want a longer line if you're float (bobber) fishing, or if you'd like to "cast"—throw—the hook end farther out into deeper water.

Fishing Line

One challenge that makes "sport fishing" sportsmanlike is to use as light an outfit as possible to take as large a fish as possible. It is an oxymoron of fishing and hunting for the sheer sport of it that participants employ the latest and most advantageous technology to accomplish getting their prey, but at the same time, willingly handicap themselves in numerous other ways.

The concept of unfair doesn't enter into survival, and keeping oneself and one's loved ones alive means that the proverbial gloves are off. A survival fisherman uses fishing line that will not break, because the joy isn't in the battle, it's in the eating. I do not use a fishing line rated for less than 10 pounds. Even 20 pounds isn't too much (this line can pull double-duty as snare line, and even for heavy-duty sewing repairs).

Fishing Hooks

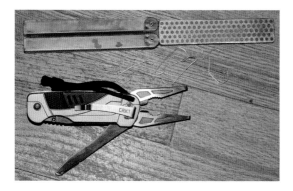

Making fishhooks from heavy metal staples.

Like everything else, fishing hooks have become almost incredibly specialized. Survival fishing is not specialized, however, and we'll concern ourselves with 3 fundamental hook types.

First are **short-shank**, trout hooks, shaped almost like a semicircle. Available in different sizes, these hooks work well, but are easier for a fish to swallow entirely, and more difficult to extract. The ability to get a hook out of a fish's mouth, so that it can be used again, is essential.

Long-shank hooks are more stereotypically hook-like, with a radius at the bottom, and a long, straight shank that extends from it to a fishing line eyelet. Long shank hooks are pretty much universal; they come in different sizes, and will catch everything from perch to sharks. A long shank makes them easier to extricate. All hooks in my personal kits have always been long shanked.

Treble, or triple hooks, are snagging hooks. A favorite method among poachers is simply dragging a weighted hook through the water until it encounters a fish's body, then giving your line a hard yank, driving the sharp hook into a fish's body. This decidedly inhumane practice is illegal in most places, so it should be reserved for survival purposes, and snagging is more difficult than it would seem, in any case.

Choosing the best size hook is best done by carrying an assortment, because different manufacturers tend to use different sizing criteria—a 4/0 Mustad hook might not be the same size as a 4/0 hook from a different manufacturer. Remember, a too-small hook can catch a larger fish easier than a too-large hook can catch a smaller fish. An assortment of inexpensive hooks from a department store will serve you well.

Carrying fishing hooks can be a dangerous proposition. If one penetrates into your skin past its barb, the easiest, least painful method of extricating it is to push it all the way through, then clip the shank in two with a wire-cutter (multi-tool), and pull it free—do not try to pull backward, against its barb.

Always try to carry hooks in a bottle, to keep barbs safe. Barring that, fold the hook and barb portion of each fishhook between a short length of tape. Pulling a hook out of the tape for use is as simple as gripping tape between thumb and forefinger of one hand, and a hook's shank between thumb and forefinger of the opposite hand, then pulling them apart.

Making Fishing Hooks

A homemade fishhook.

Fishhooks have been around for a long time, long before manufactured steel types have been sold in bait shops. Fish are relatively dumb animals, and, like a child, if it looks enticing enough, they'll try to eat it. A fish hook exploits that weakness to embed a sharp, barbed spike into prey's mouth, enabling an angler to then pull it from the water.

The simplest and oldest style is the straight hook (which isn't a hook at all), a length of bone, wood, hard plastic, or metal that has been sharpened to a point at either end, preferably with a barb or two notched into its length, to keep it embedded in flesh. A fishing line is tied to the sharpened section, slightly off-center to help ensure that it will up-end in a fish's gullet when the line is pulled, and a bait (a worm, grasshopper, strip of summer sausage . . .) slid over it and the lowest portion of the line—see illustration—to make it easier to swallow.

Alternatively, it's fairly simple to manufacture conventional-style fishing hooks from stiff wire, or—better—steel staples. For example, staples with a "crown" width of ½ inch can be fashioned, using needle-nose pliers (or a multi-tool), and a small mill file—or any abrasive surface—into a hook capable of catching fish up to 2 pounds, even more.

Fishing Bait

The setting sun glared from the water of a large beaver pond, where it emptied into a small stream, and, ultimately, Lake Michigan. Few anglers fished in this remote place, because it took a hell of a 4-wheel drive to get through areas of mud along the old telephone throughway. The trip was worth it, though; this pond contained schools of trophy-sized largemouths, and they usually fought each other to take a spinner bait.

Not right now, though. Maybe the sun was still too high. After more than a dozen retrievals, I glanced at my pre-teen nephew, who was munching earnestly from a large bag of cheese popcorn.

"Let me have a piece of that popcorn," I said.

I selected a fat, orange kernel from the bag he inclined toward me, but, instead of eating it, I fastened it as securely as I could to the spinner bait's treble hook.

The kernel had barely touched water on my next cast when its surface exploded, and, after a good fight (I was using 20-pound test line), I pulled in a bass weighing almost seven pounds.

The moral of that story is that bait is whatever a fish will take into its mouth, and the best bait is the one that works at any given time. It's no more complex than that. Fish might be wary, and well-endowed with keen senses, but they are not smart, by any means.

A few fish are like creek chubs, which will attack a naked hook, but most need enticement. Earthworms dug from damp shorelines, or from under wet leaves, are traditional. Grasshoppers, crickets, bees, and most other insects work as bait, too. Most caterpillars, millipedes, beetles (with the exception of fat June beetles)—anything with a natural bitter taste, or a chemical defense, do not work well as bait.

Revolting to some, larvae, like this June Beetle grub, are highly nutritious.

In winter, freshwater clams migrate close to the shoreline, and can be pried open, then cut into pieces most species of fish find irresistible. And, after the first fish is caught, even if it's too small to constitute a meal itself, it can be cut into chunks, and used as bait to catch more fish.

Many backpacks already contain fishing bait: I've seen some pretty impressive fish caught on a raisin. Likewise, pieces of summer sausage have proved to be good bait for even trophy-class pike), and Gummy Bears, Twizzlers, and other hook-able soft candies may also catch fish.

I once watched a number of steelhead anglers on the shores of the Betsy River, south of Traverse City, Michigan, landing some very nice catches using nothing more than a few inches of red, orange, or yellow yarn tied to a hook and floated on the current. Colored closed-cell foam earplugs threaded onto long-shank hooks have caught surface-feeding bass and trout. Bottom-feeding species, like catfish and suckers (and turtles), have been caught for generations by a few inches of shoelace soaked in bacon grease. Other natural baits that have proved effective include discarded feathers, fur—or your own hair—tied onto a hook to form a fly, and at least one large-mouthed bass has gone for a dandelion floated on the water.

Handfishing

Using only one's hands to take a fish is, ironically, illegal in some places. Spawning fish that congregate seasonally in streams—suckers, trout, and humpback salmon in spring, pike in early summer, brook trout, king and Coho salmon in the fall—are good prey for handfishing. The technique is simple, and easily mastered.

Handfishing can be done day or night. Lay your open hand, flat and palm-up, against the stream bottom, then slide it into likely hiding spots—under logs, undercut streambanks—move slowly and smoothly and you'll seldom disturb sheltering fish. When you feel a fish's belly against your palm, close your hand hard around its body, driving your fingertips into its flesh. Don't try to hold a slippery, flopping fish, but immediately arc your hand toward the bank, tossing your catch far enough inland so that it can't flop back into the water.

If the method sounds simple, that's because it is simple, and that's also why handfishing is outlawed in so many places. Game wardens hate it, because the only the evidence against a perpetrator (especially if he dumps his catch back into the water) is that he has a burlap "gunny" sack.

Making a Bobber

If you're an angler, you probably know that sometimes it's preferable to have your fishing line suspended from a float, or "bobber." A bobber holds your fishing line vertically from a point some distance from shore, instead of at an angle, the way line that isn't suspended has to be. A bobber also can hold your hook at whatever distance between the bottom and the surface that you desire; above potential snags, and in plain view of any fish that swims near.

This essential component of any fishing kit is available inexpensively at any department store or tackle shop, but a bobber is so easy to make that you may never buy a manufactured version again. Probably the simplest homemade version is a plastic pill bottle with a watertight top (I used to get 35mm film canisters for free from film processors, but these have gone the way of the cameras that used the film they held). Whether pill bottle or film canister, the container itself is ideal for making a self-contained fishing kit, complete with hooks, sinkers, and a coil of fishing line. A heavy rubber band (I use a "Ranger Band" cut from a section of bicycle inner tube—very tough) wrapped around the bottle and the line enables it to be slid to the desired fishing depth.

In the field, whatever the environment, nature provides the materials necessary to make a good bobber quickly and easily. To begin, select a dry, dead stick, broken to a 6-inch length. Place a folding knife blade (thin) with its cutting edge across the stick's diameter, and, using a firm, careful, downward pressure, split the stick less than halfway down its length. Lay your fishing line across the split, then pull it down into the split until it is wedged there securely. Slide it along the fishing line to a desired point; the fishing line will be held in place by friction. Coil the baited hook, line, and stick bobber loosely into your favorite hand and toss it onto the water where you want to fish.

Alternatively, a tightly capped pill-type plastic bottle can be affixed to a fishing line, using a rubber band or a strip of tape. Until it is needed, the bottle itself can serve as a complete fishing kit, containing several yards of coiled fishing line, several hooks, and split-shot sinkers.

Pill-bottle types tend to lay on the water on their sides. When a fish strikes, it pulls the bottle onto one end, then underwater. A stick type, depending on its age (dryness), its length, and the point where fishing line is attached, may lay flat upon the water, or float vertically; either way, its crazy performance when a fish takes the hook below will be obvious.

There's a little lag time with a bobber, so keep the line as taut as possible. Don't try to "set" the hook on the first bite, but wait until the fish actually takes the bobber under water, then yank forcefully against the pole to drive your hook into the fish's mouth.

Spearfishing

Since the era of *Homo habilis*, spearing is an effective means of taking fish in shallow water. Any sharpened stick will do, but refraction makes it more difficult to aim, so most spearheads have multiple prongs to help counter that problem. Prongs should be barbed, to help keep skewered fish in place.

A working spearhead can be whittled from the crotch of a green sapling that naturally branches in two, or especially three, directions, but be sure that the tines are stout enough to pierce and hold a fighting fish pinned to the bottom until it stops struggling. Whittle one or two barbs (backward-facing notches) into the length of each tine, near its point, then harden the green wood by charring it in a fire.

Better is the steel four-tine frog spearhead found at department stores. The head is easily friction-fitted to a shaft that can be cut on the spot from a straight-ish sapling, and it will suffice to take fish more than a foot long, yet is small enough to be effective on smaller fish, even crayfish, snakes, and rabbits hiding in their burrows. Most retailers sell 3- or 4-tine frog spearheads (sometimes called "gigs"), for under $4, sans handle shafts. Larger fishing spearheads retail for about $8. A frog gig can take larger fish, and one of these has been a permanent component of my own backcountry pack for almost four decades. For safety's sake, the spearhead's sharply pointed tines are embedded in a strip of soft wood (usually a section of pine branch), and held there by an inner-tube rubber band.

Several manufacturers make fishing spears, or replicas of more conventional types, but my personal favorite is the wholly reinvented line of working spears from Schrade. Dubbed *Phantom* spears, these handy survival tools boast a 3-foot glass-filled nylon fiber shaft, with *Enhanced Flexibilizer* design that allows it to bend dramatically without breaking. The shaft is wrapped in 2 places with 3 feet of genuine 550-pound parachute cord, and 16-inch handle extensions are available to increase the spear's 44-inch overall length to 60 inches. Protective coated, double-edged stainless steel spearheads are very sharp, right out of the box, and available in 7-inch dagger and arrowhead configurations. The butt unscrews to reveal a 6-inch storage compartment containing a ferro-rod sparking fire starter, a small fishing kit in its own capsule, and plenty of room for other small possibles. A snap-on rubber cover protects the blade, permitting the spear to be employed as a hiking stick. Schrade's retail is $107, but it pays to shop around.

Again, spawning fish offer the most opportunities to spear dinner, but river and lake fish can be speared from undercut banks and other hiding spots. Bring the spearhead as close to the fish's body as possible before lunging hard to drive the prey against the stream bottom. Hold it tightly against the bottom until it stops struggling, then toss spear and all ashore in a single motion.

In lakes and ponds, larger fish keep to cooler deep spots until sundown, then come to shallower waters to hunt. The lunkers' approach is telegraphed by schools of minnows and crayfish scurrying into shallows where large fish can't go. Predator fish who follow them often come quite close to shore, so it pays to have a long spear shaft that can reach out ten feet, or so.

Fish can also be speared through ice. Inland lakes are often home to pike and other fish that can be speared through an ice hole in waist-deep water. "Chumming" the water with pieces of clams that gravitate to shallow water in winter, or the innards of previously caught fish, even

Field Expedient Artificial Fish Baits

Foam Earplug Popper

Parachute Cord Jig

Feather Wet Fly

Flower Surface Bait

Yarn Stream Bait

Scented Shoelace Bait

Field-Expedient fishing lures.

left-over pasta or rice from your own meals, helps to ensure that hungry fish pass under your hole.

Knife Fishing

More effective than game wardens would like it to be, knife fishing has taken many a large salmon, trout, or pike during their spawning runs up rivers and streams. Spawning is hard work, and often an exhausted fish will ignore a person who approaches it slowly, knife held low, below the surface of the water, in a tight fist, ready to stab forward. Cutting edge should be held upward. Stab hard, with a purpose. When the blade penetrates as far as you can drive it into the fish's body, just below the spine, behind its gill, raise upward, as though trying to lift the fish out of the water with your knife's blade. In most cases the fish will fall free, back into the water, but too badly wounded to swim more than a few yards without turning belly-up.

Be prepared. Killing with a knife is not the fun activity that some tactical-type magazines would have you think it is. Use a knife with the stabbing power to do the job—for example, the esteemed Tom Brown Tracker knife is a poor choice, because of its very wide blade. Schrade's BT-01 survival knife is so effective, though, that it's scary. Do not be tentative; you're killing a live creature, not chipping ice for a highball.

Trigger Line

The trigger line, taught to me by an Ojibwa grandfather before I was a teenager, is sometimes the most effective method of harvesting fish. Essentially a cross between spring snare and fishing pole, a trigger line automatically sets its hook in a fish's mouth when it grabs the bait. Once hooked, the fish remains at the end of the line, alive, but securely caught, until retrieved. The advantage in a genuine survival dilemma is that trigger lines will catch and hold fish while you sleep, helping to conserve energy and time that might be better spent doing other things.

The working principles of a trigger line are simple enough for a child to understand. Required materials for a single trigger line consist of 1 fishhook, 1 or 2 split-shot sinkers, 6–8 feet of at least 10-pound test monofilament fishing line, a springy green sapling, and a stout stake chopped from dead wood. Since more sets usually equals more fish, the fishing kit that resides permanently in my own daypack (inside a plastic videotape case) contains a 50-yard spool of fishing line, 2 dozen assorted sinkers, and 100 assorted fishhooks safely contained inside a metal cigar tube.

The stake acts as an anchor for the springy pole, and is best made from dry dead wood because it can be notched more cleanly with a knife than green wood. An ideal candidate will be about 10 inches long by 2 inches in diameter. Sharpen the end that will be pushed into the ground, then cut a sharply squared notch (see illustration) about halfway through one side about 2 inches below the top end. Drive the stake about 6 inches into the ground at the very edge of a streambank, notched side pointing downstream, or away from shore in the case of ponds and lakes.

Next, rig the pole, which should be made from a springy green willow or dogwood sapling (both common on streambanks) about 3 feet long and with a base of about 1 inch. Tie on the line about 2 inches above the pole's narrow end with a fisherman's slipknot, attach hook and sinkers, then drive the butt end of the pole firmly into the ground about 2 feet behind (inshore from) the stake.

Finally, bait the hook, toss it into the water, then bend the pole downward and wedge it gently into the stake's notch. There it will remain bent over until a fish tugs against the baited hook, pulling the pole from its restraining notch and allowing it to spring forcefully in a direction opposite that of the fish. The force of its release sets the fishhook's barb deep into the fish's mouth, and in nearly every case the fish will remain there, securely tethered to shore, until retrieved by the fisherman.

Tips for making the trigger line work more efficiently include knowing what types of fish are likely to be encountered, and then setting the trap accordingly. Small trout hooks (I prefer long-shanks) are necessary for catching the smaller fish species that are likely to be most available, like brook trout, creek chubs, and sunfish.

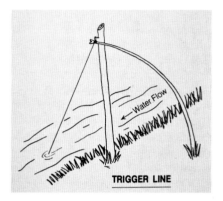

TRIGGER LINE

Likewise, the notched pole should be under enough tension to securely set the hook when it springs free, but not firmly enough to allow a fish to strip it clean of bait without also releasing the pole. As with all spring-type traps, this is the tricky part. Sharp, flat-sided notches make for a smoother release, and a little gentle knife work can make a custom near-perfect fit between restrained fishing pole and anchoring stake notch.

Bait is always available where there are fish. Moist logs along shorelines and embedded in wet humus can be rolled over to reveal earthworms, or they can be dug from the wet ground at water's edge. Grasshoppers and crickets work well as bait, and even in winter I've used cut-up freshwater clams found just under the ice in shallow water.

One of the best all-around fishing baits is a food item often found in backpacks and daypacks: raisins. A few years ago a camping companion discovered that an ordinary raisin skewered onto a fishhook was almost irresistible to brook trout, and since then I've used raisins to catch most species of freshwater fish. Perhaps it has something to do with a high sugar content, but fish that refuse to bite on other baits seem inordinately attracted to dried grapes.

Be warned that the trigger line fishing technique is illegal to use in most places, except under actual survival conditions. Like many too-effective hunting and fishing methods, this one could virtually wipe out the fish population in a body of water were it allowed, and I've seen for myself that a few ignorants have abandoned trigger line sets—sometimes with fish hooked to them.

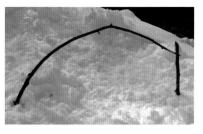

Fish are native to all permanent bodies of water, and nearly all species are edible.

Bow Fishing

Essentially a variation on spear fishing, bow fishing is considered sport by many, and there are a whole bunch of arrows, tips, reels, and other gear associated with the activity. When regarded as a sport, it can be pretty complicated.

But spearing fish with an arrow propelled by a bow is, in fact, not a complex undertaking. First, make a bow. The springy willows that grow next to sources of water across the globe are ideal, but almost any springy green wood (with the exception of white pine, and a few other weak-grained woods that snap in two under stress) will work fine. The ideal bow stave is at least 6 feet long, and requires 20 pounds, or more to pull. It should be around 2 inches in diameter at the thickest. In days past, a bow was strung with a strip cut from animal hide, but today we have nearly ageless, nearly indestructible, super-strong synthetic cord and string, and a length of that should be in every survival kit—indeed, every pocket of every jacket.

Arrows do not, should not, be complicated, either. Fletching is actually a hindrance to performance, because a missile flies better through water if it's rudderless, and a fishing arrow needs only travel a few inches in most cases. It does need to be extraordinarily long; candidates are, of course, as straight as possible, and about 4 feet in length to give you maximum reach. Cut them from inch-thick saplings that are usually numerous on stream and lake shores, cut flat at the butt end, then whittled to a sharp point at the narrow end. If possible, whittle a barb or two into the sharpened end. Nocking is not necessary.

To take a fish, first get as close to the prey as possible. Fit the butt end of your arrow against the string, and, pinching its butt end between forefinger and thumb, draw it back to your chin. Place the pointed end of the arrow as close to the target fish's body as possible, and let loose.

I prefer not to anchor an arrow to my bow, because a skewered fish with a 4-foot arrow through its body cannot swim well, even if it has been only wounded, and is less likely to escape.

Gaff

Familiar to deep sea anglers as a tool for boating large fish, a gaff hook is very effective for large-size spawning fish in streams, too. In times past, chinook salmon, especially, were important to getting my family through hard northern Michigan winters, and it is no exaggeration when I tell you that I took many tons of these big fish from rivers and sometimes surprisingly small creeks.

Some guys liked to snag them with a very heavy "meat stick" fishing pole and an Ocqueoc hook. Named for the township of Ocqueoc (pronounced *ock-yock*), Michigan, where it was invented, this was a very large treble hook over which a heavy lead bell sinker had been molded.

Others tried using a heavy 3- or 4-tined steel spear to take large spawning fish in shallow water.

I tried both methods, and went to a sturdy gaff hook after discovering that either of the other methods was inefficient and destructive to the equipment used—a large salmon can weigh in excess of 45 pounds, and it can twist the tines of a spear into pretzels.

My own best gaff hook was made from a 4-foot length of 1.5-inch I.D. (internal diameter) iron water pipe, into which a 1-inch diameter solid steel rod had been driven, leaving 2 feet of the rod sticking out. After welding the two components together, I sharpened the end of the rod to a keen point. Then, with assistance from an overweight friend, we wedged the rod into a truck bumper, and bent it into a big hook, with a diameter of about 8 inches. I'd wade out into the chill October water, reach across the back of a large spawning salmon, and pull back hard, driving the hook clean through the fish's body. There never was a one that got away, and it was not without reason that our smoker was built to handle 400 pounds of fish.

Smaller gaff hooks are built to handle smaller fish. Most efficient of these is a large (#8 or #10) triple hook, brazed to a 5-foot steel rod. This hook is well suited to brook trout or suckers, during the spring spawning run, but has also worked to take bass off of their spawning beds.

Again, be aware that the techniques described here are for survival only, and usually run afoul of game laws.

Net Fishing

In early spring around here, you've got to watch your driving speed on roads along the shoreline of Lake Superior. Anywhere there's a creek emptying into the big lake, there are smelt (and suckers, and, sometimes humpback salmon—imports from Alaska) swimming upstream to spawn and lay eggs in the streams where they were born. The mouths (outlets) of these streams are clotted with mostly tourists (often identifiable by their fires) during these annual fish runs.

Dip nets, with long handles, and often made from coiled steel wire, have been in use for generations. They have been so efficient for taking every species of spawning fish—including pike, and bass on their spawning beds—that gaming laws outlaw them in many places.

The main difference between a landing net and a dip net is that the latter is bigger, and has an extended handle to enable it to reach out and scoop in fish. A good dip net can be had for around $20, and it's a worthwhile addition to a home or cabin survival outfit.

CHAPTER NINE

MEAT HUNTING

Hunting

Often depicted as a wily escape artist, a whitetail deer is not so difficult to get in one's sights.

I killed my 200th deer in 1980, and it occurred to me that it was wrong to keep tally of the lives I'd taken. I mention this because the majority of people living in the New Millennium do not hunt, which is ironic when you consider that hunting for meat might be essential to getting enough to eat.

Personal experience has shown that a 100-pound whitetail can feed a family of five for at least a week.

Pig-Stickers

The 260-pound hog came toward me through a narrow chute, herded along from behind by the farmer, who tapped it on the flanks with a short stick to keep it moving. Beyond the chute, in a plank-fenced holding pen, I waited with a cocked-and-locked Colt Commander and a Schrade Extreme survival knife. When the hog had entered the holding pen, the farmer closed the gate, then stepped away several paces.

I disengaged the Colt's safety, and, when the pig turned toward me, I fired a .45-caliber Winchester SXT bullet through the top of its skull from a range of ten feet. The 230-grain expanding bullet exited through the underside of the hog's jaw with explosive force, plowing harmlessly into the dirt floor below. The animal collapsed in a heap, dead before it hit the ground.

But the nerve-wracking part was yet to come. I snapped the gun to safe, and quickly exchanged it for the already unsheathed knife. I'd been butchering "winter" hogs every autumn since I was a kid, and I knew the hard way that only about five seconds would pass before the creature's nervous system caused it to thrash wildly for about two minutes, until its heart ceased beating. To keep blood from coagulating inside major blood vessels, and imparting an unpleasant taste to the meat, a pig has to be bled-out before its heart stops. It's a race with time, and there's no time to be tentative; you really don't want a big hog to start kicking while you're holding a shaving-sharp blade.

The hog collapsed onto one side. With my left hand (I'm a southpaw), I thrust the tip of the Extreme hard into the side of its neck, just above the rib cage. There was slight resistance on penetration, then the blade slid in effortlessly to its hilt. I grasped my left hand with my right, and drew forcefully across the throat. It was a cold day, and the initial gush of aortal blood felt hot as it washed over my hands, but the blade easily parted a chasm as deep as its seven-inch length from one side of the neck to the other. I had just finished the job and stepped back when the big hog began thrashing, its violent gyrations accelerating blood loss from the huge gash my knife had made.

If that description sounds repulsive, imagine being the guy who does the shooting and cutting. But there was a saying in my family, "Sometimes you've gotta do the hard stuff," and before we could eat the pigs, cows, chickens, and occasional goat we raised for meat, someone had to kill and butcher them. It was a lifestyle that gave kids a more grounded, less narrow perspective of the world than most get today, and a genuine, firsthand understanding of the realities of life and death.

Butchering animals also impressed on me at a young age the very real power a sharp blade has to pierce and rend flesh. The wound created to bleed a hog or cow would be horrific to a human body, far more damaging than a gunshot wound; the almost effortless way a sharp edge slices through the rib cage of a whitetail makes onlookers cringe; and the ease with which a large animal can be instantly dispatched by a slender-blade knife driven upward through the jaw, the upper palate, and into the brainpan is no less than frightening.

Contrary to one myth, a knife embedded in flesh is not held there by suction, nor is it the purpose of the so-called blood groove, or fuller, to break said suction. A fuller, which has gone notably absent in modern knives, is put there to stiffen a blade that might otherwise flex when pressure is applied against its point. As for the suction myth, one old-timer observed that if a blade can cut its way in, it will also cut its way out.

As a weapon, only a shotgun can match a sharp blade in the amount of tissue damage it can create, and in a close-quarters, home-defense scenario no firearm is more likely to injure some part of an assailant. A single, blind strike in a dark room can eviscerate, or cause sufficient trauma to swiftly put a much larger opponent out of commission. James Bowie's brother, Rezin, has been credited with adding the handguard to his namesake knife after nearly cutting his own thumb off while using his belt knife—as the tale goes—to kill a charging bull.

Whether you buy that story or not, it was clearly the effectiveness of edged weapons that spurred the invention and evolution of projectile weapons, because the only safe defense against

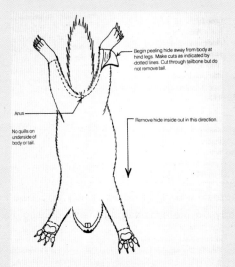

Begin peeling hide away from body at hind legs. Make cuts as indicated by dotted lines. Cut through tailbone but do not remove tail.

Anus

No quills on underside of body or tail.

Remove hide inside out in this direction.

GENERIC TUBE-SKINNING METHOD
(PORCUPINE SHOWN)

The tube-skinning method shown here, sometimes with a lengthwise cut down the abdomen (to gut an animal), is typical for every game species on Earth.

a determined assailant with a knife is to bring him down before he can reach you.

One federal officer tells me that during training he was instructed to shoot a knife-wielding assailant as soon as he or she approached to ten feet, because within that radius a knife was judged to be on par with a handgun in terms of lethality.

In reality, few of us are likely to use a knife as a weapon in our lifetimes, and, based on personal experiences with animals, I believe that is a blessing. Most of the folding and fixed-blade knives carried in public or in the wild will spend their existence performing mundane cutting chores; but, like the claws they emulate, intent can turn any of them into a ferocious weapon.

Advanced weapons technology has not lessened the decisive lethality that a keen cutting edge has demonstrated countless times over many millennia. If you have a knife, you're still very well armed.

Understanding Animal Behavior

Caught, a porcupine turns its back in defense mode, ready to lash out with its spiked tail. (Photo courtesy of the National Parks Service)

According to Jim Williams, Assistant Director of the International Wolf Center in Ely, Minnesota, being attacked by a wild animal ranks as the greatest fear among hikers and campers. The extreme drama accorded animal attacks has made many nature lovers afraid of the woods, and real or imagined animals moving unseen in the shadows makes every first-time camper afraid of the night.

A porcupine's winter den, inside a hollow tree, marked by an abundance of predator-repelling scat pellets around its ground-level entrance.

A porcupine is an irony: easily caught and killed by an unarmed human, but dangerous to the most powerful of predators.

In a disaster scenario, you might or might not have to deal with wild animals, but starving dogs have frequently banded together into packs in urban environments, and, unlike a wolf or coyote, *Canis familiaris* has no instinctive fear of humans. Then there's the very real possibility that wild predators from a local zoo can escape into the streets. You *may* have to deal with animals, and it pays to have some insight into how an animal's mind operates.

The vulnerability a person feels in wild places isn't wholly unjustified: We can't see in the dark, our sense of smell is impotent, our hearing is limited, and, pound-for-pound, humans are physically inferior compared with wild animals. We run slowly, climb poorly, and lack natural weapons or armor. If some mean and nasty creature were waiting to lunge from the darkness, we couldn't know our peril until it was too late.

Docudramas aside, the possibility of being attacked by a wild animal is about the same as none at all. Except under conditions of extreme starvation (a situation in which even humans have eaten one another), land carnivores do not consider humans edible, not even ones already dead.

Observations of radio-collared animals show that nearly all withdraw at the first scent of an approaching human, proving the maxim that a thousand bears will see you before you see one of them. Add to that many millennia of learning to respect Man, the weapon-maker. Even today, whole prides of African lions will avoid the long spear and shield carried by Masai tribesmen.

Recreational campers have lost some of the respect our usually armed forefathers inspired in creatures that had learned to equate human presence with danger. But a few pointers about animal behavior and body language can still give you the upper hand in a chance encounter. Many predators have scared hikers by scrutinizing them from a distance—evaluating their threat potential—but eye-to-eye contact is abnormal. If you are facing a wild animal within fifty yards, it probably has possession of something worth defending—like food or offspring. A staredown does not indicate aggression, only assertiveness, but proper response may be important to ensure that an encounter ends as nothing more than a treasured memory.

Bloody fights make good television, but conflicts between wild animals are normally resolved without violence, because neither combatant wins in a knock-down, drag-out battle that inevitably injures both. Instead, challenges are made and met with body language and displays of strength. By understanding how an animal communicates through gestures and posturing, you can defuse a tense confrontation before it figures out that you aren't as dangerous as it might believe. Knowing how a particular species usually acts enables a person to react accordingly.

The universal response to any encounter in which an animal stands its ground is to back away slowly. Avoid sudden movements that might be construed as aggressive, and never turn your back to the animal until you're out of its sight. Some authorities recommend avoiding eye contact, claiming that could be perceived as a challenge; others maintain that eye contact instills doubt about how dangerous you might be, making you appear able to defend yourself, without demonstrating overt aggression.

One absolute rule is: Never run from a wild animal, regardless of species. Fleeing labels you as the weaker animal, exciting the hunting instinct in carnivores, and giving normally peaceable omnivores a pleasurable feeling of territorial power—even marmots have pursued people who ran from them. Few of us can outrun even a raccoon, and the animal that inevitably catches you will be jacked-up on testosterone, so it is imperative that this situation never be allowed to occur.

Beyond these generics, it pays to know some of the behaviors that are unique to the species most likely to display aggression toward humans.

Black Bear

This is the animal most feared by campers, even by noted brown bear researcher Doug Peacock, who points out that rare black bear attacks on people are usually predatory, for the purpose of nourishment. But healthy black bears do not eat people, not even corpses, and individuals who break that rule are always sickly and underfed, usually old and arthritic (the token bear killed for such transgressions has not always been the guilty bear). Starving, unable to travel the long circuit required to keep abreast of seasonal foods, and too underweight to survive a winter in the den, aged bears may become desperate for nourishment.

Wildlife experts agree unanimously that a person should never show fear to a bear, even while withdrawing from a confrontation. Black bears are inherently peaceful, and it's imperative to make the animal believe you are dangerous. Always stand upright, and try to make yourself appear as large as possible by holding your jacket open, or your arms wide. Never crouch or kneel, because in black bear language that position is a prelude to an attack. Should a physical confrontation occur, the recommended defense is to fight back enthusiastically, a strategy that has caused black bears to break off an attack.

Gray Wolf

When geology student Kenton Carnegie was killed by an animal in Saskatchewan in November of '05, the incident was initially blamed on wolves. This caused a real stir, because never in history has a healthy wild wolf preyed on a human. A more expert examination of the evidence by biologist Dr. Lynn Rogers proved that the killer had been a black bear, probably old, sickly, and too undernourished to survive the coming winter. By then, three faultless wolves had been shot, but the fact that wolves do not prey on humans remains true.

Rarely seen even where they are abundant, gray wolves are highly intelligent, intensely curious, and loath to risk injury to themselves. Hikers have been frightened to glimpse a wolf shadowing them through woods, sometimes "tasting" the air for spoor, with mouth open and teeth exposed.

Again, it's important to never show fear to these hunters. Equally important with this species, according to veteran wolf-handler Cheanne Chellis, is to avoid starting a fight; never kick at a wolf, as that is an act of overt aggression. A long walking stick or branch struck against trees or the ground is frightening to wolves, who cannot comprehend an ability to transform objects into weapons.

Cougar

On America's west coast, the cougar is feared most of all. The number of attacks on humans varies almost wildly among official sources, as do population estimates and geographic range, but the bottom line is that these superbly adapted hunters are again ranging across North America. Like all predators, the cats instinctively select prey that is unlikely to harm them; horrific as it is to our sensibilities, the preferred human target is small-statured, including children, and usually alone. In many respects, a cougar is like a housecat, easily excited, and possessed of the ultra-sharp hunting instincts needed to survive without help in an unforgiving environment.

Avoiding a cougar attack begins with not looking like prey. A lone jogger or biker who is gasping for breath is, to a cat, an animal in distress; likewise small children running and shrieking at play, or a hunter or angler who smells like blood, or a camper running in apparent panic to seek shelter from hard rain. More than any predator in North America, it is imperative that a puma facing a human be convinced that this adversary is too strong to tackle. Never hike alone in remote country, avoid gasping for breath, and do not drop to all fours or lie down in the presence of a cougar. Most cat attacks are sprung from hiding, and from behind, and the most recommended response is to fight back with any weapon available; if a victim can inflict pain on the cat, it will probably break off and flee.

In a normal world, few people will see a large carnivore, let alone be assaulted by one, but realizing that the possibility exists is enough to make the most sensible of us fear shadows. The intellect that causes that fear is our greatest weapon, because only we possess the power to win a confrontation with animals stronger than ourselves through intelligence and bluff. By knowing what is in the shadows, how it behaves, and how to respond to a face-to-face meeting, you take away the mystery that detracts from the joy of just being there.

Pot Hunting

It was November in northern Michigan, and I was supposed to be deer hunting, but it seemed I'd brought the wrong gun that day. The deer I did see were moving constantly, and those that weren't—mostly does and fawns—were lying in the center of large hayfields, where they could detect approaching hunters from far beyond the range of a 170-grain 30-30 bullet. Should've brought the aught-six.

In contrast, there seemed to be small game everywhere, and I carried a license to take them, too. I slung the empty-chamber Winchester muzzle-down across my back, and drew the Ruger .22 pistol at my hip. I went home that evening with a grouse, a gray squirrel, a cottontail, and a porcupine, all of which contributed to a pretty good wild game dinner.

This experience demonstrates the original meaning of terms like *pot luck* and *pot shot*, from the earlier times when every rural teenaged boy (and a few girls) learned sometimes impressive marksmanship skills from shooting small animals for the dinner table. Most started with a single-shot .22 rifle, sometimes a .410 shotgun, not because those guns are safer than large calibers, but to make sure that proper shooting skills became a conditioned response before introducing youngsters to a hard-kicking big-bore.

On the premise that an empty gun is beneficial only to prey, I still prefer the .22 long rifle as a survival firearm, particularly with explosive hyper-velocity ammunition. But when it comes to real-world meat hunting, it really isn't what you've got so much as how you use it. Any firearm that shoots with reasonable accuracy can pot game, but one NRA study also concluded that a typical sport hunter was most likely to get into trouble in the woods, and least likely to survive it. Having a gun can induce an unfounded sense of security, compounded by conventional sport-hunting techniques that burn more calories than they net. Having a gun and ammo is no guarantee you'll eat.

If your goal is to shoot dinner, follow the philosophy that generations of successful after-school hunters used: Small game is more plentiful than big game, usually easier to get close to, and easier to kill. Schoolboy pride and an ammunition budget made rural American kids into efficient hunters (that was illustrated in both World Wars), and the meat in many families' diets came from a mix of smaller species, few of which were not considered fair game.

The best thing about pot hunting, especially in a genuine survival situation, where success may mean the difference between eating and going hungry, is that it requires little hunting skill. An involuntary survivalist who becomes snowed-in at a remote cabin, or the survivor of a light plane crash in the northern Rockies, will usually see the most wildlife simply by walking quietly through the woods. As many birdwatchers know, a surprising number of wild animals seem more reluctant to flee at the unhurried approach of a single person, and hikers often get within a few feet.

By definition, pot hunting means that most encounters are a surprise, so you have to be ready to shoot as you walk—game animals can often tell from body language that you are in predatory mode. The gun must be in your hands, at the ready—but always pointed in a safe direction, the most holy rule of gun safety. Never touch the trigger unless you mean to pull it, and keep the safety engaged, but be prepared to mount the stock to your shoulder as soon as you see a game animal.

A telescopic sight, set to its lowest magnification, makes the job easier, because you have a clearer sight picture and a single sight (crosshair) to place on-target. With a little practice, you'll find that this process becomes automatic and fast.

In one comprehensive study, all brands of .22 LR ammo held 5-shot groups within 2 inches at 50 yards, and under 4 inches, with a 3.5-inch drop, at an honest 100 yards on a windless day. Standard high-velocity, 1150 feet-per-second ammo can punch through 4 inches of pine at 50 yards; hyper-velocity, 1500 fps ammunition blasts through 6 inches of pine, and delivers explosive results against live tissue. To put it bluntly, a Remington Yellow jacket bullet will gut a rabbit at 50 yards.

The problem with being stranded in a wilderness is that there is no one around to help; the upside is that local game is less likely to flee at the sight or scent of human, because they probably haven't been hunted. As you get closer to civilization, game will become more wary and tougher to draw a bead on, but in untrampled wilderness—the kind of places you want to get out of—some short-lived species might just stare, having never seen a human before. Refrain from actually going after any animal; stalking is a high-intensity exercise that burns more calories than it nets, especially against prey that is alert to your presence.

There has always been argument over which caliber or gauge is best suited for survival, but most disturbing in recent years has been the gradual shading of any armed woodsman as suspicious, at least. In some places the decision to carry is made for you by local regulations prohibiting firearms, but in places where help might be a day away, and being armed might, in fact, save one's life, local laws often require no more than a small-game license to be armed in any season.

Sliding a rifle into your kayak might draw stares, and a longarm strapped onto a backpack will be questioned, but being politically correct and unarmed is no help if your boat has been hulled on a rock, or if you turn an ankle. Let good sense dictate whether or not a survival gun is needed, and always conduct yourself as an ambassador for gun rights, but I for one am not going to diminish my own chances of survival because some folks have seen movies like *Deliverance* too many times.

Processing Game

Before any animal can be used as food, it must first be skinned and gutted. The methods described here are easy to master, and almost universal for quadrupeds, whatever their size or species. They have been used by aboriginal peoples from Asia to North America since before recorded history.

The first step is to suspend an animal head-down by its hind legs. The hunting magazine depiction of a deer hanging from a noose on a "buck pole" by its neck serves no purpose except to display the antlers. It is impracticably difficult to remove an animal's hide from this position, and among peoples who process animals as food, it has never been seen.

Skinning

With this method, the hide is removed from the animal in one piece, ideally without opening the stomach cavity, and releasing foul smelling digestive tract gases, guaranteed to raise bile in the throats of the uninitiated.

It's essential to note here that if you do happen to puncture the gut or the urine bladder, it in no wise "ruins the meat," as an all too commonly believed myth says it does. Certainly, you wouldn't want to ingest fecal matter or urine, but make no mistake, it will wash off with clear water (do not use soap or any cleaner, because those will indeed make you sick). The truth of this assertion is validated by generations of rural dwellers for whom flesh in cellophane-wrapped Styrofoam trays was never available.

A feature of many quadrupeds that can impart an irremovable unpleasant taste to their meat are the tarsal glands, located at the inside of the *talus* (knee) joint of either hind leg. These glands are the usual culprit behind the "gamy" or "wild" taste on which so many have mistakenly based their dislike of venison and some other meats.

Identifiable as darker patches of fur, located directly on the inside of the knee joint, where urine can dribble over them, the tarsal glands' natural function is to exude an oily, pheromone-laden excretion that has a powerful musky (skunk-like) odor, particularly during the species' mating season. Removing these glands should be done as soon as you take possession of a carcass, because I have learned the hard way that their musky secretion can render an entire hind quarter inedible in just hours. Some hunters even carry a small knife whose sole purpose is to remove tarsal glands, although I've personally never found that to be necessary.

Removal of offensive tarsal glands is simple: Pinch the discolored area of furred skin that contains them firmly between thumb and forefinger, and pull it outward, away from the joint. With a sharp knife, slice off that section of skin completely, as close to the bone as possible. Discard, or save it for drying; dried deer tarsal glands are sold as attractants for sport hunters seeking to draw in trophy bucks.

Every good old boy knows how to ground-skin an animal, but it's a lot cleaner and easier to hang it before you peel the skin off—and hanging is essential if you mean to save the pelt for other uses (our wolves and sled dogs love to use pieces of furred hide as chew toys).

In bygone times when every rural household processed the meat they consumed, most homes possessed a set of *gambrels hooks* (known to a lot of good ol' boys as "gamblin' hooks") that made hanging an animal easier. Seldom seen today, these were a pair of large steel or iron hooks attached to either end of a pipe or small timber. The hooks were inserted between the gambrels—the equivalent of an Achilles tendon in humans—and the ankle bone through a slit in the hide between them. Extreme care was taken not to cut, or even nick, the tendon with a knife, because it suspended the entire weight of a hanging animal. Having a three-quarter-ton cow come crashing earthward was deadly serious.

A 200-pound deer is less dangerous, but it is still critical not to nick the gambrel. With or without gambrels hooks I recommend securing an animal's ankles with a slipknot in conjunction with a timber hitch (see the section on Knots on page 329). I've hung deer from the trunk of a tree for skinning in the field, as aboriginal peoples around the globe have done since the beginning of humanity. So long as the hind legs are held apart with a broomstick-type spacer inserted through the gambrels, secured with a slipknot/timber-hitch combination, you're ready to skin the animal. At this point, I recommend placing a large (about 50-gallon) plastic trash can under the animal, head and legs inside the can if possible.

Presuming that you're using the gambrels tendons to help to support an animal's weight, you must first remove the skin from around those tendons. This is a delicate process, because even a slight nick can cause a carcass to come crashing down. For this, a very sharp knife is best. Grasp the skin around each tendon and pull it away. Insert the tip of your knife between skin and tendon, its cutting edge facing away from the tendon, and sever the skin. Severed skin will split apart, revealing the tendon. Repeat the process until the entire tendon is exposed as a thick white cord.

With gambrels exposed, sever the remainder of the skin around each hind ankle and pull the hide away. Then make a cut through only the skin like an inseam, along the inside of each leg, across the anus, and up to the opposite ankle. The finished cut should be one continuous incision through the skin that permits the entire bottom portion of an animal's hide to be peeled entirely from its hind quarters and anus area at once. When you reach the tail, just cut through that small segmented bone with a hard downward pressure of your knife, leaving the tail itself attached to serve as a handle for pulling against the hide.

Leaving the tail in place is especially critical if the animal that you're skinning is a porcupine, because their 30,000 barbed quills make them painfully dangerous to mishandle. (In most cases, a porcupine is skinned without hanging.) With a porcupine, when you get the skin inside-out past the hind legs and tail, step on the tail to anchor it, and pull upward hard on the hind legs, rolling its hide off in one piece, with quills safely inside.

But with less dangerous animals, work hide away from muscles until the entire hind quarters is exposed. After that, there is little knife work as skin is separated from muscle and sinew with just a hard pull. To make the process easier, a slice down the center of the belly enables the skin to split apart there as you pull it down, making the process easier; the danger is that only a few experienced skinners can make that cut without puncturing the abdominal muscles (or the stomach itself), spilling out foul-smelling innards.

Probably most deer hunters "gut" their deer in the field, ostensibly to lighten the carcass, so the abdomen is split, anyway. In either instance, whether hanging or lying down, sever the ribs at either side of the sternum with a forceful, twisting motion of your knife blade (this is why a lightly built kitchen knife cannot serve as a field/hunting knife). Severing the ribs allows a rib cage to be opened fully to better enable entrails and blood to fall out.

Internal organs are fastened by sinew primarily to the inside of the spine and to a membrane at the abdominal muscles. A hard yank is often sufficient to tear the organs free; if not, a touch of your knife's cutting edge is sufficient to remove them. If your taste buds allow, heart, kidneys, and liver are edible and nutritious.

Being leaner, deer and other wild game animals need not be bled out. Pigs and cows must be "stuck," with a long, slender knife through their heart right after being shot to allow drainage of blood vessels (20 miles of them per pound of fat). Otherwise, blood can clot in the meat, imparting an unpleasant taste. Deer and other wild game may be simply hanged and processed into meat.

Quartering

Once a carcass is skinned, it can be rendered into edible meat. Begin by removing the head with a saw (meat saws are made for this purpose, but even a crosscut carpenter's saw works). If a saw isn't available—and your aim permits—bones can be severed with a small axe (my preference) or a knife that is heavy and sturdy enough for the task.

Next, remove the legs at the largest, middle joint. You can now separate hide, with head and legs attached, from the carcass. Ontario Knife's SP-8 Survival Machete is typical of a knife made for this task, but be aware that chopping through bone demands the utmost of any knife. One small knife-making company in Michigan's Upper Peninsula goes so far as to state that "No knife is made to chop bone." Except that some are, sometimes a bone must be severed. Like "batoning" wood, chopping bone demands tremendous strength and toughness. One cutting tool that is purpose-made for such abuse is the Redi-Axe from Rapid River Knifeworks (rapidriverknifeworks.us). A little light for my tastes, the Redi-Axe is virtually unbreakable, forged of A2 tool steel that can be chiseled through any size bone without damage, while remaining sharp enough to skin a deer.

The first step in quartering is to remove the shoulders, which requires no cutting of bone. Quadrupeds have "floating" shoulder blades that are attached only by tendons and ligaments. By making long slices into what would be the underarm on a human, between the scapula (shoulder blade) and rib cage, an entire shoulder can be separated from its torso using only a small knife.

Next, take the tenderloins, or "backstraps." These are universally the most prized cuts of meat from a deer. Remove them by making an incision down the length of the *spinous process* (the dorsal ridge) on either side. Another cut along the *transverse process*, about 2–3 inches (depending on the size of the animal), cutting inward at about 45 degrees, on either side will remove a pair of long strips of lean meat that extend from the neck to the pelvis. Inside the entrails cavity, opposite the tenderloins, are a pair of short muscles known in good ol' boy vernacular as "sweetmeats," and these too are worth removing.

Removing the meaty hind quarters involves severing the spine, just below the pelvis, so the rib cage falls free. There is precious little meat on the ribs of a deer, and an abundance of foul-tasting fat, so rib cages are generally discarded. That leaves the two hind quarters (haunches) hanging alone, attached together by the pelvis.

It is possible to separate haunches from pelvis at the ball joints, but that is far more difficult and slow than simply chopping through the rectal channel, like virtually everyone does. The job needs a hefty cutting tool, like a hatchet. Remove haunches by sawing or chopping them off at the knees. Be aware that when you remove one haunch the other will drop quickly, like a playground seesaw when weight is suddenly removed from one end. It's not much more than a painful whack if you're skinning a deer, but if the hind quarter is from a cow, the force can be crushing.

Butchering

Begin by washing the meat free of dirt and hair that it might have acquired during the skinning process. Always use cold, clean water, never hot, and never with any sort of soap added. A thin membrane of sinew, most of which can be pulled free with only thumb and forefinger, aids in removing foreign particles that are stuck to it from the meat.

Cutting meat with pieces of bone in it became normal in the twentieth century, because electronically operated power saws made it possible and, most importantly, inedible bone added mass to a product that was sold by weight. Soup bones, which today fetch astounding prices, were only used by impoverished people to add the taste of meat to soups that had none in them. Rural people who butchered their own meat typically boned it, donating skeletal remains to grateful dogs.

Cold meat is easier to cut than warm meat, so before you begin cutting meat, it helps to refrigerate it for an hour or two. Do not freeze the meat entirely, though, or ice crystals within the tissues may impart a musty tasting *freezer burn*. Freezer-burned meat is identifiable as washed-out-looking grayish areas.

To butcher an animal without its bones, simply cut along the lines—really. If you lay a shoulder or a haunch upon a work surface, you'll note an irregular white line of sinew separating the muscle groups—equivalent to triceps and biceps. This white line describes the bone beneath it, and if you plunge the point of a butcher knife straight in from any point along that line, it will make contact with bone.

Drive the knife completely through the leg muscle, and follow the bone from one joint to the other, cutting the muscle free at either end. The resulting mass of meat can then be sliced across the grain (never cut meat along its grain, lengthwise, or it will be tough) to render it into steaks, cut into small pieces to make stew meat, or left in a larger roast-size hunk to serve as Sunday dinner.

Birds

Preparing a bird for cooking is easy: Lop off the head, make an incision from the anus to the breastbone, and pull out the entrails; do not cut through the breastbone, as the edges can be very sharp. Traditionally, birds have been plucked of their feathers, and then singed over an open fire to burn away tiny down feathers that escape plucking. This was done in a day when fat was a scarce commodity to "seal in the juices," but I seldom pluck birds. Skinning is easier, and bird skin rips using just the fingers. Larger tail and wing feathers will have to be pulled free, but skinning keeps the number of down feathers that go up your nose to a minimum. When skin and feathers are gone, wash the carcass, and you're ready for cooking.

Cooking Birds

The simplest method of cooking any bird is to skewer it through on a green sapling suspended across a low fire by crotched (Y-shaped) stakes drilled into the earth on either side. A cook fire should be more heat than flame, with a coal bed broad enough to surround the bird with radiated heat. Rotate the bird every few minutes to ensure even cooking, and when the breast meat peels away cleanly from bone, the bird is ready to eat.

If cookware (including cans found on the trail) is available, birds can be cut up and boiled until the meat literally falls from the bones. Cook bird carcasses with fiddleheads, burdock roots, or wild carrots, pick out the bones, and you have a wilderness "chicken" soup to rival grandma's.

Cleaning Fish

Basic fish-cleaning is simple enough to master on the first try. Do not bother scaling or skinning, as the skin will slide off after cooking. Make a cut with your knife or sharpened rock from the anus hole near the underside of the fish's tail to its gills. Remove the entrails from the body cavity, and pull out the gills by hooking a finger through them, if you desire. Finally, wash the fish, and it is ready for cooking.

Cooking Fish

Fish must be cooked before eating. That's practical advice for avoiding infestation by parasites that might be contained in the flesh of fish not raised by humans. Worse than being in a survival situation is being in a survival situation with fever, cramps, diarrhea, and vomiting.

There are several methods for cooking fish in the field: You could wrap it in layers of large green leaves (like an ear of corn), coat it with mud, or both, before tossing it onto a bed of red coals to cook slowly. The easiest method is to bend the cleaned fish into a U-shape, and skewer it with a sharpened stick. Cook the fish evenly over a low fire until the flesh becomes flaky and white, and the skin peels away easily. The most common mistake is trying to cook the meat too fast over too hot a fire.

The faster you can get a fish from water to fire, the better it tastes. Fish flesh spoils very quickly, but you can extend its edible life by drying it thoroughly over fire, making it into a sort of fish jerky, and salting it if possible.

You can also extend its edible life by smoking it. Surround a low, smoky fire with a teepee-like shelter. Hang fish flesh inside, suspended far enough above the fire to not actually cook, just dry in the warm smoke. The fish is done, and preserved for the next several days, when the flesh is dry enough to peel away in strips.

CHAPTER TEN

SURVIVAL TRACKING

Tracking and Reading Sign

As you walk quietly through a woods, even in a city park, you'll often chance upon one of the animals that live there. When I was a kid, and children (God forbid) actually took their .22s and shotguns to school, for the walk home after classes, the practice was called "pot shooting." An animal, fish, or fowl (sometimes all together) that made it to the dinner table that night fell to "pot luck," the victim of a "pot shot." Today, those expressions are used generally to define very different things, none related to hunting. But when many American families regarded "What's for dinner?" as a serious question and not an invitation to choose from among a cornucopia of prepared foods, it held genuine gravity. Just as Pot Hunting, as an aside to other activities, rather than being a pursuit in itself, can have real value to a wilderness or urban survivalist.

The National Rifle Association has recognized that, in general, the person least able to feed himself in a survival situation is an armed sports hunter, because the techniques of sport hunting are kept at ineffective levels by game laws. The concept of fair doesn't enter into survival hunting, and the hunter who is most successful at it is the one who knows the most about his quarry. Tracking and reading sign are essential skills for anyone who intends to take wild game on its own turf, and the most expert hunter is not the best marksman, but the best educated. You can't shoot it if you can't find it.

Porcupine (*Erethizon dorsatum*)

Porcupine (Erethizon dorsatum) tracks

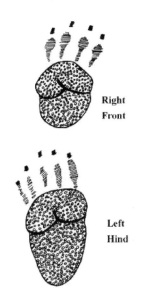

Right
Front

Left
Hind

Porcupine tracks are often faint, but unmistakable.

Long known as a gift to the lost woodsman because it is one of the only animals a human can run down on foot. (A hard blow across the rostrum kills it.) Suitable environments always include tall trees where this able climber can often be spotted as a lump sleeping on a large horizontal branch during daylight hours. In winter, it often dens in standing hollow trees, the entrance of which are marked by a collection of curved, sawdust-like scat pellets. At dusk, the porcupine climbs down to forage for grasses and forbs. It is a strict vegetarian, and eats a variety of plants in summer; in winter, it prefers to dine on pines, and is especially fond of white pines. It will often spend several winter days in the same large pine, leaving clues to its presence with needle-bearing twigs nipped off and dropped on the snow around its base. Defended by approximately 30,000 needle-sharp, barbed quills (except on its head and neck), a porcupine under assault will always turn its back, ready to lash out with its spiked tail.

Rabbits and Hares (*Leporidae*)

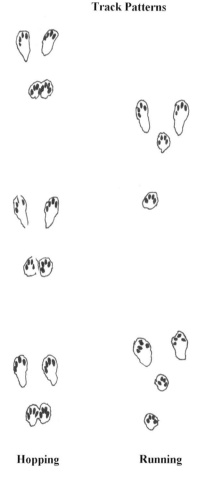

**Eastern Cottontail (Sylvilagus floridanus)
Track Patterns**

Hopping   **Running**

Typical rabbit and hare track patterns.

Eastern Cottontail Rabbit
(Sylvilagus floridanus)

Rabbits are plentiful wherever there are edible ground plants.

This family of lagomorphs is a large one that includes numerous species across the Americas and the world. All are fast runners, but none are capable of running long distances, and all species are a staple of predator diets. Classed as strict vegetarians, snowshoe hares especially have been noted to eat insects and small animals when food becomes scarce, and trappers have caught them trying to steal meat from their carnivore sets. Having simple digestive systems and typically rough diets, rabbits and hares employ a digestion process known as cecal fermentation: partially digested plant matter is defecated as green balls, eaten again and then excreted a final time as brown balls.

Being prolific is a family trait, and rabbits and hares breed year-round, with females often nursing one litter while being pregnant with the next. A rabbit's best defense against predators is motionlessness, and many a sharp-eyed hunter has taken them while they lie quietly in the brush.

Snowshoe hare
(Lepus americanus)

Snowshoe, or Varying, Hare in its all-white winter coat. Snowshoe hares in southern latitudes may remain brown all year.

A snowshoe hare in its northern winter coat; those in the southern range might not turn white at all.

Extremely near-sighted, rabbits cannot see well at 50 feet or less, but will pick up on motion at twice that distance. In winter, rabbits and hares make packed trails in deep snow, where they can run flat out while predators with a wider stance must try to run on top, where their speed is hampered.

Tree Squirrel (*Sciuridae*)

A diverse family of arboreal rodents that is found in forested places across America, with cousins throughout the world. Prolific breeders (spring and fall), gray squirrels, which are often black, were purposely transplanted to Great Britain and mainland Europe, where they've since become destructive pests. Except for flying squirrels, all species are active only during daylight hours, and have poor night vision. They have very short attention spans, about 15 minutes, and squirrel hunters with firearms have often taken their limits by just sitting quietly in a single spot. The alarm call is a staccato "kuk-kuk-kuk!" becoming slower as a squirrel becomes less agitated. Note that the normal hopping track pattern is

Typical tree squirrel running track pattern

Track pattern shown here is typical of all tree squirrel species, and denotes a hopping gait similar to that of rabbits and hares.

Tracks as they might appear on snow or in soft mud. On firmer ground heels may not register.

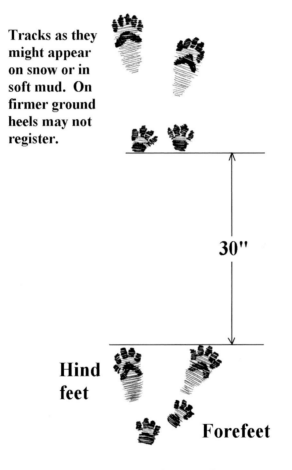

30"

Hind feet

Forefeet

Running gait

Typical tree squirrel track patterns.

similar to that of rabbits and hares, but smaller, relative to the size of the animal. Squirrels are often noisy, especially during morning and evening hours, during mating seasons, and when danger is approaching. Signs include pine cones and acorn-bearing twigs littering the ground under their parent trees, and feeding stations on elevated places that are littered with husks of eaten nuts.

Marmots (*Marmota*)

This broad family of large ground squirrels includes well-known species like woodchucks (groundhogs), hoary marmots, and Olympic marmots. Unlike tree squirrels, these much larger cousins have powerful forelegs designed to excavate the multi-chamber burrows where they take refuge in summer and hibernate in winter. Marmot dens extend several feet underground and even include a separate chamber for relieving itself without contaminating living space; when the indoor latrine becomes full, the rodent walls off the old one with dirt and digs a new one. Predators include badgers and bears that have the digging ability to excavate down to dens. To help counter them, marmots have at least one escape tunnel that surfaces several yards from the entrance. Escapes are failures most of the time, because a predator's objective isn't to catch a rodent in its burrow, but to leave it no place to take refuge. Neighbors are too territorial to allow a fleeing marmot to take shelter in their burrows, and marmots are poor tree climbers. It has been said that the badger and coyote hunt together, because while an industrious badger excavates a burrow, coyotes have learned to guard escape exits.

Raccoon (*Procyon lotor*)

Raccoons are found almost everywhere in North America, from deserts to forests to swamps, but are almost never far from fresh water. They have an omnivorous diet, much like a black bear, and will eat almost anything that has food value. Raccoons often make pests of themselves by raiding garbage cans, and they've long been the bane of farmers. Possessed of long, articulate finger-like toes, they can open most latches and even unwind wire. A single raccoon can take a chicken a night from a hen-house, and a family of the animals can destroy a corn crop by breaking stalks to reach the ears. They are able climbers and will devastate apple and other fruit trees. When cornered, a raccoon turns into a vicious and capable fighter, so only the largest predators make it part of their diets unless very hungry. Raccoons are very edible, with fur that has been prized for centuries for warmth and fashion, but typically have a thick layer of fat between hide and muscle. Fat is foul-tasting and is usually scraped or parboiled off before the carcass is consumed, but a survivor in the real-real world is likely to regard it as valuable to his diet.

**Virginia Opossum
(Didelphis virginiana)**

Not a rodent at all, opossums have been food wherever they've lived.

American Opossum (*Didelphis virginiana*)

The only native American marsupial, the housecat-size "'possum" has been a classic staple of working-class Southerners' dinner tables since the United States were under British rule. Not to be confused with the possum of Australia and New Guinea, the opossum is well known as an omnivorous scavenger that will eat virtually anything that has nutritional value. It is also known for "playing possum," or playing dead when attacked by a stronger enemy.

Opossum walking track pattern

Opossum track patterns.

Opossum (Didelphis virginiana)

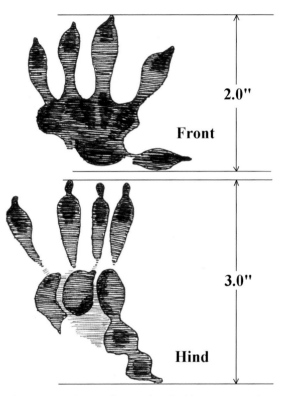

2.0"

Front

3.0"

Hind

Opossum tracks are often confused with raccoon tracks.

The opossum is far from defenseless, having 50 sharp teeth—the most of any North American mammal—with canines that identify it as a predator. But the opossum isn't a fighter, and will refrain from tackling any food animal that isn't incapable of putting up a fight or already dead. Opossums are active at all times of day or night, but mostly move about at dawn and dusk (crepuscular). Survivalists who mean to render them into food are probably best advised to arm themselves with a stout club, and then charge the animal in the hope that it will fall over and play dead while the hunter delivers a decisively fatal blow.

Grouse (*Phasianidae*)

Ruffed Grouse Bonasa umbellus

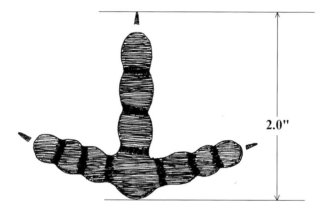

2.0"

Track similar to that of a wild turkey, except much smaller, and almost never found in the open areas frequented by turkey flocks. Also, hind toe may print faintly to the rear of tracks on soft sand or snow.

Ruffed grouse tracks.

One species or another of grouse is found across North America. They mate in spring, when birds announce their presence with drumming (ruffed grouse) or clucking as they advertise for mates from elevated positions. The typically robust birds are excellent table fare. Their importance to a survivalist isn't limited to their flesh; these ground-nesting birds leave nests of about 5 small eggs in (typically) May. Fast flyers, they're usually hunted with shotguns on the wing, but a patient rifleman can take them while sitting. They are easily captured with foot snares laid atop the ground.

Turkey (*Meleagris gallopavo*)

American Turkey (Meleagris gallopavo)

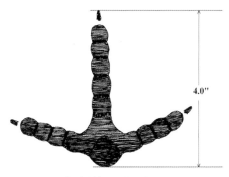

4.0"

Note lack of rear toe in track.

Wild turkey tracks.

One of the most widely distributed game birds in North America, turkeys have been an important source of food since Colonial times. The birds avoid thick woods that inhibit their five-foot wingspans, preferring large trees where they roost at night, and open fields where they forage for a variety of foods, from insects to plants. Turkeys are one of the fastest fliers, but are too heavy to fly much farther than is necessary to get out of sight. They congregate in noisy flocks as they move to and from feeding and roosting areas. A hunter armed with a firearm can take them by walking quietly into roosting woods and shooting the birds silhouetted against the sky. Eggs from ground nests in May are a valuable source of food as well.

CHAPTER ELEVEN

SURVIVAL GUNS

Firearms

Half a millennium ago, an Iroquois chief complained that his braves no longer knew how to hunt with a bow-and-arrow because more powerful and accurate flintlock muzzleloaders had replaced them. Used properly, a firearm is the most efficacious hunting weapon ever devised. It *is not* an automatic superpower, though. To be perfectly honest, most people have greater survival rates in a confrontation if they concentrate on running speed.

Used judiciously, like the farm boy of old who got one box of .22 ammo a month, and like the aforementioned Iroquois, a gun can be the most effective meat-getter in a survival outfit.

Rifles

A rifle is the ideal for survival purposes, and for the very reason that a rifle is not a pistol or a shotgun: It has the capability of driving a single projectile, at usually high velocities, a long distance, with precise accuracy. Velocities and calibers (projectile diameters) vary, depending on whether a weapon is a .50-caliber sniper rifle that can kill a 5-ton truck at half a mile, or a .177-caliber air rifle that can pierce a squirrel's brainpan at 75 feet, a common characteristic among them is an ability to deliver piercing power with pinpoint accuracy.

For this author's money, a small-caliber rifle is the ideal survival weapon. You can carry a lot of ammunition in a small space—any gun is useless if it's empty—yet you possess the power to bring down game that is otherwise out of reach.

This .177-caliber Remington air rifle fires a pellet faster than the speed of sound, holds a steady pressure in its cylinder for long periods of time, and possesses the accuracy to drive nails at 25 yards.

Shotguns

A dolled-up 12-gauge shotgun.

Put bluntly, a shotgun, of any gauge, is a poor choice as a survival weapon, regardless of circumstances, environment, weather, or any other conditions. The worst disadvantage is its ammunition, which is too large, too heavy, and lacks the power, range, or accuracy of even a small-caliber rifle, or handgun.

As a fast-shooting, close-range home defense weapon at ranges of around 50 feet, the shotgun is unmatched. A single shot can take down several adversaries, and although the wounds from perhaps numerous small pellets can be horrendous, a shotgun lacks the penetration to pierce several walls and furniture, and poses substantially less collateral threat to other occupants in a home.

Shotgun pellet diameters vary, but the most popular defensive loads use larger pellets known colloquially as "buckshot," because they have historically been considered to be adequate for taking deer-size game. Nominal diameters of individual pellets range from .38 caliber for Quadruple-aught (0000) buckshot, to .33 caliber for the infamous Double-aught buck, and .24 caliber for #4 "Duck Shot." Most firearms experts recommend the latter of these for home defense, because a load of 41 pellets in 3-inch magnum 12-gauge round enhances the likelihood of stopping intended targets.

How many pellets a shotgun shell contains depends on length of the shell (traditional 2-3/4 inches or more modern 3 inches), and bore size. Shotgun bores are measured by gauge, which become smaller as numerical values ascend—for instance, a 20-gauge is smaller than a 16-gauge, and a 12-gauge is smaller than a 10-gauge. Only the diminutive .410 is measured by its caliber.

Shotgun projectiles achieve maximum velocity (speed being a major constituent of power) from an 18-inch barrel—thus the federally mandated minimum length of 18 inches. To a point, a longer barrel in a rifle or pistol results in increased velocity, although too long a barrel can actually decrease velocity through friction. It was once thought that the same applied to a shotgun—which resulted in designs such as the famed Marlin model 55 "Goose Gun," with its extraordinarily long 36-inch barrel.

The Goose Gun has no advantage over a barrel half its length. Most important is the "choke," that is, the way a barrel tapers from chamber to muzzle. An open choke means that a barrel's bore diameter is the same as its chamber diameter, resulting in a maximum spread of projectiles. Open chokes aren't usually desirable, unless you're hunting whales at very close range.

A full choke means that a barrel tapers to a small size at its muzzle, constricting shot into a smaller, tighter group, and resulting in maximum range. A full-choked gun must be aimed like a rifle, or a shooter might miss his target altogether.

Most preferred for all-around use is a modified choke, which is a happy medium between the aforementioned extremes.

One irregular choke is the duckbill, so called because it has an oval shape, and is wider than it is high. This configuration sprays out shot projectiles at maximum width, and reportedly saw its first use in the jungles of Vietnam. A shotgun fired from the hip across a large room will cut everyone in front of it virtually in half at their abdomens. Be warned that the sporting use of duckbill chokes has been questioned, and it may be illegal to possess one in certain municipalities.

Pistols

The deputy had just arrived back from the Federal Law Enforcement Training Center, in New Mexico, where governmental experts had trained him in the latest gunfighting techniques, including things like shooting while on his back, over his head, and in other positions. But today he'd set his paper target 10 yards away, because his instructors had told him that most gunfights occur at ranges of about 7 yards. All of his marksmanship training had been at what I considered to be very short ranges.

His gun was a Glock, chambered for the rather outstanding (I think) .40-caliber Smith & Wesson. Being a hunter more than a gunfighter, I asked him why he didn't set his target at the 50-yard mark to give himself, his gun, and the cartridge a little workout.

He looked at me, and said, in all seriousness, "You can't shoot that far with a pistol."

I took his gun from him, and printed a 3.5-inch, 3-shot group into the target I'd set up for the .22 rifles at the 50-yard range. The group wasn't perfectly on-target, its nexus printing about 4 inches to the right of the bullseye, and about 3 inches low, but with the latest generation of expanding bullets, any one of those shots would have inflicted a mortal wound on a whitetail deer.

Think of a pistol as an abbreviated, more portable, rifle. I knew a deer hunter who got his deer with the .38 Special on his hip, after he'd leaned his 30-30 against a tree while he dropped his trousers to relieve himself.

Remember, the advantage of a gun—any gun—is that it can disable and kill at a distance. Turning a handgun sideways, gangsta-style, is both ineffective and foolish, because you negate that advantage by making its sights virtually impossible to use. Likewise, the action-movie habit of putting a gun to someone's head, where they just might be able to move out of the way and take it away from its wielder.

Having taken 3 deer with an autoloading "combat" pistol has convinced the author that it has all the attributes of what whitetail hunters call a "brush gun."

Teach Your Children Well . . .

One of my favorite pastimes has always been to go into local coffee shops or bars a day or so before deer season opens, and eavesdrop on hunters who gather there. The challenge is not to guffaw at what I hear. I described one such spying incident in my book *The Log Cabin*, but I didn't really give justice to the outrageous conversations I'd overheard.

Hunting is difficult, because it requires many, many skills to achieve any level of competency; that's why the preferred candidates for Marine Corps Sniper School have always been rural good ol' boys, who grew up hunting. As Major John Plaster (73 kills) observed, anyone can learn the mechanics of shooting accurately in a few weeks, but twenty years of hunting experience takes twenty years to acquire.

But shooting skills have to be learned, too. Braggadocio aside, no one is born knowing how to shoot. You can learn enough from the following paragraphs to take a deer at 100 yards, though. First, the single worst hindrance to marksmanship I've ever witnessed: Some adults think that it's funny to place a hard-kicking shotgun or rifle into the hands of a first-time shooter, and then laugh at how badly it hurts them. This bit of ignorance is not only despicable, it has resulted in giving more shooters than I can count a permanent flinch, one that all but guarantees that they can never be taught to shoot.

Again, I'll make my point with an example: I once took a childhood friend to the local rifle range (every town had at least one big, open field that went by that title), to try out his shiny new Winchester lever gun. I sighted-in for him, then handed over the carbine for him to try. After spending half a box of cartridges, it was clear that the only shot that had touched the paper had been accidental.

"Here," I said, "let me try something."

Without his noticing, I unloaded his gun, then handed it back to him. "Try this," I said.

He yanked back the trigger on an empty chamber, and it was clear to the world that when the hammer fell, his eyes were squeezed shut, and he was braced as if against a blow. He was afraid of his gun, because his father had thought it hilarious for him to take his first shot, a decade earlier, using a 12-gauge shotgun. That was forty years ago, and that guy never did learn to shoot, even though he goes hunting every year.

The kid who doesn't make a fatal mistake with a gun is the kid who knows firsthand, in real life (not a video game), what a bullet does to flesh. That was a big reason why, in an era when kids pot shot game for the dinner table, every boy or girl knew how to properly handle a firearm. Start them off with a BB gun, a pellet rifle, or a .22 rimfire, and you might just have a crack shot on your hands—the way many of our ancestors did.

ABCs of Marksmanship

Shooting a rifle isn't all that difficult. The principles of marksmanship are essentially the same for every projectile weapon, be it a rifle, pistol, or slingshot, even if the techniques for shooting the launcher differ. In this instance, we'll deal specifically with a rifle.

First, nestle the butt of the gun's stock comfortably in the hollow of your shoulder. Not against your collar bone or your deltoid, as is so often seen in movies, but naturally into the indentation between those two points. When you lower your cheekbone onto the stock's upper surface, or comb, the rifle's front and rear sights—or the crosshairs of your riflescope—should appear easily in front of your sighting eye, the eye that's on the same side as your trigger hand.

It has long been argued whether you should shoot with both eyes open, or with one closed. It doesn't matter, so long as you can focus your vision through your sighting eye, and see the sights clearly—seeing the sights is the only thing that matters. For the sake of continuity, though, you should learn to shoot the same way, every time.

With the gun nestled securely—marksmen might describe it as almost affectionately—against your shoulder and cheek, line up its sights as shown in the accompanying illustration. Don't think in terms of right or wrong, but in terms of how sights are designed to be used. With a telescopic or holographic sight, there's only one sight, a crosshair or lighted dot, to place onto the target; if it has been adjusted to indicate a bullet's point of impact, and if a shooter releases his shot without introducing movement that changes that point of impact, a target will be struck. Iron sights are a bit more involved, because there's a front sight, usually a blade, rising vertically from the barrel's muzzle, and a rear sight, closer to the shooter's eye, which might be a notch or an aperture (peep) sight.

Put generically, a shooter moves his gun (the same rules apply for pistol air rifles and BB guns) until the front sight blade is centered into and fills the rear notch or aperture as much as possible. For notch-type (usually squared *Patridge* or *Buckhorn* V-sights), the front sight blade should be on the same plane as the rear sight, meaning that a ruler placed across them would sit flat atop both.

With front and rear sight properly aligned, a target—the point at which you wish your bullet to strike—should appear to sit atop both sights. Sights should not cover the aiming point; the intended point of impact should appear to perch atop the center of the aligned sights.

Next, trigger pull. This is so imperative that it cannot be over-stressed. Ignore what you might have read in gun-nut magazines and periodicals that try to convince you that shooting straight demands a doctorate, and a turkey has the intellectual capability of Albert Einstein. Keep it simple.

Place the ball of your index finger on the trigger, just opposite your fingernail. This is the portion of your finger that pulls a trigger straight rearward, until its connecting mechanism disengages the sear surfaces— the machined-in steps—restraining the spring that drives the firing pin into a cartridge's primer. Forget the jargon about squeezing, instead of pulling. The objective is to gently pull the trigger until the steps that we call sears slide past one another sufficiently to release the pent-up, or cocked, force that drives the firing pin.

Finally, breath control. This simply means that you hold your breath while you release your shot. Forget everything that you've heard about shooting between heartbeats. Keep it simple. The real objectives are to (a) be sure that your properly aligned sights indicate where a projectile will strike, (b) that your trigger finger does not influence (move) the sights as you release your shot, and (c) that your breathing—and anything else, for that matter—causes no change in the sights' position. Accomplish those things, and you'll hit your target.

The same rules apply to every sort of projectile weapon. Exceptions to that assertion occur when the shooting range is extreme, crosswinds are very strong, or, sometimes, when you've changed from a light bullet load to a much heavier one. In general, though, if you keep your sighted-in weapon on-target, and do not move it while shooting, you'll drill bullseyes.

Group Therapy

Find a hunter who always hits his or her target, and you've probably found someone who has burned considerable time and ammo shooting groups into paper targets on a range. The objective of group shooting is to make every nuance of good marksmanship an automatic function, independent of the jack-hammer heart and the butterfly stomach that occur when a trophy buck presents itself. Veteran hunters often cannot recall pulling the trigger, or even seeing their sights, when making what turned out to be a fine shot, because practice had made doing those things conditioned responses, like automatically braking a car when you see deer at night.

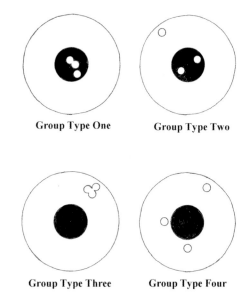

Group Type One   Group Type Two

Group Type Three   Group Type Four

If you can't use it effectively, you shouldn't pack it; group shooting is a time-honored method of sharpening marksmanship skills.

How far a shooter has gone toward achieving consistent precision is represented by the amount of space groups of 3 to 5 shots take up on a target (the folks at CCI claim the ideal group size should be 7 rounds). Plinking is great, but dedicated marksmen know that the real key to proficiency lies in punching paper. The closer a shooter can get to putting every shot through the same hole, the more accurate he will be when success rides on making a single flawless shot under less than perfect conditions.

For that reason, every shot fired into a group should be launched from a steady platform, just as it should be if the target were a trophy whitetail. All firearms should be bench rested on sandbags if possible, although shooting across the hood of a truck, rested on a backpack, has often sufficed. Rifles should be rested on the stock forend only, never on barrels, which must be free to expand from heat and pressure. Handguns should be held with a firm two-handed grip, and the forearms rested on a stable surface. The objective is to remove as much human variation from the firearm as possible, making it easier to predict where every shot will land because body motion has been mostly eliminated.

Shooting accurately offhand with a rifle or pistol—that is, without using a rest—is a skill that every hunter needs, but one that few savvy whitetailers use if a tree branch or rock is available.

Plinking offhand with a .22 at tennis balls in a vacant gravel pit is good practice and great fun, and serious riflemen even shoot 100-yard groups from that position, but there are no cases in which using a rest won't improve accuracy.

Groups are also great analytical tools if one can decipher the meanings behind a cluster of bullet (or arrow) holes. Like numbers, groups don't lie, and they provide a quantifiable, measurable means of determining how well shooter and weapon perform together. There are essentially four types of groups, all of which can have real value in determining where a shooter's inconsistencies lie.

Group Type One

A nearly ideal 3-shot group, with all points of impact tightly centered on the point of aim. This type of group indicates that sights are in proper alignment with a projectile's trajectory at this range, and that the shooter was both steady and consistent. This is the group that novices try to achieve and experts try to beat.

Group Type Two

This group, with two shots printing neatly together at the point of aim and one straying widely apart from them, is what range regulars call a "flyer" group, or sometimes a "yanked" shot. Paired holes in the bullseye indicate that human and machine were in agreement most of the time, so the likely cause of a flyer is some glitch or flinch by the shooter. It is possible to have a wild variation in ammunition that causes a projectile to fly off-target, but nowadays this is very unlikely with even cheap ammo. The remedy is usually as simple as shooting another group or two to limber up the trigger finger. Like riding a bike, it's true that a practiced marksman never forgets the mechanics of sharpshooting, but in both instances one can anticipate being a little wobbly after an extended period without practice.

Group Type Three

Nice tight grouping of all three shots, except not at the weapon's intended point of impact. This type of group suggests a marksman with real skill, even though no shots are in the black, and this is the only example in which a shooter is probably not at fault. Likely causes are sights that have been knocked hard enough to change their point of aim, or sometimes a change of ammunition weights and charges that result in different flight paths. The remedy is to adjust the sights so that point of aim agrees with point of impact.

Group Type Four

Shooting this type of group is a little embarrassing for veteran marksmen, even though everybody gets one now and then. All three shots scattered about the target like this indicates a real inconsistency somewhere between human and machine.

The most common cause is a flinch or other unsteadiness on the part of a shooter. Mechanical culprits can include loose scope mounts or, in some old military bolt-actions, a recoil lug inlet in the stock that has become enlarged enough by repeated firing to allow the action to shift on discharge. Still, the reason for a scattered group lies with the shooter nearly all of the time, so before making sight adjustments, first fire a half-dozen groups to see if they don't shrink with practice.

Although the primary focus here has been on rifles and pistols, all of the above is pretty much generic to all hunting weapons. The reasons an archer sticks arrows everywhere on a target except its bullseye are generally the same reasons a shooter has for doing the same with bullet holes. Likewise, archers, pistoleros, and riflemen who consistently hit everything they shoot at in the field or on the range are practiced group shooters. With good group analysis and regular range practice you'll know precisely what an arrow or bullet is going to do at a given range, before you even fire, and that alone will help to make every shot as accurate as it can be.

The Ultimate Survival Firearm

Attempts to identify a perfect gun and caliber have been written, read, and argued over for as long as there have been two calibers, and despite the creation of numerous cartridges along the way, the topic still livens conversations at deer camp.

My choice is a light, handy rifle chambered in .22 long rifle caliber. The overriding factor in this choice is ammunition; without bullets, all other features lose meaning. A standard "brick" of .22 lr weighs four pounds, and contains five hundred rounds, individually packaged in boxes of fifty rounds each. Sealed in Ziploc bags with moisture-absorbing silica packets, the ten fifty-round boxes can be carried in jacket pockets, or spread throughout your gear, and cartridges carried this way have remained functional for more than ten years.

The potential power of a .22 long rifle bullet is often dangerously underestimated. At the muzzle, a plain old Winchester T22 cartridge with forty-grain lead bullet has a velocity of 1,150 feet per second, and 117 foot-pounds of force. At 100 yards, the bullet retains a velocity of 976 fps, and a respectable 85 foot-pounds of energy. Loadings in the 1,150 fps category have proved most accurate for sighting-in and plinking, and they are the least expensive, but lack the killing power to reliably take game larger than a squirrel. They will, however, consistently punch through four inches of pine at fifty yards.

When the target is live game, you might switch to one of the "hyper-velocity" long rifle cartridges that were introduced in the 1970s. Souped-up to muzzle velocities of 1,500 fps, these cartridges offer premium killing power per box of fifty rounds. Perennial favorites include Remington's Yellowjacket (36-grain truncated hollow-point, 1,410 fps, 159 ft-lbs), CCI's Quik-Shok (32-grain fragmenting hollow-point, 1,640 fps, 191 ft-lbs).

For game animals under thirty pounds, you might opt for the less explosive power of CCI's expanding SGB, or Small Game Bullet (40-grain flat-nose, 1,235 fps, 135 ft-lbs).

In terms of accuracy, no caliber beats the .22 long rifle to 50 yards, and its bullet retains lethal power at twice that range. Benchrest tests using five types of ammunition, two rifles (an auto and a bolt), and two shooters revealed that accuracy decreased slightly as velocity increased, but every loading could be counted on to hold five shots within 2 inches at 50 yards. Beyond 50 yards all bullets were susceptible to wind drift. It was helpful to note that points of impact between all brands varied only a few tenths of an inch at 50 yards, meaning that you can sight-in with target ammunition, then switch to more lethal hunting cartridges, without re-zeroing your sights. If a squirrel peeks at you from around a tree at 60 yards, you can expect that your .22 can hit it in the eye.

Some claim that the .22 WMR is a better survival caliber; I disagree on the grounds that .22 Mag ammo is not as common as .22 LR, but it is triple the price. CCI's Maxi-Mag WMR (Winchester Magnum Rimfire) propels a thirty-grain, hollow-point bullet out the barrel at 2,200 fps, with an impressive 322 ft-lbs of energy, but its trajectory is matched within half an inch by the company's own Quik-Shok long rifle out to 100 yards. Compare potency, price, and availability, and I believe the .22 LR is a better choice.

Like their ammo, guns that shoot .22 LR ammunition tend to be lightweight and inexpensive.

Virtually any make or model can suffice as a survival rimfire, but many need a paint job that will allow them to shrug off the same foul weather their owners might endure. This is as simple as suspending the barreled action by a cord, then spraying it with several coats of black primer, taking care not to get overspray inside the trigger or action, and allowing each coat to dry thoroughly before applying the next. If the finish gets scraped in the woods, just spray that area again when you get home. In the quarter century since a handful of good ol' boys started using it, this protective coating has been applied to dozens of firearms that must be exposed to the elements for days at a time. You can further harden enamel paint against abrasion by coating it with several layers of acrylic-based floor wax, taking care to treat only the outside surfaces, not any moving parts.

The primary sight on any survival rifle should be telescopic (I like to keep iron sights as backup). Today's scopes are more rugged and watertight than ever, even inexpensive ones, and a $40 model will suffice, providing it has at least a one-inch tube, 32mm objective lens, and magnification of 4x to a maximum of 10x. Features of a good scope include sealed, nitrogen-filled body, JIS Class 6 waterproofing, and light-gathering metallic lens coatings (preferably phase-coated and applied to both sides). Always keep lenses covered when not in use, clean them gently with a soft cloth, and never use saliva to clean them, as the enzymes in spit are corrosive to lens coatings. Mounted properly and sighted in, an inexpensive scope can perform almost as well in the field as its high-end counterpart.

Grooved ring mounts that make gun and scope perform as one must be well-fitted and tight; I recommend sticking with name brands, like Uncle Mike's. On my own "working" guns, the fitted scope mounts are more permanently affixed to the receiver by a seam of epoxy (or, more recently, Gorilla Glue), which strengthens the mount, and makes changing scopes easier.

My preferred sling is the "Ranger sling," described later.

Creating your own ultimate survival rifle can become quite personal, like the often one-of-a-kind muzzleloaders carried by mountain men of old. Nearly every .22 rifle made today is capable of remarkable accuracy, whether it's a $1,000 Kimber or a $100 Marlin. Give them an immunity to weather, a reliable sight, hyper-velocity expending-bullet ammo, and a few practical add-ons, and you can transform almost any plinking .22 into a seriously lethal survival firearm for under $250.

Field-Expedient Riflescope Sighting

Calibrating a telescopic sight to make its point of aim coincide with a rifle bullet's point of impact at a specified distance isn't a skill anyone is born with. But it is a fundamental component of marksmanship. A hunter should know how to sight-in his or her own gun before using it to shoot at live game, because any bullet that misses its target poses a danger to something else.

Having a scoped rifle collimated, or bore-sighted, to put its point of impact "on paper" helps, but it seldom brings scope and gun to zero, where every bullet bullseyes its target at (typically, even for .22s, today) 100 yards. Being preset for an established average, a collimator can't compensate for ballistic changes caused variation in barrel lengths, propellants, elevation, or temperature.

Adjusting a rifle and scope to the setting at which both components agree at a given range requires shooting holes into a target. The technique described here enables almost anyone to mount a scope on a rifle, then zero it, without a collimator, and without the frustration of missed shots. This procedure also allows a scoped rifle to be zeroed in the field, on any fixed target, from a standard paper target to a coffee can lid nailed to a stump.

The first step is to eliminate mechanical accuracy problems. All screws used to fasten scope base to the rifle receiver must be snug; absolutely no movement can occur between rifle and scope. Rings must be fully seated onto their bases, and screws between scope and rings must be snug (check them occasionally). A loose mounting system guarantees that the rifle it's on won't put bullets where the crosshairs are, yet this is the most common cause of inaccuracy.

Position of a mounted scope should be such that a shooter can snap the rifle to his shoulder and see a clear, bright sight picture immediately, without moving his head. This distance between a shooter's eye and a scope's ocular lens is known as "eye relief," and is typically engineered to be 4 inches. A scope that is mounted too far forward or rearward presents the shooter with an occluded sight picture that has reduced size and brightness, and is surrounded by a dark circle. A properly positioned scope presents a clear sight picture that fills the eyepiece from a natural shooting position, and, importantly, doesn't thump its shooter's eyebrow during recoil.

"Your crosshairs are crooked" is a comment scoped rifle owners are sure to hear. Ideally, crosshairs should be perfectly vertical and horizontal to a rifle's bore, and the rifle should never be canted in either direction while shooting. In the real world, eyeballing crosshairs to their true position, where a shooter thinks they look straightest, is usually precise enough to keep groups inside 3 inches at an honest 200 yards, with centerfire rifle calibers.

If your bullets consistently land more left or right as you adjust the elevation turret upward, the crosshairs may indeed be cocked to one side. Loosen the ring retaining screws, and gently twist the scope barrel until the crosshairs look straight each time you shoulder the gun. To keep the crosshairs in that position, tighten each ring retaining screw a quarter-turn at a time until they feel equally snug; called "pattern torqueing" by machinists, this procedure ensures that all points of a mounted fixture remain level under pressure.

If your scope appears to be positioned correctly, but the sight picture looks blurry, the ocular lens—the lens you look through—is probably out of focus. This problem is corrected by loosening the ocular lens' locking ring, just ahead of the eyebell, and turning the entire eyebell (usually) clockwise until the sight picture becomes clear. When maximum clarity has been achieved, secure the lens in that position by turning the locking ring counterclockwise until it presses tightly against the eyebell.

The right ammunition is critical. A 220-grain .308-caliber bullet fired from a rifle that has been zeroed using 150-grain bullets will impact lower on its target at a given range, and that difference will increase with range. Even the same weight bullet from different manufacturers can have slightly different points of impact, depending on barrel length, type of action, and bullet shape. Hunters should always sight-in using the same make and type of ammunition that they intend to use in the field, and rifles should be re-zeroed following any change in bullet weights or brand.

Terrain is an often overlooked factor in the sighting process. Shooting downhill, for instance, will result in a point of impact slightly lower than it would be on level ground, because gravitational influence is greater, which causes trajectory rise to decrease. This is seldom a problem in the flat terrain of established target ranges, but it is something to bear in mind when circumstances dictate that a rifle be zeroed in the field.

Proper targets can help take the frustration out of any sighting process, particularly with a newly mounted scope. Shooting soup cans is fun with an already-sighted rifle, but attempting to sight-in for the first time using a small target can be impossible. A shooter needs to see where his bullets land, because bullet holes are the points of reference used to adjust point of impact. If you don't know where the last bullet hit, you can't determine how many clicks of the adjuster turret are needed to place the next shot on target, or even in which direction to make those adjustments. Large targets, especially those with one-inch grids, are easiest to use, but a paper plate with a cross of contrasting vinyl tape in its center suffices in a pinch. Bits of masking tape can be used to cover bullet holes, extending the useable life of your targets.

Now you're ready to sight-in your rifle. Regardless of caliber, or the range at which you intend to zero your rifle, the first 3-shot group should be fired from 12 yards—and it should be fired as carefully as if it were from 100 yards. The Rifle fore-end must be rested solidly, its barrel should touch nothing, and each shot should be aimed at the target's center, regardless of where bullets actually land. Never compensate for a bullet's point of impact by shifting your point of aim, and never shoot without a secure rest, because doing either defeats the sighting process.

Using the center of this initial group as a point of reference, remove your scope's turret caps and adjust the windage and elevation knobs to bring the crosshairs into alignment with point of impact. Presuming a traditional "1 click = 1/4-inch at 100 yards" (marked on the adjusters), crosshairs will move at a rate of 32 clicks per inch at 12 yards. If the group's center is 1 inch left of the bullseye and 1.5 inches low, adjust the windage (side) turret 32 clicks right, and the elevation (top) turret 48 clicks upward.

Next, move back to 50 yards and fire another 3-shot group. Using the center of that group as a reference, adjust windage and elevation turrets at 8 clicks per inch. If the group center is 2 inches high and 1/2-inch to the right, adjust 16 clicks down and 4 clicks left.

The next, usually final, group is fired from 100 yards, the optimum range for most whitetail hunting. Again, the group should consist of 3 shots, minimum, and should be placed with as much precision as its shooter can muster. At 100 yards, 4 clicks of the elevation or windage turrets is equal to 1 inch of movement on a target. If your group's center is 1.5 inches high and 2 inches left of the bullseye, adjusting 6 clicks downward and 8 clicks right should place your bullets' point of impact directly on the target center.

While the above holds true for scopes marked "1 click equals 1/4-inch at 100 yards," do not expect that it will be exact for all telescopic sights, because all scopes are not created equal. If your rifle is sporting a tactical sight that retails for $1,000, it had better move the point of impact exactly .250-inch per click at 100 yards. But if your gun wears a low-end model that sold for $50 at a department store, it cannot be expected to contain the same clockwork precision. An inexpensive scope can get the job done very well once it has been sighted-in, but you may have to twist 5 clicks to equal 1 inch of movement on a target 100 yards distant.

Experienced marksmen recommend that turret adjustments be made using a procedure known as the "there-and-back" technique. With this method, a shooter who determines that his scope needs, say, 4 clicks of adjustment will actually turn the turret 6 clicks in the desired direction, then come back 2 clicks. This practice helps ensure that tiny adjustor gears inside fall into place completely.

If you can't seem to change your bullets' point of impact, no matter how many clicks you adjust, try rapping the scope tube lightly around its turrets with a soft tool (a rubber-handled jackknife). The delicate inner workings of a telescopic sight can become sticky with time and exposure to heat and cold, causing the crosshairs inside to hang up. Rapping the turret area gently is usually sufficient to free the mechanism.

Keep scope lenses clean using a soft cloth, like those made for cameras, and keep them covered when not in use. Never use saliva to clean lenses; digestive enzymes in saliva erode the metallic coatings responsible for gathering and transmitting ambient light to a shooter's eye, resulting in a less vivid sight picture. Treat your telescopic sight well, regardless of its price, and it will reward you with years of accurate shooting.

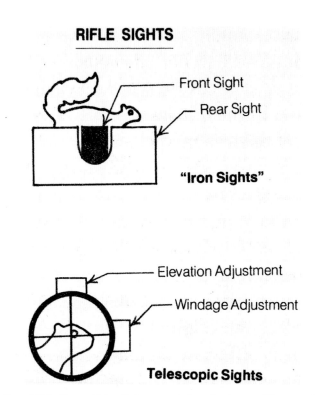

RIFLE SIGHTS

Front Sight
Rear Sight
"Iron Sights"

Elevation Adjustment
Windage Adjustment
Telescopic Sights

Shooting skill isn't something that anyone is born having, and if you can't use it effectively, a gun should not be part of your survival outfit.

Telescopic Riflescope Sighting Chart

Yards to target clicks per inch 1 click equals

12.5	32	1/32" (.031)
25	16	1/16" (.063)
50	8	1/8" (.125)

100	4	1/4" (.250)
150	3	1/3" (.333)
200	2	1/2" (.500)
250	1.75	2/3" (.666)
300	1.50	3/4" (.750)
350	1.25	7/8" (.875)
400	1	1.0" (1.00)

Air Guns

Today's pneumatic pistols and, especially, rifles are the stuff of dreams for your grandfather, with the power and accuracy to kill rabbit-size or larger game to 50 yards, and an ability to carry thousands of rounds in your pockets.

When I stepped off the bus in Traverse City, Michigan, in 1982, I carried a duffel bag, a grant to attend Northwestern Michigan College, and a wallet containing $450—all that I owned in the world. I rented a windowless room at a seedy downtown hotel that had an open kitchen, and stowed my few possessions. Then I walked to a nearby hardware store where I spent fifty precious dollars on a then state-of-the-art Crosman American Classic .177-caliber pneumatic pistol that could drive a lead pellet up to

600 hundred feet per second with ten pumps. I didn't know how long it would take me to find a job, but I had a good idea of how long it would be before I got hungry.

As it turned out, I landed a living-wage job in less than a month; until then I attended classes at night, and when I wasn't studying or sleeping I roamed vacant buildings, shorelines, and tree-lined side streets with the Crosman tucked inside my book backpack. Urban game was plentiful: pigeons from abandoned factories, gray squirrels in city parks, and ducks or geese at the shores of Boardman Lake. I knew I was afoul of the law, but hunger is a powerful need, and hunting was a solution that I'd grown up using to remedy it. Kills had to be swift and surreptitious, and head shots were the order of the day. Prey was slid into reused plastic bread bags and into the daypack along with the pistol. Then I'd saunter nonchalantly behind a convenient bush, preferably near a shoreline, to quickly skin and clean my dinner.

Today that worn but still serviceable pistol has been replaced by highly improved telescopic-sighted, break-barrel air rifles that cock and power-up in a single stroke, deliver bone-breaking energy past 25 yards, and boast the accuracy of a fine target rifle. Nitrogen-filled pistons enable these guns to deliver consistent compression and velocity when left charged for long periods, and especially in subfreezing weather that has always made conventional air guns lose enough power to be useless as hunting weapons.

Quieter than even rimfire .22 BB and CB caps, Remington's NPSS is one good example of how grandpa's air gun has evolved into a genuine hunting weapon that impresses even big-bore rifle shooters. Mine wears the synthetic digital-camouflage stock, with pistol grip for enhanced trigger control, and a soft-rubber cheek piece that nestles comfortably under your cheekbone. The bull barrel and receiver wear no sights, but the rifle includes a very strong groove mount with integrated rings to securely hold a Center Point 3-9 × 40 scope with target turrets, adjustable objective lens, and Mil-Dot range finding reticle. The Nitro Piston power system generates up 1,200 feet per second from a standard 10-grain .177-caliber lead pellet, and with its adjustable target trigger this gun can consistently head-shoot squirrels beyond 25 yards. Remington rates this gun adequate for rabbits, but I believe head shots would be in order for any game larger than a snowshoe hare. With a length of 44 inches and weighing in at 7 pounds, this gun is a serious shooting platform. Retail is around $400.

The rifle that resides on my porch here in the wilds of Lake Superior State Forest, replacing the venerable .22 Long Rifle that had stood there guarding against rabid animals and predators since my earliest memories, is a .22-caliber Benjamin Trail NP break-barrel rifle. Powered by a more powerful Nitro-Piston, this beautiful beast wears a synthetic black pistol-grip cheekpiece stock that is comfortable enough to elicit praise from most shooters. In terms of performance, this gun is a hammer, driving 14-grain lead pellets up to 950 fps, with 23 foot-pounds of muzzle energy, 16 percent more downrange energy than a .177-caliber, and enough terminal force to take game larger than hares. The Trail NP also wears a Center Point 3-9 × 40 air rifle scope with target turrets, adjustable objective lens, and Mil-Dot crosshairs. Length is 43 inches, weight is 8 pounds; a handsome black cushioned rifle sling with the Benjamin logo embroidered in gold makes the Trail NP easy to carry for pot-hunting and survival. Retail for this survival rifle is about $300.

In 2010, Benjamin introduced the Trail NP XL 725, a break-barrel .25 caliber that can drive any of the existing array of 14- to more than 30-grain pellets that already exist at velocities up to 800 feet per second, with more than 30 foot-pounds of muzzle energy. Like the two rifles described above, this large-bore model uses a smooth-shooting Nitro-Piston drive that delivers reliably consistent velocities in cold weather, or when left cocked-and-charged for long periods. With 8 percent more downrange energy retention than its .22 counterpart, and prairie dog kills reported past 80 yards, the 725 might be the better choice for some.

Adding to the value of any of these calibers as a survival weapon is the fact that with pneumatic rifles power is derived from the gun itself, not externally from a cartridge. All you need are the bullets; there are no spent casings, there's no smoke or odor, and no loud noise. More than a thousand rounds can be carried in jacket pockets, and thousands of rounds can be carried afield if need be. If you subscribe to the philosophy that no gun is a good hunting caliber when it's empty, then the latest ideal survival rifle might well be an air rifle.

Ranger Sling

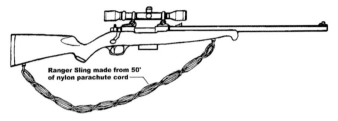

Ranger Sling made from 50' of nylon parachute cord

Everything in a survival kit should perform multiple tasks, and the Ranger Sling is prime example of that philosophy.

Among the gun handling lessons I learned as a kid—a few accompanied by a smack to the head to emphasize their importance—was the real value of a rifle sling. A properly slung long arm is a safe gun, because its barrel must always be pointed either upward or downward, and muzzle-down carry is always sound wisdom in falling rain or snow. "Getting into" a sling by wrapping it around the forearm until taut helps to enhance a shooter's accuracy, particularly in situations that call for making long shots from an unsupported offhand position. And of course a sling is handy for just carrying the gun to which it's attached, leaving a hunter's hands free to negotiate tangled brush, or to drag a whitetail from the woods.

The problem is that conventional rifle slings have always been little more than a strap between forend and buttstock swivels, good for carrying and shooting the gun to which they're attached, but not much else. Attempts by manufacturers to increase utility by adding cartridge carriers, pouches, and other accoutrements to their slings have for the most part detracted from their usefulness by making them difficult to wrap around the forearm, cumbersome, and sometimes pendulously heavy. The rifle carrier that has best served me personally over the past 20 years is a simple homemade outfit called the Ranger Sling, named after the elite military unit to which its invention is credited. Comprised entirely of rope or cord—my own consist of 100 feet of 550-pound test parachute cord—the Ranger Sling is soft against the shoulder, the quietest of any sling I've used, and easy to get into for offhand shots.

In addition to working very well as a gun carrier, the Ranger Sling can have tremendous value as a ready source of strong cordage. I've taken lengths from my slings to replace broken bootlaces, to make a fish stringer, to lash together a shelter frame, and on a few occasions I've hung adult whitetails from a single strand of parachute cord and skinned them. Strap-type slings can't match a Ranger Sling in terms of versatility or use-fulness, and "working" long arms adapted for use in places where civilization is far away are often carried by this design. So long as 4 feet of cord remain, a rifle or shotgun has a functional sling, but I've yet to noticeably deplete the first Ranger Sling I made, more than twenty years ago.

The first step in making a Ranger Sling is to measure it against both the firearm and user. Slip one end of the cord or rope you'll be using through the forend swivel of your unloaded gun (open the action), then tie that end off securely to the buttstock swivel. Pinch together the dou-bled cord from either side of the forend swivel to keep it from sliding freely, and shoulder the gun in barrel-up and barrel-down modes to get

Ranger Sling rifle sling detail

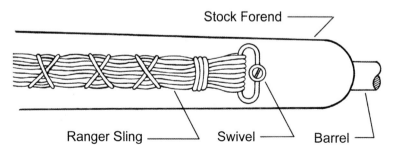

A Ranger Sling's simplicity and ease of manufacture belies its value.

a fix on how long subsequent loops of cord will need to be, adjusting the length as needed.

I recommend allowing 3 to 4 inches of latitude when determining how long your Ranger Sling will be from swivel to swivel, because the finished project will be about 2 inches in diameter, and for those times when terrain or conditions dictate secure hands-free carry of a long arm across your back, with the sling running diagonally across your chest. The finished Ranger Sling is not adjustable, but then, not many hunters need to adjust a sling once a comfortable all-around length has been determined.

When you've determined the desired length, cut this "master loop" free of the rest of the cord and tie it off securely to the forend swivel. The master loop never leaves the gun because it serves as the most fundamental means of carrying it, and because it serves as a gauge for applying a new Ranger Sling should you deplete the original's supply of cord.

Suspend your gun upside-down by the master loop from a convenient, secure protrusion (I like doorknobs), again making absolutely certain that its chamber is empty (you can't be too obsessive about gun safety). The gun's weight will pull the master loop taut. After freeing it of tangles along its entire length, tie one end of the remaining cord to either swivel, then run the opposite end through the opposite swivel. Pull the cord through until this first loop in the Ranger Sling is parallel to and identical to the master loop. Double the free end back through the opposite swivel, and add another identical loop over the doorknob.

And so on. This is the tedious part, threading consecutive loops back and forth between swivels until they've consumed a hundred feet of cord. But be comforted by knowing that with every loop you add, the remaining cord grows shorter. When you've threaded all but 10 feet or so onto the gun, it's time to wrap up the project.

Literally, because the final step in assembling a Ranger Sling is to bind together the strands of all those loops so they can't snag against brush. Start by winding the remaining cord around the massed loop strands in a wide spiral, with about 4 inches between each turn. When you've spiraled to the opposite swivel, thread the free end through the swivel and wind another spiral in the other direction. Repeat this spiral binding process until only enough cord remains to tie off securely to the nearest swivel. The final result should have a cable-like appearance, with no loose ends or loops sticking out.

You can also add to a Ranger Sling, as well as take from it. A short length of cord or light rope can be looped and spiraled over top of the existing sling. One example I saw incorporated several types of cordage, from fly line and nylon string to parachute cord, which doubtless added to its versatility in the wilderness.

While a completed Ranger Sling isn't repulsive, neither will it enhance the showiness of a favorite deer rifle on the gun rack. A nice compromise between keeping that Browning or Remington looking good in the den, yet functional in the field, is to make your sling using spring-loaded detachable swivels, preferably with screw-down locks to keep them fastened to your gun in rough country. That way you can dress your finest rifle in a hand-worked leather sling for a day at the range, but quickly convert it to field readiness by changing over to the ranger sling.

CHAPTER TWELVE

OTHER HUNTING WEAPONS

Archery

Although the hemorrhage-inducing power of a modern broad head far surpasses anything a medieval archer could have used, an arrow lacks the hydrostatic shocking power of a bullet that travels 3 to 4 times faster than the quickest of them. It would be bad for business if archery hunting magazines admitted it, but the cleanest archery kill is no less gruesome than the old pig-farmers' practice of sticking a hog, then letting it walk around until if fell over from blood loss. The principle is identical; a deer pierced through its heart with the most efficient hunting broad head just runs until a critical amount of blood spills from the rent into its chest cavity.

This is not an indictment of bow hunting, but it is a statement of fact, and a fact of life that anyone who needs to hunt game or fish for food should be aware of. Hunting isn't (or shouldn't) be done for points. I've never met a sane person who didn't make his or her first kill with a little remorse at having taken a life. Be prepared, killing is not enjoyable to an average person.

Yet, we—humans—are predators, and an arrow launcher was super-seded only by the advent of firearms. It does no harm to have an archery weapon on hand for squirrels, muskrats, rabbits—even birds. Not many animals are, in fact, inedible, and your tastes in what you consider to be food will expand proportionally with how hungry you become.

An arrow launcher need not be complex, and should be simple enough to demand minimal maintenance. The compound bow, favored by deer hunters and Rambo is not a good candidate, because its pulleys and cables require maintenance, and its numerous parts may be impossible to replace or repair in post-disaster confusion. Another drawback with compound bows is that the quest for ever faster arrow speeds has made them unable to use traditional wood arrows, because the flex an arrow endures during its acceleration stroke is often sufficient to cause wood grains to shatter apart; that, of course, makes improvising arrows in the field an impossibility.

Although a compound hunting bow is easier to master, with its adjustable sights and tunable system, the best bowshots in the world have always used conventional recurve or long bows that are essentially just bent sticks with a string at either end. These are instinct shooters; they aim with a brain that can calculate all of the variables it sees and feels, and use that information to deliver an arrow with sometimes incredible precision. This takes practice, and can be obtained through no other means.

While not the sniper weapon portrayed in some movies, a crossbow is a potentially effective hunting weapon; but keep the model you select simple enough to keep working in the field.

Easier to master, because it possesses sights, is the crossbow. Again, it needs to be a recurve, because you can make your own arrows in the field, if necessary, and a length of parachute cord will suffice as a bowstring, if necessary. If you can hit them, small game animals can be killed with field- or target-tipped arrows, and even a low-powered beginner's-class bow has adequate power.

Making a Bow-and-Arrow

Every kid used to make a bow-and-arrow to play with, and their sometimes unfletched stick-arrows actually took a fair amount of small game. Like any hand-crafted item, you can make the weapon as complicated and labor intensive as you want, but a basic bow, with arrows, can be constructed in less than an hour. Again, don't make the job more complicated than it needs to be.

First, select a bow stave. Flexible green wood, like willow, cedar, even maple, works. Try to select a stave that is naturally bent like a bow. Ideal candidates are at least an inch in diameter at their thickest point, and as long as possible—between 5 and 8 feet.

Using a timber hitch knot, tie a strong cord to one end. Then, place one end of the stave against the ground, over the inset of one foot, with the stave between your legs, near your crotch. This positions the other end of the stave behind your opposite hip. Bend the upper end of the stave over your hip, and circle the end once with the bow string (to make it easier to hold under tension), then tie it off using another timber hitch, and a couple of half-hitches.

Arrows should naturally be made from as straight a sapling as you can find, cut as flat as you can on their thicker, butt end. If you can do it, a small notch cut crosswise into that end serves as a nock to accommodate the bowstring. A few wraps of thread (held in place with tape or pine sap) keeps the end from splitting.

This field-expedient bow, made from a green maple sapling, and strung with parachute cord, took just 15 minutes to make.

A field-expedient arrow can be manufactured anywhere, and the simplest way to make sure that it flies straight is to fletch it with duct-tape vanes.

Whittle the opposite, business end of the arrow to a sharp point, and, if possible, char it in a fire to harden the wood.

Fletching, which causes the tail of an arrow to drag like an air brake that keeps a projectile straight as it flies through the air, has traditionally been made from feathers. A feather is split down its center, then attached in 2 or 3 equidistant locations around the arrow shaft, just ahead of the nock. In olden days, a feather half was affixed by pine pitch and sinew, but you can use wraps of thread at either end with glue. A quick and easy modern alternative is duct tape (see illustration), trimmed with scissors.

Slingshot

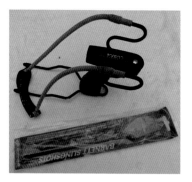

A slingshot has been taking game since before a diminutive sheep herder named David used a centrifugal sling to fell a Shaq-size Philistine named Goliath. A heavy, hard projectile propelled at an accelerated speed can deliver bone-crushing force to victims impacted by it.

A modernized version of David's sling is the Wrist-Rocket, a type of slingshot. Introduced in the early 1970s, this weapon employs super-elastic surgical tubing to propel steel bearings (or marbles, or just stones) at lethal velocities.

Like a traditional bow-and-arrow, aiming is purely instinctive, because there are no sights, and accuracy must be learned. Practice makes perfect, and the secret lies in repetitiveness; typically, the pouch, loaded with a projectile, is pinched between thumb and forefinger, and drawn back to the chin. Release at the same point every time, as smoothly as possible.

And, like a bow, firearm, or any distance weapon, the trick with either is to get as close to your victim as possible. There's no such thing as cheating or being unsportsmanlike when the objective is survival. Every advantage needs to be employed, and if you can shoot a victim from a foot distant, do it.

CHAPTER THIRTEEN

TRAPS AND SNARES

Traps and Snares

Spring snares release a restrained force to violently yank a noose tight around its victim's neck, even lifting it off the ground, or decapitating large animals, depending on spring force and type of snare line used. By providing their own killing force, instead of relying on an animal's struggles to kill itself, spring snares are decidedly lethal.

The weakest link in every spring snare is its trigger, the mechanism responsible for releasing pent-up spring force when tripped by a gentler outside force. Ideally, the trigger can restrain a force sufficient to guarantee a quick death, yet releases that force with only a light pull, while being impervious to elements (wind, ice . . .) that could cause it to hang-up, spring prematurely, or otherwise fail.

Pencil Snare

In terms of simplicity, reliability, and effectiveness, the Pencil Snare is the best survival snare for every environment. With two release points, or "sears," the pencil snare is twice as likely to trip, while remaining stable enough to resist the forces of wind and rain. It can be constructed from any environment that supports woody growth, and the design works

A pencil snare, shown in its entirety.

well on every size game. With a little creativity, the pencil trigger can be employed for a variety of "sets," including trip wires, deadfalls, and even booby traps.

Components of a pencil snare are simple and easy to construct using only a knife; they consist of the snare cord, two notched anchor stakes, and the "pencil" trigger that fits into and is restrained by the notches in the anchor stakes. Wooden components are best made from dead wood that is dry, but still firm enough to whittle; green wood is more difficult to shape. Size of the snare and its parts are dictated by the size of the animal it is intended to capture, but generally the anchor stakes are at least two inches in diameter, or at least twice the size of the pencil.

When cutting notches, first observe the classic wisdom of not cutting toward yourself. With the knife in your preferred hand, press the cutting edge into the wood by pushing against the blade's unsharpened spine with the opposite thumb (another example of why a survival knife is not double-edged). For anchor stakes, use this method to shave thin layers that extend progressively deeper into the wood, each shaving extending an equal distance. Every three or four layers, place the cutting edge across the top of the shavings, and press down hard with a rocking motion that cuts the shavings free, and leaves a flat bearing surface to better hold the pencil in place. Continue shaving and cutting (don't try to take too much wood at once) until the anchor notches are at least one-half-inch deep, and clean and flat at their tops.

A pencil snare can be quickly set in any environment, in any season.

The pencil dictates how far apart the anchor stakes will be set, and, in general, too wide is better than too narrow. The pencil should be straight and even, and stout enough to restrain the amount of spring force being used. Gently shave the upper ends to give them flat surfaces that mate well with the anchor stake notches.

The best snare cord is man-made. Rawhide and braided plant fibers cannot match nylon cord for strength and toughness, or for the slipperiness that is critical to smooth, fast noose operation. Tensile strength should be matched to the weight of the animal being snared, as are noose diameters and snare heights. For smaller game, 10 feet per snare is more than sufficient.

With notched anchor stakes, pencil, and cord in hand, first tie a noose loop of the desired diameter—about eight inches for most small animals. Next, using the pencil length to determine how far apart to place them, push the sharpened anchor stakes into the soil in unobtrusive spots at either side of a likely animal trail; drilling them down with a hard, twisting motion. In most soils, with most game, stakes are anchored well enough at 3 inches. In snow, anchor stakes for snares and fishing sets are held in place by packing snow around their bases, then pouring a little water on the mounded snow to lock the stakes in ice.

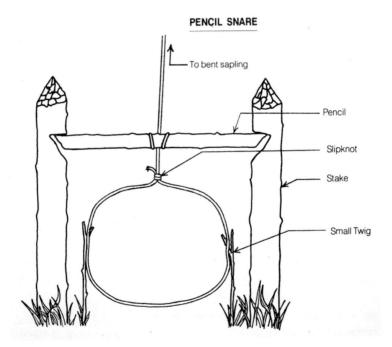

PENCIL SNARE

To bent sapling

Pencil

Slipknot

Stake

Small Twig

Simple to manufacture, fast, and secure, while being easily triggered.

Next, with noose held open to the desired diameter, tie the cord, just above the slipknot, to the pencil's center. Wrap the cord around the pencil twice, and tie it off with a square knot—the type of knot used isn't important, except that it must be able to restrain a strong pull from above without pulling against the noose suspended from the pencil's underside. Set the pencil into the anchor stake notches to see how everything fits, and make adjustments as needed (noose diameter and height, stake height, notch angles and such).

When everything fits, all that remains is to "cock" the trap by connecting it to lethal force, usually in the form of a green sapling at the side of an animal trail, or a live branch overhead. If no suitable spring is available at the desired location, one can be created there by drilling a long, stout sapling into the ground. Again, no need for complexity; the spring needs only to be capable of exerting a strong upward pull against the pencil when it is bent over and held under tension by the pencil in the anchor stake notches. When everything is cocked and in place, spread the noose to hold it open by hooking either side over blades of grass or tiny twigs. The noose's bottom should be suspended at least two inches above ground, to ensure that an animal passing in either direction will push against it with legs or chest when its head passes through the noose.

With a little ingenuity, a pencil snare can be made into a booby trap, or an alarm system.

Snare Placement

Snares are not as productive in the real world as movie writers might have us believe. Every fur trapper of old knew that his prey, whatever its species, would be intimately familiar with every stick and stone in its domain, and would probably avoid any noticeable changes made to a regularly used trail. Keep that in mind when selecting a location for snares; if possible, use a snare cord that does not contrast with the surrounding terrain, and make as few changes to the environment as possible.

Game trails are the most likely places to set snares. Try not to leave your scent in the area, or to leave obvious sign, but the best plan is to set as many snares as you can before nightfall, then "run" them in the morning to retrieve caught animals. If the snare is empty, reset it, and—survival strategy permitting—check them all again the next morning.

When making any survival tool, no technique is written in stone, and imagination is a powerful design tool. Available materials can be very different from one environment to another, or from season to season, and there is no right or wrong way to do anything; there are only methods that do or do not work. Practice the skills described here to understand

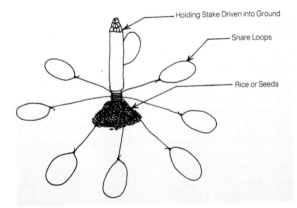

This foot snare for birds is an ages-old method of entangling a bird's foot, and holding it until it can be dispatched; bird-foot snares may be baited, but ducks and geese, for example, group together on shores during migrations, and may become unsnared in unbaited traps.

their workings, and to get tactile experience, but do not be befuddled if an environment doesn't provide precisely the materials you've practiced using. For humans, fight-or-flight is a useless instinct; our adaptability relies on abstract thought and an ability to combine dissimilar products into the assembly of complex machines that make life easier. You belong to the most successful species on this planet, and if any animal can figure out how to stay alive, you can.

CHAPTER FOURTEEN

LIVE-GIVING WATER

Water

Who does not remember residents of New Orleans who ignored FEMA's order to evacuate, only to find themselves begging for drinking water from their rooftops the first day after the storm? Not to mention the epidemic of cholera and other aquatic diseases that occurred in the following weeks—because you *will* drink the water, however polluted it is, if you get thirsty enough. No one lasts more than a few days without water.

Finding Water

Like someone watching the victim in a slasher movie bumble around while you know the killer waits behind a door, I cannot sit through most survival-type shows while experts attempt to find water—it makes me crazy.

Finding water is not a challenge in most environments where animals live. They get moisture from somewhere, and in most cases, that somewhere is a water hole. Remember that water runs downhill, and that the lower you go, geographically, the closer you are to water. Elephants dig into the sand of dried-up streambeds to find water lying, at times, a foot below the surface.

Where there are green plants, there must be water close. Low places that are permanently shaded probably have water closer to the surface.

Moist soil under a rock probably means the same. Water-loving trees, like birches and willows, are another indication that the water table is close.

Humans have been digging wells for millennia, and any place that has hosted human civilizations must—*must*—also have water. An added benefit is that water taken from a hole in the earth, even if it's muddy, is almost certainly free of parasites and microbial pathogens.

Obtaining Water from Plant Tissue

A stopgap measure that can keep you alive is to crush any green foliage into a wet, pulpy mass in your hands (or—better—inside a plastic bag), then drip the usually bitter juices into your mouth.

What's in the Water?

The most dangerous threats cannot be seen with the naked eye. Most recognized by name is the free-swimming flagellate *Giardia lamblia*, the parasite usually blamed for "beaver fever" outbreaks. Most common, according to the Centers for Disease Control, is a tough intestinal cyst named *Cryptosporidium parvum*, which the CDC estimates will infect at least 80 percent of Americans in their lifetimes. Another cyst that is common around human habitation, particularly refugee camps, is *Cyclospora cayetanensis*. These aren't the only dangers lurking within a drop of water, only the most common in North America.

Like most parasites, neither the Giardia flagellate nor the Cryptosporidium cyst are normally fatal to their hosts, because it's not in any parasite's best interest to kill a host. Both colonize a victim's lower intestine, taking nourishment while reproducing, causing intermittent bouts of fever, nausea, and diarrhea, until live eggs and expired adults are expelled after about two months. If you suspect you've contracted a parasite, seek medical help. Do not take antacids, as these may mask signs of a parasite's presence in a stool sample.

Other hazards—seen in the aftermath of almost every natural disaster—are chemicals and raw sewage that leach into groundwater as a result of spills and flooding. Gasoline stations, fertilized farmlands, industrial sites . . . all of these are to be avoided when looking for drinking water. Chemicals are not usually an immediate threat, but it should be presumed that there will be cholera, typhoid, E. coli, and other sewage-borne pathogens present downstream of such places.

Water from Toilets

On more than one sci-fi movie, survivors have been depicted taking drinking water from the bowl of a toilet. This is dangerously inaccurate. Toilet bowls, no matter how clean they appear, are petrie dishes of *Escherichia coli* (E. coli), *Vibrio cholerae* (cholera), and host of other dangerous communicable diseases. Toilet bowls are not acceptable sources of water.

A typical household flush toilet carries an elevated reservoir tank on its rear, containing (typically 1.3 to 1.6 gallons) water that, in fact, is the same quality as the water that comes from your kitchen faucet. Rust and other sediment may make water in a reservoir tank appear "dirty," but this water is as safe to drink, without treatment, as that from any faucet in the house. Should it become necessary to drink water from a toilet bowl, it should be treated by boiling, or with 2–3 drops of *chlorine bleach* or *tincture of iodine* per quart.

Making Water Safe

Boiling is the classic method of destroying harmful organisms in water, because you can't see 180 degrees, where most pathogens die immediately, but you can see a rolling boil (212 degrees Fahrenheit).

A rolling boil for two minutes kills every living thing. *Boiling doesn't remove chemicals or other contaminants.* One "survival" docudrama on an educational channel depicted a doctor who made water from a truck radiator potable by boiling it—this is dangerously untrue.

Iodine was the chemical "purifier" of choice for decades, until it was discovered that no concentration that is safe for human consumption will kill cysts like cryptosporidium or cyclospora. Iodine does kill giardia, bacteria, and viruses.

Chlorine, often marketed as a water disinfectant under the name *Halazone*, possesses essentially the same qualities as iodine; it kills giardia, bacteria, and viruses, but is ineffective against cysts.

Both chlorine and iodine have recently been made obsolete as water treatments by tablets made from s*odium chlorite* and s*odium dichloroisocyanurate dihydrate*, like the Micropur MP1 tablets from Katadyn (about fifty cents per tablet). The only EPA-registered water purification pill on the market, each tab treats one liter of water, killing giardia, bacteria, and viruses within fifteen minutes, but even they require a four-hour wait to ensure the demise of cysts.

Katadyn's Combi filter can even be purchased with an attachment that connects it to a house faucet.

Katadyn's Vario water filter uses a combination filter element.

MSR's (Mountain Safety Research) *MiOx* disinfectant tool ($140) employs raw water, ordinary salt, and electricity from wafer (wristwatch) batteries to create a super-oxygenated cocktail that kills giardia, bacteria, and viruses immediately, but also requires four hours to ensure the death of cysts.

The MSR (Mountain Safety Research) MiOx purifier uses raw water, salt, and electricity to create a "super chlorine cocktail," similar to Katadyn's Micropur tablets.

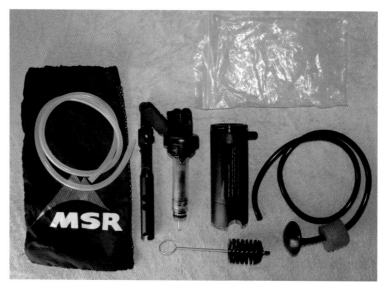

MSR SweetWater microfilter.

One of the first, and still favorite, portable water filters, MSR's MiniWorks filter typically works long enough to become an heirloom.

One of the most overlooked maintenance procedures for any water filter is simply to thoroughly dry its component parts.

Basic Solar Still

The simplest distillation device, passive solar stills are an old standard on US Navy life rafts, and they've been recommended in virtually every wilderness survival manual. A solar still uses sunlight to evaporate untreated water, trapping its component gases against a transparent waterproof membrane. There they cool and condense back into water, which drips into a container below.

A solar still can be as uncomplicated as digging a hole in the ground, setting a metal soup can at its bottom, and covering the hole with a sheet of Visqueen (clear plastic). Moisture trapped in the soil will produce some condensation, but for best results the bottom of the hole should be saturated with raw water, seawater, or even urine or sewage-contaminated flood water. As temperatures cool after sunset, warmed oxygen and hydrogen trapped by the membrane condense against its underside. A stone placed in the membrane's center makes it cone-shaped, and gravity causes condensed droplets to slide downward to its lowest point, then into the container below.

A solar still is most effective when constructed with a clear plastic membrane that permits maximum sunlight to penetrate. It works best in arid conditions, where air isn't so humid that moisture won't evaporate. Under desert conditions, a solar still—or several of them—can keep a person alive.

A container, half-filled with untreated water, then heated by hot sun or weak flame to a point of condensation, will output distilled, potable water from an exit hose at its top; a condensation still, like the one shown, could have prevented the epidemic of disease that followed Hurricane Katrina.

Condensation Stills

A more efficient variation of the excavated solar still is the solar condensation still. A metal or plastic gasoline can with a pour spout is ideal, but even soda bottles can be made to work. Fill the can half full of contaminated water, and slide a 6-foot section of garden hose over the can's pour spout; on many cans the hose will fit snugly without modification, but it may be taped or clamped to the spout to ensure that vapors can escape only through the open end of the hose. Wrap the hose into a coil, tying or taping it to hold that form. Make sure that the coil is at the bottom, as shown, to further trap heavier-than-air particles. Set the half-full container onto a roof, or another sunny, hot surface, and place the open end of the hose into a container.

Heated Condensation Still

A solar still is passive, reliant on sunlight and humidity, but a heated condensation still uses a small fire under a metal can to continuously evaporate water, producing drinkable water even in subfreezing temperatures. Fundamentally the same as the solar type, it needs a steel gasoline-type can that won't melt. Again, the can's pour spout is an output for condensed water, and should be lengthened with a garden-hose extension that is long enough to accommodate a particle-trapping loop.

Because it can operate nonstop twenty-four hours a day for as long as fuel and raw water are available, a heated condensation still is ideal for producing larger volumes of clean water for a group. And in a community setting, like post-Katrina New Orleans, it should be no problem to round up enough gas cans and garden hoses to generate as much drinking water as needed. Safety warnings include never heating water to a boil, and never permitting the container to go dry; either could cause unsafe pressures inside the container. If the can bulges even slightly, remove it from heat immediately.

Water Filters

The most effective and surest means of making water safe to drink is to remove whatever harmful contaminants it might contain. The stuff of science fiction a couple of generations ago, water filters have been around long enough to have been thoroughly tested, improved, and to have become an integral part of every well-supplied backpacker's kit. Mandated by the EPA to remove pathogens—meaning that it has to work, or it cannot be sold as a water filter—they can also reduce chemical contaminants by as much as 80 percent.

Powered by hand pump, gravity, or a hard squeeze, water filters employ a process known as reverse osmosis to force raw water through a microporous filter, where it emerges on the other side free of pathogens and most contaminants. Filter elements are replaceable and may be comprised of ceramic or fiber. Both perform equally, but fiber cartridges (about $70) are cheaper and rated to filter up to two hundred gallons before needing replacement. More expensive (about $100) ceramic types require frequent disassembly and cleaning, but essentially last forever. Replacement filter cartridges typically cost two-thirds as much as a new filter.

The filter shown is perhaps a prime example of long-term, quality-made water filters.

Just fill it with untreated water, screw on the filter cap, and squeeze potable water into your mouth.

Water filters take many forms today, and there is no justification for contracting a waterborne parasite, although tens of thousands of hikers—and even city dwellers—persist in doing so every year.

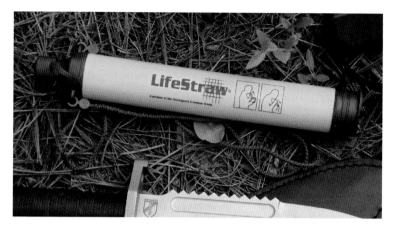

The LifeStraw; perhaps the lightest, most inexpensive way to avoid intestinal parasites.

Driving a Well

A 5-gallon bucket, with lid, and a (clean, of course) toilet plunger has served as a field-expedient washing machine for generations.

At some point in early human history someone figured out that water drawn from below ground didn't carry sicknesses like open surface waters, and it has been a practice since biblical times to obtain fresh water from underground aquifers. Before pumps and pipes became common hardware items, wells were made by simply digging a narrow hole down to the water table, then drawing the water that seeped into its bottom to the surface in a bucket attached to a rope. A seepage well required that a low, unscalable wall be constructed around its perimeter to keep water-seeking mice, frogs, and other small animals from falling in and drowning—and fouling all the water below. It also needed a roof over it to fend off contamination with bird guano. Fortunately, a shallow seepage well can be emptied and cleaned by steadily pulling filled buckets of water to the surface, where they are poured out, until the well bottom is empty; unfortunately, many bone-dry wooden towns of the Old West were burned to the ground because the village well went empty in the middle of a fire.

An improved version of the open seepage well that has been in use since the first cast-iron water pump was forged is the driven well. This method of bringing groundwater to the surface uses a rocket-shaped "well point" to drive downward through soil until it reaches the water table. The well point is hollow, with (usually) slotted holes along its barrel to allow water to flow into it. Inside, these holes are covered with a heavy-mesh stainless-steel screen to keep out coarse sand and gravel. By driving a well point into the earth until it is entirely submerged in subterranean water, then fastening on lengths of pipe with sealed joints as the well point drives deeper, a simple piston-drawn, hand-operated pitcher pump can easily bring up a gallon of drinking water that in some locations has a better taste and more biologically usable minerals than any water sold in a bottle.

The first step is to determine as precisely as possible where will be the best place to sink your well—where the largest deposit of water lies, and where it is nearest to the surface. The most time-honored method for accomplishing that is through "divination." This still inadequately explained yet remarkably effective technique for locating subterranean water was once practiced by well diggers using a green willow "twitch."

Water "witchers" would walk a selected area holding their twitches—which weren't necessarily made from willow—parallel to the earth; when the twitch began to vibrate or dip toward the earth of its own accord, there was water present underfoot, and the more forceful the dips, the closer the water table.

Today's witchers most often use a pair of L-shaped steel wires with equal-length sides about six inches long. To eliminate any chance of being influenced by the user, one side of each wire is placed inside a plastic PVC (water pipe) tube, and the tubes held vertical so that the free end of each wire is parallel to the ground. With tubes held at an even height with about four inches between them, the witcher walks his chosen area until the wires swivel toward one another and form an X. Below that X there is water close to the surface. The physics of water-witching have frustrated scientists for more than a century, but the fact is, it works, and the technique is still used by professional well drillers today.

Other witching methods include the time-honored willow "twitch," a Y-shaped switch cut from the branches of a living willow tree. Holding the Y by its two shortest legs, with their crotch and the longest leg facing forward, away from the user, a diviner simply paced off likely areas for a well. When the long leg began to vibrate, then dip visibly downward—sometimes with real force—a witcher was standing atop water. An almost humorous alternative is to hold an ordinary crosscut saw by its handle, with its blade pointing forward at belt level, held even and horizontal to the ground. For those who have the divining gift, the saw blade will vibrate up and down with greater energy the closer its holder gets to water.

While every first-time water witcher always believes that the technique works, even if they can't explain it, it doesn't seem to work for everyone. When I needed to dig a well at my 1800s-style log-cabin homestead, I paced off ten paces from an exceptionally large multi-trunked white birch, then dug down ten feet until I'd created a narrow hole with three feet of cold, sweet water at its bottom. Other visual indicators that water probably lies near the surface include cracked mud at seasonal water holes, the valleys created by even long-vanished riverbeds, and the presence of reeds, and marsh grasses. The lowest point in elevation is nearly always closest to water, while hilltops are always the farthest away.

There are several methods of getting a well point down to the water table, but the one most used by people in remote places today is the driving method, in which the point is driven downward like a nail. A pipe cap screwed snugly, but not tightly, onto the threaded end protects it from being damaged or deformed while being pounded from above. It is critical that neither the open end nor the threads below it are harmed while the point is being pounded into the earth.

Begin by digging a clean pilot hole at least two feet deep using a hand auger or a shovel; the auger will make a pipe-size hole, but the wider shovel hole will require that soil be tamped around the well point to help hold it straight when pounding. A PVC casing placed over the well pipe—but kept above the point so that it doesn't inhibit water flow—keeps loose dirt from falling in around the well pipe as it is driven downward.

Well hammers can be as simple as a sledgehammer, or—more preferably when soil density permits—a large wooden mallet that is less punishing on the end of the soft-iron pipe being pounded. When punching through harder earth, some well drillers employ a pile-driver weight (often just a large-diameter iron pipe filled with concrete) suspended from a tripod where it is hoisted upward via a pulley, then dropped from a height of about four feet onto the capped upper end of the well pipe. More physically demanding versions include "slam hammers" comprised of a heavy, flat-bottom iron weight with a long steel rod that extends from it and into the uncapped well pipe, using it as a guide when the hammer is dropped from a height of about three feet. Another form of well hammer slides over the pipe, and can work with the pipe end capped or open.

When the well point has been driven down until only about ten inches remains above ground, remove the protective pipe cap and screw a four-inch nipple (a collar with internal threads) over the exposed threads. Use pipe joint compound or Teflon plumber's tape (wound in the direction of the threads, clockwise) to ensure a watertight seal. Screw a six-foot pipe that is threaded on both ends into the nipple—actual length of the pipe can vary, but it has to be short enough to reach the upper end (you'll probably want a stepladder). Cap the upper end of the pipe, and pound it down until only about ten inches remain above ground. Remove the cap, apply joint compound to the threads and screw on another nipple, then screw another length of pipe into the top of the nipple. Pound this pipe down, and repeat the process, making sure to seal every threaded connection with joint compound or Teflon tape.

The pipe should move visibly downward with each blow from your hammer. If it stops and refuses to sink further after several blows, you might have hit a large rock. Do not continue hammering, or you might damage the well point—maybe even bend it, making it virtually impossible to pull back to the surface. It's easier to pull up an undamaged well point by gently wobbling the pipe back and forth to widen the hole as you pull upward, then to move the operation to another location.

When you reach the water table you will hear a hollow "bong" sound that issues from the pipe with every blow. To test it, remove the cap and drop a long string with a weight tied to its end (chalk line works well) down the well pipe until slack in the string tells you that the weight has reached the bottom of the well point. Draw the string back up, and measure how much of its length has been wetted to determine how deeply the well point has penetrated into the water table. To ensure good suction at the pump, it is important that the entire length of the perforated well point be immersed, and preferably at least 2 feet beyond that to account for seasonal variations in the water table.

When the drop-string is wetted to a length of at least 5 feet, it's time to screw on a pitcher pump (remember to seal the threads, or it might not draw efficiently). Prime the pump to create suction for its vacuum cylinder by pouring a cup of water into the pump's top, and jack the handle until water spurts from the pump with each down stroke. To be sure the well point is fully immersed in water, remove the pump, replace the cap, and hammer the pipe another two feet. Replace the pump, and jack the handle roughly 100 times to create a hollow filled with clear water around the well point. Alternatively, you can use a portable electric water pump to create a water-filled cavity around the well point, and to test for a benchmark flow of five gallons per minute. When only clear water comes from the well spout, remove the pump and thread on a "check valve" between the well pipe below and the pump above; this will help to prevent water in the pipe from draining back down, and reducing the need to prime the pump.

How deep your well needs to be of course depends on how deep the water table might be in a particular place. The depth to which manual pumps can operate is limited, depending on the type of pump, by the force of gravity, and the length of its drawing stroke. In general, pitcher, jet, or centrifugal hand pumps are effective to a depth of twenty-five feet; larger stand pumps with draw cylinders will work to a depth of fifty feet.

Finally, check with authorities to be sure that there are no laws prohibiting wells where you live, and that the groundwater is not contaminated by toxic chemicals that have leached into it—this is not uncommon in more developed areas. Even where home wells are permitted, you will probably need to buy a building permit, and maybe have the finished well inspected and approved. Even with the red tape, a driven hand-pumped well is worth the hassle for the peace of mind it brings knowing that you can never run out of drinking water, come what may.

Seepage Well

Seepage wells have been supplying homes, and once whole villages, with safe drinking water since before recorded history—since someone discovered that digging straight down to the water table netted a stable abundance of cold, potable water. So important were village wells of old that stone walls were erected around them as a barrier against runoff, a roof was placed above to keep out bird guano, and community wells became renowned as places to find friendly conversation.

What makes well water safe to drink are many tons of soil and rock compressed under its own weight. This natural filter removes infectious organisms and, with the exception of a few heavily polluted areas, groundwater is safe for drinking. Woodsmen have always known that water drawn directly from a springhead is safe to drink, because springs are essentially holes from which trapped groundwater escapes.

A survival seepage well taps into groundwater at levels where one to two feet of earth separates topsoil contamination from the underlying water table. The principle isn't much different than a Bedouin obtaining potable water by digging a shallow hole at the lowest point of a seemingly dried up water hole. A seepage well's advantage is that it not only fills with water kept uncontaminated by layers of soil, but makes bodies of water that would otherwise be unsafe to drink from into good places to cook a meal and fill a canteen.

The best sites for digging a seepage well are at least four feet back from a waterline, preferably in sandy or rocky soil that settles quickly to the well's bottom. Using whatever tools are at hand, from a stout knife to a slab of wood broken from the outside of a rotting stump, excavate a hole there. Be especially sure to scrape all topsoil outward from the intended hole first, as this is the layer of earth in which infectious organisms are most likely to be concentrated. At a depth of about two feet, the hole's bottom will become watery, but dig at least six inches more to help ensure a good pool.

Like any open well, the potable water that seeps into the hole will at first be murky. It is drinkable right away, but silt can trigger the body's gag reflex. Larger particulates can be filtered out through a shirt or other cloth. If no container is available, an article of clothing can be saturated, and moisture sucked from its fibers. In a few hours, after all silt has settled to the well's bottom, the clear water in your well can be used to fill water bottles, for cooking, or drunk directly without filtering or boiling, and without fear of parasites or other pathogens.

CHAPTER FIFTEEN

BREATH OF LIFE

Air

Survival experts have always liked to debate which element or piece of gear was most vital to maintaining life. Like the never-ending argument over which gun works best for deer hunting, or which fishing fly is most effective, the thing you most need is entirely dependent on the situation. But it goes without saying that if the thing you need is air, then that is definitely a critical problem. It might take days or months to die of thirst or starvation, but hypoxia will positively kill you within four or five minutes.

Concern over breathable air is pretty far from paranoia. On December 3, 1984, a leak of deadly *methylisocyanate* gas at a Union Carbide chemical plant in Bhopal, India, killed 5,200 people outright, and permanently maimed or temporarily injured several thousand more (by comparison, the number of casualties in the World Trade Center attack was 2,752). The dangers of air that is suddenly made toxic has been confirmed many times since Bhopal. CNN reported: "The 2005 railroad chlorine spill in Graniteville, South Carolina, killed 'only' nine people, but it illustrated the difficulties of achieving adequate capacity to handle no-notice evacuation for hazardous materials incidents." The So Cal Company's methane gas leak that occurred in 2015 forced the evacuation of 6,000 households. Dangers from increasing industrialization are so widespread as to make man-caused disasters inevitable.

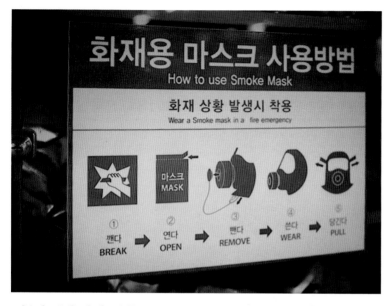

A train station in South Korea, where the possibility of airborne contaminants being released on the public is recognized and guarded against—as it should be in the United States, and any nation that cares about its citizenry.

Then there's the Yellowstone Caldera, among others. When—not if—that super-volcano blows, its ash fallout will encompass practically the entire United States. As the Icelandic eruption of the Bardarbunga volcano (2014–15) demonstrated, abrasive volcanic ash is like a sand-blasting a jet turbine, and attempting to fly through it borders on suicidal. When the Yellowstone volcano goes, scientists predict that the weight of its ash alone will collapse buildings for hundreds of miles in every direction, as it did to buildings at Clark Air Force Base in the Philippines, when Mt. Pinatubo erupted in 1991. Likewise, breathing volcanic ash causes the linings of lungs and respiratory tracts to hemorrhage, causing pneumonia, bronchitis, and death, particularly in asthma sufferers.

Scientists are unsure about when, but they are unanimous that the Yellowstone super-volcano is going to blow.

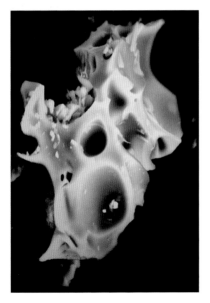

Volcanic eruptions are becoming almost commonplace everywhere in the world, with ash similar to the magnified particle shown here filling the air in concentrations that cause the roofs of strong buildings to collapse under their weight—this is not something that most parents would like their children to breathe.

Then, of course, there's that good old standby, war. *O-isopropyl-methylphosphonofluoridate*, better known as Sarin, or Agent GB, is a very old, extremely potent form of nerve agent that was invented "accidentally" by Nazi scientists in 1938, while they claimed to have been looking for an insecticide. In March 1998, Saddam Hussein used a toxic cocktail containing Sarin to murder 5,000 Kurdish civilians. Sarin has already been used twice for terror attacks in the Tokyo subway in 1994 and 1995. There are very real, non-paranoid reasons to fear that the air you breathe might be suddenly made poisonous by other persons who have evil intentions.

Lastly, living in the midst of forests, I've spent a few sleepless nights watching nervously as the woods around my home filled with smoke, and a raging wildfire came too close for comfort. The boondocks tend to be sparsely populated, and evacuees got out in time, but if a human were caught within a mile of the inferno, he could be asphyxiated long before it got hot enough to burn him.

The situation is even worse in an apartment building, where unlighted hallways (power is cut as a matter of procedure) are too black to navigate without a light, and usually filled with choking smoke that can't be pierced by the brightest flashlight. Firefighters confirm that most deaths in a house fire aren't caused by heat, but smoke inhalation. Smoke from a building fire is deadly, because of toxins produced by burning foam, plastics, and other common, yet hazardous, materials.

Reasons to have a respirator among your survival equipment are numerous, and it's more than likely that it could be the single item that saves your life.

A cautionary statement about respirators from the 3M Company: "Diseases that may be caused by inhalation of airborne biological organisms include *tuberculosis* (TB), *Hantavirus*, *anthrax*, *Sudden Acute Respiratory Syndrome* (SARS) and *influenza*. Biohazards may become airborne; perhaps as the agent itself such as an anthrax spore, the agent riding on some other material that becomes airborne such as dusts, mists or droplet nuclei (a sneeze). Hantavirus infection has been caused by people inhaling soil dust that became airborne after rodents shed the virus via urine, feces or other materials into the soil. In fact, it is generally thought that airborne viruses are normally attached to other particles, and rarely exist as naked organisms.

"Inhalation of these bioaerosols may be reduced by wearing respirators. The *Centers for Disease Control and Prevention* (CDC), the *World Health Organization* (WHO) and many National Health Authorities have made numerous recommendations for respirator use where they believed the potential for the spread of disease through the airborne route exists. Considerations for selection and use of respirators for exposure to bioaerosols include filtration, microorganism survival on the filter, potential reaerosolization of the bioaerosol, reuse of the respirator, fit and the assigned protection factor of the respirator."

Types of Respirators

For her help in composing this vital section, the author wants to personally thank Ms. Javiera McGuiggan of 3M. Her assistance has been essential to making the reviews and recommendations presented here as comprehensive as possible.

Except for *forced-air* types, which are basically self-contained apparatuses, with their own air supply—not drastically different than a SCUBA outfit—a respirator is an air filter. It prevents most harmful contaminants from reaching the lungs when its wearer inhales. There are different types and grades of respirators for different purposes.

Volcano, asteroid, radiation, viruses, toxic gases, even a building fire: Any of these are very real possibilities that might make the very air around you unbreathable without a respirator.

Respirators are available in many forms, for many airborne hazards.

It has never been paranoid to have a good respirator on hand, and today, it's pretty short-sighted not to have one, with replacement filter canisters, for every person whose life you care about.

Filter Levels

N95: Filters at least 95% of airborne particles. Not resistant to oil.

Surgical N95: A NIOSH-approved N95 respirator that has also been cleared by the Food and Drug Administration (FDA) as a surgical mask.

N99: Filters at least 99% of airborne particles. Not resistant to oil.

N100: Filters at least 99.97% of airborne particles. Not resistant to oil.

R95: Filters at least 95% of airborne particles. Somewhat resistant to oil.

P95: Filters at least 95% of airborne particles. Strongly resistant to oil.

P99: Filters at least 99% of airborne particles. Strongly resistant to oil.

P100: Filters at least 99.97% of airborne particles. Strongly resistant to oil.

Respirator Use Tips

- Be sure that respirator masks seal well to a user's face; masks do not seal well around beards.
- *Do not* share respirators.

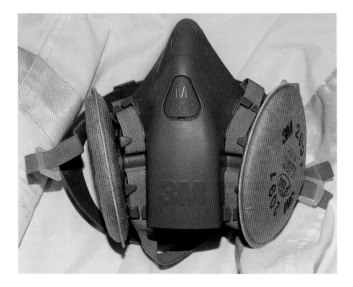

- Change filter canisters (where applicable) between uses.
- Decontaminate (wash and disinfect) face masks between uses.
- Do not reuse disposable masks.
- Do not remove mask while in the presence of contaminants.

CHAPTER SIXTEEN

ELECTRICAL POWER FOR SURVIVAL

Electricity

Survival in the new millennium is a whole lot more than building a fire.

The romantic image of a survivalist as a martial artist gunfighter with rippling muscles, and the stealthy lethality of a Bengal tiger is patently fantastic. In the twenty-first century, a survival expert more resembles a Renaissance Man than he does Tarzan.

Electrical appliances have become a permanent part of survival under adverse conditions. Just as bolts, nails, pliers, solar panels and semiconductor components are not going to disappear from human civilization, a basic understanding of electricity is as essential as righty-tighty/lefty-loosey.

If you're thinking that a basic knowledge of electrical theory has no importance to you, consider buying a portable generator that can keep your refrigerator running during a brief power outage, and keep food inside it from spoiling. How many watts does your generator have to output? What if you need to run a refrigerator, and an oxygen generator for an asthma victim?

Resistance

Electricity acts much like water in the way it flows through wires and other conductive areas. DC, or Direct Current, flows in one direction, from negative to positive, from hot to ground, from black wire to red wire, when a circuit is wired correctly. Resistance is the innate quality that a conductor has to inhibit the passage of electrons through it. By regulating resistance in a circuit, we can help to regulate how that circuit behaves. A lot of resistance—as in an incandescent light bulb filament— creates heat. A smaller wire, like a smaller water pipe, offers greater resistance. Resistance is measured in units called *Ohms* (pronounced like "homes," without the H).

Voltage

Electromotive force (EMF) is measured in units called volts. Volts are units of electrical pressure. Again, to use the analogy of water in a pipe, the smaller the pipe, the greater the pressure needed to move a given amount of electricity through it. The bigger the pipe, the less pressure is needed. Voltage is measurable as either *Alternating Current* (AC—household electricity) or *Direct Current* (DC—like your car's system)—or static electricity, like lightning; most of what a survivalist deals with from solar panels, crank generators, and windmills is Direct Current.

Even fifteen years ago, this simple solar/battery system was keeping the author's backwoods home running during power outages that were frequent enough to be regular.

This 1kw solar panel was a disappointment to its buyer, because the energy a solar panel is capable of putting out is not generally what it does generate.

Innovations like this folding solar panel have made electronic devices independent of the power company.

Amperage

The volume of electricity flowing through a conductor is measured in Amperes, usually just called Amps, for short. The old axiom "It's the amps that kill you" simply means that the amount of electricity that flows through a victim is the decider of how much damage is incurred. A sudden blast of water (high voltage) is less dangerous than a constant high flow of water that can drown you.

Watts

Wattage is a unit of work that can be done by electricity. Based on the Horsepower unit (1 horsepower equals 746 watts), wattage is determined by multiplying voltage in a circuit with its Amperage. This is generally made easier, because household voltage is a constant 110 volts;

automotive voltage 12 volts (14 volts, actual). Wattage is the most commonly used indicator of an appliance's power.

Basic Electrical Formulas

The basic formula for calculating each of the above values in a circuit is called Ohm's Law, after its inventor. This law shows that there is an integral relationship between the three major properties of electricity, and that you cannot change one of them without also changing at least one of the other two. The basic formula reads $E = I \times R$. E is Electromotive Force, or voltage; I stands for Inductance, measured in amperes; R is Resistance. If $E = I \times R$, then E divided by R must equal I, and E divided by I must equal R. Using real values, if current measures 2 amperes, through a resistance of 30 ohms, then voltage has got to be 60 volts.

It is very likely that at some point, a basic knowledge of the principles of electricity will be needed in a survival situation. For example, if you try to run a radio receiver designed to operate on 6 volts directly from a 12-volt car battery, you'll burn up the radio. But if you insert a light bulb that requires about 6 volts to operate into the circuit, only 6 volts remain to reach the receiver, and it will function without being damaged.

CHAPTER SEVENTEEN

DEFENSE OF LIFE

Self-Defense

It is a trademark of my books and articles that they do not deal with harming other human beings. When I was a field editor for the now defunct *Tactical Knives* magazine, that penchant literally cost me a substantial amount of money, because I refused to write what I regard as macho-dude pornography.

I'm breaking that self-imposed rule now, after more than three decades, because a real-life survival scenario, according to FEMA, is a near certainty for most of us who are alive today, and because Hurricane Katrina, for one, surprised me at just how fast a highly cultured society can revert to barbarism when feces impacts the oscillating turbines. When times get desperate, and luxuries become scarce or impossible to come by, neighbors you've known for years might turn selfish and vicious.

How I know the subject that I'm expounding upon in this chapter is, quite frankly, dear reader, none of your business. Just be assured that if I've written it, it is a fact. Not conjecture, not something I've referenced from *Soldier of Fortune* or another testosterone-powered magazine. There's nothing heroic about hurting anyone, and there is absolutely no glamour in being a killer, in a uniform, or not, however you might justify the sin as patriotism or self-defense. Make no mistake, if it becomes necessary to employ force, it's a serious mistake to hesitate, but the safest way out of any confrontation is always to avoid it in the first place. Endanger yourself out of foolish pride if you like, but if you have someone depending on you, you don't have the option or the right to act like John Wayne.

Do not depend on Officer Friendly, Big Brother, or any other governmental entity to come riding to your rescue in the event of a nationwide or global catastrophe. Confidential interviews and a long history of actual disasters have shown indisputably that when times get tight, members of clubs tend to take care of their own first, regardless of rhetoric about public duty during good times—and when times get really hard, those alliances will splinter into smaller, more close-knit groups, like precincts, organizations, families, and gangs. Every convict knows that when real trouble comes, officers are going to lock the doors, and go home to their families. Faith can give you strength, but every Jew who marched into a gas chamber probably thought that what happened to mothers and children couldn't possibly be allowed to happen by a civilized world. Bottom line: You are your own savior.

With violence, there are never any guarantees. It's a contest, as much a gamble as any poker game, and odds of success always favor the swift. Every MMA fighter and Kung-fu sifu will tell you that a lucky shot can come from the most outmatched opponent, so always try to stack the odds in your favor. A percentage of people have always hesitated, and those who are armed are sometimes killed by their own weapons because they did. Even in a society that has not been broken down by a disaster, where most people are not hungry, thirsty, or homeless, there are criminals who prey on anyone who happens into their domain, and who seems weak enough to subjugate. Three or more people are safe from mugging. A single dangerous-looking individual (most experienced criminals can tell, because they, too, live by rules of survival) is left unmolested. It's the defenseless-looking guy who's in danger of being accosted, even in normal times, because appearance counts—for and against.

One thing you can count on is that if you're accosted by a greater number of people in a place where there are no witnesses, you are in danger. Like a rapist, whose motivation is not sex, but power, street predators are not primarily robbing you to get whatever possessions they say they want; there's a sadistic mentality that drives people who have the nature to personally take someone else's belongings.

History shows that you cannot reason with this type of mentality, but this is where no one can advise you. If you strike, be it with a gun, knife, or club, you must do so with resolve. A half-hearted defense will, without any doubt, result in severe retaliation—a thug who might have only beaten you senseless and raped your wife might now murder the both of you (there is no politically correct way for me to get that point across).

It is a fact of human nature that we tend to evaluate anything according to our own experiences, and what we would, could, can, or cannot do. A lot of young men think that they're combat experts—until they walk into a VFW Hall. It seems to be true that most people are good and decent, but there are a few who would gleefully commit atrocities normal folks don't even like to imagine, and they have free rein after a catastrophe.

The Fortress Mentality

Stocking up on stores of food, water, and medical supplies is always recommended, and it may well become necessary to shelter-in-place, as suggested by the Federal Emergency Management Agency (FEMA), to avoid fallout from radioactive, viral, or chemical agents. But it may, at some point, become necessary to move. Take note that **No Fortress Is Impregnable**. Fantasies of holing up, Road Warrior style, and fending off marauders is simply not possible, unless you possess an army, and even then, only until challenged by a larger army. It can be hoped that humanity is, or will become, sufficiently mature to avoid the habit of self-annihilation that it has religiously displayed thus far, but the aftermath of Hurricane Katrina showed otherwise.

Wild animals lack the luxury of living in a den, unchallenged, relaxed and comfortable. Be ready to pick up and move at a moment's notice. A warm, secure home can become a death trap almost instantly.

The life of a nomad is very hard, but it is the habit of mankind to rebuild itself into a stable situation after each catastrophe. Until then, staying alive might mean staying mobile.

Dogs

The secret to survival is to avoid any scenario that could injure you or take your life. A sensei once told me, "The first rule to living through any confrontation is to run away." Knowing that a danger exists before it swoops down upon you is important. For nearly half a century, at home and away, my very best personal alarm system has been my dog. It is impossible to approach me without my knowing that you're there. The enhanced auditory, olfactory, and unidentified senses of a dog have worked for millennia to make that animal worthy of the title Man's Best Friend.

A good dog who loves you will defend you from harm, even to the point of sacrificing its own life; that's just the nature of the beast. Some breeds are more amenable to the job of protector than others, but it is an indisputable fact that a person who relies on a dog for physical protection is a fool. Don't kid yourself: A man can kill a dog, and he doesn't need a gun to do it.

I cannot state that without explaining why and how. Despite its strong teeth and powerful jaws, a dog is a fragile animal. Animal trainers of all types, and especially sled dog "trainers" of a bygone era knew that very well. An unarmed man who keeps his senses can seriously injure a large dog with a kick to the ribs or jaw, he can break a leg by snapping it over a knee, or he can permanently disable the beast by gripping upper and lower jaws, and twisting them in opposite directions. Some blood will be shed, but in the midst of a fracas, you won't even notice. It will hurt like hell the next day, though; after washing, before dressing a bite wound, you need to squirt an antiseptic directly into the punctures (steel yourself, this also hurts like hell).

Exploit your dog's strengths. Treat it as the wonderful friend that it is, and employ the animal as the sometimes incredible early-warning system it is. The instincts of *Canis domesticus* are of a pack animal; it lives to serve its pack, even to the point of repressing its own reproductive instincts and relinquishing food. If your dog believes you and it are pack members (in our lingo, if it loves you), it will never abandon you.

The Fragile Human Animal

The owner of a popular knife-manufacturing company makes a good living out of promulgating the fantasy of humans battling one another with edged weapons. Aside from the fact that this guy's girth belies his claim to living an austere warrior's life, he fails to recognize the proven fragility of the human form. In real life, a knife fight is over in seconds—few can continue with a perforated lung, or a severed intestine—and no one can keep fighting with a punctured aorta. Being disemboweled is a fight-stopper, too.

An axe in the hands of a lumberjack can punch through any armor yet invented—and if it isn't sharp enough to penetrate, it will severely damage anything it hits, as well as what lies beneath. If the tool can batter down a locked steel door in the hands of a firefighter, it can do incredible harm to flesh.

As old a weapon as mankind, an axe has no respect for body armor.

Likewise, a wooden baseball bat, as so aptly demonstrated by gangster Al Capone when he executed one of his lieutenants with a single blow to his head, is capable of removing the biggest man from a fight.

A single blow from an untrained fist can break a big man's collar bone, and literally cripple that side of his body. A knuckles-down uppercut to the short ribs, just below the sternum, is not just painful, it can snap off the short ribs, and puncture heart or lungs. Applying force, by any means possible, to push a joint in a direction it's not designed to bend, can result in severe tendon and ligament injury. The main strategy of Master Bruce Lee's *Jeet-Kune-Do* style of Kung-Fu was not to anticipate what an adversary *might* do, but to respond to what he *did* do. Bruce Lee understood the value of training, but he also knew that it didn't require a lifetime of commitment to learn to strike with lethal force.

Any number of easily inflicted injuries can take the fight out of a presumed warrior, and render him easy to finish off. Guerilla fighters make an art out of merely debilitating members of superior enemy forces, forcing them to reduce their fighting strength to care for their wounded. No one is too big, too strong, or too tough to be rendered helpless. To believe oneself is invincible is a serious weakness in itself; that's one reason that no military Special Forces training is complete without showing a trainee where his breaking point lies—every Green Beret and SEAL has been broken.

To learn an opponent's weak spots, look in a mirror. Does it hurt when you're poked in an eye? How about when you barked your shin? A skull is actually one of the stronger and better-protected areas; but a hard blow to a man's kidneys might kill him. Does anyone ever gripe about that old football injury to his knee? A secret to success in any martial art, with or without weapons, is action. If you deem it necessary to strike an opponent, you need to do it with vigor. As any ghetto kid can affirm, he who strikes first, if he strikes hard, will probably win a fight.

Gunfighting

As this photo of a government-sanctioned militia trainee depicts well, using a firearm is a skill, and like every skill, it requires work and discipline to achieve expertise.

This is the moment when the mundane, boring repetition of proper stance, sighting, grip, and other practice you've been doing at the range does or does not pay off. Rely on nothing, but know that most guys are "spray-and-pray" types; they'll fire in your direction as fast as they can, discharge their magazines, then they'll fumblingly try to reload.

Wild Bill Hickock was more than a comic book icon. He stands as the greatest gunfighter who ever lived, and toward the end, ironically, he was losing his eyesight. He wasn't lightning fast, and he didn't carry revolvers that had been modified. He was simply well-practiced and good with a brace of comfortable big-bore pistols that enabled him to plant a bullet where he wanted it to go, well beyond the range of a normal pistolero. He rarely fired that he didn't hit the man he was shooting at, even if that man was already shooting at him. Even with today's high-capacity autoloaders, accuracy remains the single most important component of gunfighting, or hunting.

Self-defense is regarded as almost a sport in many magazines, but it is a bloody, violent proposition that few people would willingly engage in if it could be avoided; there are no winners, only survivors.

Knife Fighting

A problem with using a knife in a fight is losing your grip on it; the fighting lanyard, shown here, makes a blade integral to your hand.

Opposite view of a fighting lanyard.

A single swing of a sharp jackknife can eviscerate the strongest man. As Rich Davis, the man who invented the Kevlar vest almost found out personally (his son convinced him to try it on a mannequin, first), a hunting arrow cuts clean through a "bulletproof" vest. The *Nighthawk* knife from Buck Knives—according to a telephone conversation I had with the late, and great, in my opinion, Charles T. (Chuck) Buck—was designed with an eye toward punching through ballistic vests. The difference lies in the penetrating dynamics of a soft, blunt bullet and a hard, pointed cutting edge—it would require a great deal of force to run a man through with the end of a 2 × 4; but if you whittled its end to a point, not so much.

That old saw about the stupidity of a person who brings a knife to a gunfight merely demonstrates the ignorance of the person stating it. A police officer friend tells me that he was trained to draw his sidearm at the first sight of a knife, and to shoot a knife wielder before he could close to within 10 feet. Studies have shown that an assailant with a knife can cross that distance and inflict a fatal wound before a gunfighter can clear his holster. Aside from that, a gunman has to actually hit his target with a projectile measuring less than half an inch across; a sharp knife can disembowel its target with a wild, unaimed swing in a dark room, from 4 feet.

To illustrate that point, a knife named the *Hisshou* (pronounced *he-show*) was designed by martial artist James Williams, after the United States Army commissioned him to design a fighting knife that could be used by combat troops during house-to-house searches in the Middle East. The problem was that troops entering a darkened building from a sunlit street were temporarily blinded, while a building's occupants, whose eyes were already adjusted to shadows, were able to inflict damage onto them with the long-bladed knives preferred by citizens of the region. The wickedly curved 18-inch Hisshou shortsword, manufactured by *Columbia River Knife and Tool* (CRKT) resolved that dilemma nicely.

Most people of today would gasp, and the more hedonistic would probably outright swoon, but it wasn't that long ago that no farmer or rancher would waste a valuable cartridge just to kill a livestock animal for meat. After all, a large animal needs to be bled out, anyway, lest blood clot in its major blood vessels, and ruin the taste of the meat. Chickens had their heads lopped off, and were allowed to run around frantically, blood spewing from the headless stump—to the delight of small children present—until they just fell over, ready for scalding and plucking. Cattle received a single two-handed blow between their eyes with an 8-pound sledgehammer; when the bovine dropped to its knees, a long, deep slash across the top of its brisket opened its heart and, if the hammer blow wasn't fatal, it bled to death with a little unconscious kicking and little pain. I recall very well one old German widow who made her living from pigs; when she wanted one for meat, she simply walked up to the chosen hog, plunged her narrow-bladed "pig sticker" knife to its 8-inch depth, and swiftly drew it across the animal's chest. The hog continued to walk around in a daze, until it fell over from loss of blood and lack of oxygen, it kicked its legs for a few seconds—a common involuntary nervous reaction—and became a candidate for butchering.

Citizens, especially in urban areas, have long been inventive about pressing everyday tools into service as defensive weapons, from nunchaku rice-threshing sticks to oven cleaner aerosol sprays; the pulled-pork meat shredding claws shown here are one of the more vicious examples. (Photo courtesy of Cave Tools)

There are a few basics that every prospective knife-fighter should know: For stabbing, a shorter blade requires less wrist strength to control—a 3-inch blade can reach heart, lungs, kidneys, esophagus, and liver. Likewise, a narrow blade penetrates easier than a wide one, as does a stiletto- or dagger-style with at least the tip of its blade sharpened on both sides. Penetration force is maximized in blades whose point is on the center line of its handle.

Longer, wider blades are less effective for stabbing. The added weight and length work to increase inertial power for slashing, though. Ironically, it requires greater wrist strength to slash forcefully with a short blade.

If you find yourself in a position where you must use a knife as a weapon, it pays to be as efficient as possible. Do not give the other guy a chance, because he probably won't give you that same courtesy. Do not be tentative: Don't poke, stab; don't cut like you're slicing bread, slash. The first strike need not be instantly fatal (and it probably won't be) but it should be as bloody and painful as you can make it, to discourage further aggression.

Staff

One of the most lethal, most underestimated weapons ever invented is the staff—known in its various forms as a walking stick, shillelagh, and shovel handle.

As a woodsman, this is one of my favorite stealth weapons. Largely because it is so disregarded as to be ignored. It can be taken into almost any public place without raising an eyebrow. Known as the Ko-Budo-Bo by Japanese martial artists, a long staff replaced the outlawed sword as a practice weapon, and soon became a capable weapon in its own right. In Sir Walter Scott's legend of *Robin Hood*, a wooden staff was the preferred weapon of Little John.

In real life, in 1596, Miyamoto Musashi, who was thirteen years old, and not yet the swordmaster he would become, accepted a public challenge from a wandering samurai named Arima Kihei.

Young Musashi knew that his opponent was both a hothead, and insulted at having his open challenge met by someone so youthful; Musashi further enraged the samurai by showing up without so much as a sword, only a 6-foot quarterstaff. Exploiting the impetuous anger of his adversary, who did not see the wooden stick held by a teenager as much of a threat, he met Musashi's attack with his Wakisashi shortsword. Kihei underestimated the reach of Musashi's staff, and was knocked handily to the ground, where Musashi killed him. There are important morals to this story for the modern survivalist.

In Ireland, a shortened staff, usually made from an irregular branch with a bulbous growth at one end, is known as a shillelagh. Other variations include the Battle Mace, and the police baton. In any form, a staff can become a deadly weapon, and capable of delivering lethal force to a distance of more than 5 feet. Practice is required to swing it smoothly from one hand to another—and almost everyone whacks themselves on the skull, so be especially careful not to exceed your ability—but it takes no skill to use this deadly striking weapon. Perhaps best of all, a staff is provided by virtually every environment.

Nunchaku

Made famous by Bruce Lee in his final movie, *Enter the Dragon*, the Ko-Budo-Nunchaku, and known incorrectly as a "nunchuck" in popular slang, the nunchaku is actually an ancient rice-threshing tool. Like many classic Asian martial arts weapons, it was co-opted to the role of a close-quarters weapon when tyrannical emperors tried to disarm the

*Even in untrained hands, a nunchaku (colloquially known as a "nunchuck")
can be a fearsome impact weapon.*

populaces they ruled. History has shown repeatedly that it is impossible to deny weapons to a creative citizenry.

You can currently purchase a hardwood (the most popular models are foam rubber) nunchaku for under $20 from martial arts supply outlets, but these are lightweight models of the old weapon.

Homemade nunchakus, fashioned from saplings, even iron pipe, are easy to make, and with a little weight (i.e., inertia and power) behind them, they are decidedly deadly, able to shatter a 1-inch by 6-inch pine board with little effort, and capable of delivering that force to a distance of more than 5 feet.

Practice is required to swing a nunchaku smoothly from one hand to another, and almost everyone whacks themselves on the skull, so be especially careful not to exceed your ability. But it takes no skill at all to use them as a deadly weapon. Someone who has never used them can swing the sticks at 90 miles per hour, to strike a target with sufficient force to shatter a humerus or break several ribs with a single blow. In short, a novice armed with a nunchaku can disable or kill an opponent with a single blow. Gender, size, and physical strength don't matter, and with a little practice, a wielder is more than a match for multiple adversaries.

A lesser-known use of a nunchaku as a weapon is called the "nutcracker," after the tool that it resembles. In this instance, the two sticks of the weapon, joined together at one end by about 6 inches of rope or chain (I prefer rope), are placed on either side of an opponent's neck, even his skull or thigh, and their free ends squeezed together, toward one another. The effect is like squeezing a walnut in a nutcracker. For a very short duration in the late 1970s, police agencies in California experimented with trading in their traditional batons for nunchakus, but the trial was pronounced a failure after an exuberant officer seriously injured an inebriated motorist while dragging him through a car window by his neck.

Spear Fighting

As old as humanity, a spear is the most important weapon ever devised. It taught wild predators that a naked ape that had previously been virtually defenseless now possessed an ability to inflict fatal wounds before a predator could reach it. Neither making nor using a spear requires skill;

any green sapling that was mostly straight could be whittled or abraded on a rock to a sharp point, then made hard by charring it in a fire. Even without a stone or metal head, it was able to pierce flesh, and deliver a mortal wound.

Except as sport, a spear was seldom thrown. Instead, it was braced against a hip, or against the ground, and used as a distance stabbing, or—if it had a sharpened knife-like head—a slashing weapon. Fitted with a dagger-style head, sharpened on both sides, a spear had a reach advantage over the longest sword.

Medieval combat experts recommend that beginners start with a short, more easily handled spear, like the 2-foot Assegai of southern Africa, or the slightly longer Irish Short Spear. Held at its balance point, to make it more dexterous to handle, a short spear uses both blunt and tipped ends to strike a blow.

One common strategy is to grip the spear from above at its balance point, hip-high, with its sharpened tip pointed toward the enemy. Then, the spear is rotated at the wrist to deliver a strike to the opponent's ribs with its butt end. The "bounce" from this strike's impact is used to swivel the wrist and reverse the spear to power a hard thrust with its tip to the adversary's midsection. If you intend to use a short spear as a weapon, medieval combat experts recommend that this combination blow be practiced.

More reach can be achieved by holding a spear farther back, closer to its butt, but doing so sacrifices agility, because the spear demands more wrist strength. Greater striking power is achieved by holding underhand, little finger toward its tip and shaft above the shoulder, but, again, at the expense of dexterity.

Booby Traps

Whether a booby trap is acceptable or not depends on who's using it. This favorite tool of outmatched guerilla fighters is primarily used to wound, not kill, enemy soldiers, removing them from the fight, and sapping the other army's resources by forcing them to care for their wounded.

With a little imagination, the pencil snare, described earlier, can be converted to become a number of traps. But, as with everything survival, simple is better. One of the best is a variation on the Viet Cong's *punji sticks*, sharpened lengths of bamboo shoved into the earth and smeared with feces, so that anyone impaled by them would contract a nasty infection.

That old saw about it being dumb to bring a knife to a gunfight is not necessarily true. (Photo courtesy of Jame Williams)

A simpler version of the punji stick is to hammer numerous 8D-size nails through a 2 × 6 board, and then bury the board, nails-up, under a thin layer of soil, camouflaged to resemble the surrounding terrain. Feces are optional.

A favorite of illicit marijuana growers consists of 10# monofilament fishing line tied to large triple-hook fishhooks, and strung through undergrowth. Police officers searching for the crop would encounter the lines, causing them to slide along their bodies, and impaling them on the barbed fishhooks.

Simpler yet is a cord tied, ankle-level, between trees across a trail. Few people will not trip, or at least stumble, over it. Adding the 8D-nail punji board mentioned above, positioned where a person who trips will fall onto it provides an audible alarm, too.

Evasion

It is no coincidence that the original Special Forces troops up to today's elite snipers have always been woodsmen. A person who can sneak up on a whitetail deer and is at home in wilderness terrain has an advantage that no weaponry can provide.

Learn as much as you can about wilderness survival, and then, if you find yourself needing to escape an enemy, disappear into whatever natural environment is available. If pursuers are governmental agents, it's likely that they'll be extremely overloaded with body armor and weaponry. If they're an urban mob, they'll probably hesitate to get themselves lost in the woods, as it were.

Just as the trick to winning fights is to avoid fighting, the trick to successfully escaping any unpleasant situation is to remain below an enemy's radar. Butch Cassidy once remarked that the reason his Hole-in-the-Wall hideout remained undiscovered was because its occupants weren't worth the trouble of looking for them. Take his advice to heart, and "stay gray." A pigeon on a statue in New York barely gets noticed; whereas a peregrine falcon is a headline. A beige sedan is a favorite among criminals, but undercover narcotics officers are often "made" because they dress like they're on the set of *Miami Vice*.

CHAPTER EIGHTEEN

DRESSING FOR SUCCESSFUL SURVIVAL

Clothing

Layered Cold Weather Outfit

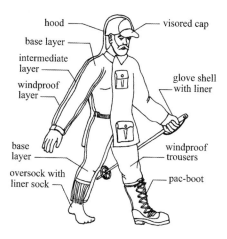

hood

base layer

intermediate layer

windproof layer

visored cap

glove shell with liner

base layer

oversock with liner sock

windproof trousers

pac-boot

The rudiments of an effective survival outfit in cold weather.

Clothing is one of the most vital survival accoutrements anyone can possess, regardless of environment. In a very real sense, it can be survival equipment in a nightclub, where whether or not you're "stylin'" can have a genuine impact on how well you achieve goals that might range from closing a business deal to just getting lucky. The purpose of clothing has always been multifold: an American soldier gathering intelligence from a marketplace in Afghanistan wears a keffiyeh, not a helmet. The little black dress that every single girl keeps in her closet will not be seen at Easter Mass. And only the dumbest of bow hunters would wear the fluorescent colors of a downhill skier.

You might not have the option of choosing the apparel you wear when the asteroid strikes, or when a tsunami washes away everything. A department store clerk in a skirt and nylons, or a taxi driver wearing shorts and a T-shirt—or, God forbid, an executive in pumps with fishnet stockings—genuinely needs a change of clothes to change into. This is an excellent argument for the coming section about survival kits in an automobile "bug-out bag" or in one's home. You can never be overly prepared, but you need to cover as many bases as possible—that is the essence of the survival philosophy.

Cotton

This is a poor choice for any garment that might need to serve you in an outdoor or survival environment, whatever the season, environment, or weather. Cotton absorbs several times its weight in moisture, dries slowly, mildews and rots, and it tears easily. Cotton is an ideal material for washcloths, towels, and char-cloth, but not for any garment outside of a nightclub or mall. Some argue that its absorbent quality makes it ideal for hot weather, but, in fact, it is outperformed by other fabrics in that respect, too.

Wool

This fabric made from woven animal hair—usually sheep or llama—is still nearly perfect for survival purposes. Wool's hollow fibers retain "dead air," which is the true quality of an insulation, it repels most water, and what it does absorb dries quickly. Wool is tough, it won't burn easily, and it both warms and cools in all but the hottest climes. The great thing is, wool is out of fashion with the younger generation, and you can pick up hundred-dollar sweaters for a few bucks in resale shops.

Microfibers

Generally recognized as *Polar Fleece* or *micro-fleece*, this synthetic material is essentially man-made wool. Constructed of plastic fibers (a selling point of Patagonia's *Capilene* fleece in the early 1990s was that it was made from recycled soda bottles), this material absorbs minimal moisture, it drips dry, and it retains up to 75 percent of its insulative properties when wet. As sleeping bag insulation, plastic fibers are outstanding, but fleece breathes (lets out perspiration vapors) slightly less efficiently than wool.

Ripstop

The self-proclaimed Vietnam vet who walked into my wife's Army-Navy store insisted that the summer-weight BDU (Battle Dress Uniform) cloth was not ripstop, because its mesh of nylon fibers made it look different than winter weight. Ripstop is not a fabric, but a type of weave that unlike denim does not continue to rip when torn. Tents and sleeping bag shells are ripstop; *Fire Hose* fabric trousers from Duluth Trading Post are tough, and they're ripstop. Blue jeans are not.

Layering

A great deal is made of the practice of layering, but public service announcements have never been adequate, in my experience. *Cotton kills* is an old adage that should be heeded—the material is okay for the outermost layer, when an outfit consists of three or more layers, but it should never be worn close enough to affect skin in any way. Each garment, even thin ones, adds a layer of motionless air between the skin and the outside, providing insulation that both retains heat and cools somewhat—like a wolf's fur coat.

Rain Gear

Ask any veteran of the Vietnam War, and he'll tell you that remaining dry in monsoon weather is simply not possible. It doesn't matter if you're wearing Gore-Tex, Sympatex, or old-fashioned rubber-and-canvas storm gear. This is not a debate, it's a fact, and whatever anyone claims, if you've been out in the rain for more than a few hours, and you're not hermetically sealed from the environment, you're soaked to the bone.

As any Vietnam veteran can attest, there is no such thing as garments that can keep you dry when you're exposed to rainy weather for more than a few hours.

Being wet won't hurt you (unless it's for a very long period), but being cold is extremely dangerous. Wear layers of synthetic, water repellant fabrics, a jacket with a hood, and find shelter as much and as often as possible. Being wet lowers felt temperatures by at least 15 degrees (40 degrees and rain is the most lethal weather you can encounter, especially if it's windy—it can kill you within hours), so dress accordingly.

Underwear

This section doesn't address jockeys, boxers, or other skivvies, it deals with "long johns"—underwear that covers both legs and arms, usually with top and bottom garments. Even in warm weather, a good synthetic long john set is critical for keeping a body warm *and* cool. Long under-wear dissipates perspiration—better than skin, in some cases—while providing a layer of insulation. There was still snow on the shore, and ice floating on the water, when my wife (through her own silliness) capsized her kayak; thanks to her long johns, she remained comfortable enough to continue paddling for the rest of the day.

They might not be stylish, but a good set of long-john underwear is vital whenever temperatures fall below the freezing point of water.

Trousers

Some TV survival experts wear denim blue jeans, or, worse, shorts. I ask that you just consider this: Your legs are likely to be exposed to scrapes, scratches, insects, rats, and slime, from an environment filled with rub-ble, fire, mud, and an innumerable assortment of sharp, filthy objects that can not only make you bleed, but can give you tetanus and other infections. Pants need to be long, tough, and as much a tool of survival as any other component of your kit.

My own trousers are a survival kit in themselves, even during every-day wear around my rural home. (Following is a description of what's in my trousers right now.) In a back pocket resides my wallet, which not only carries money and credentials, but a folding razor knife, a P-38 can opener, and a handcuff key (you never know . . .). My left hip pocket carries a disposable butane lighter, an assortment of loose stuff, like rubber bands and string, and a pocket-clipped folding knife. My right hip pocket contains a key ring with a key to every lock I might need to open, along with a pocket-clip AA flashlight (that used to be on my belt). My left thigh pocket contains a Ziploc bag loaded with cord, fire wicks fire starters, more rubber bands, a penknife, and a Zippo lighter. My opposite thigh pocket carries a folding diamond hone knife sharpener and a pocket-clip multi-tool. There's room for a lot more stuff, and sometimes I add gloves, screws and nails, or tools. Mine is presently empty, but I used to carry a few things there, too, and I could again.

Shirts

Your shirt, like trousers, should be a functional component. Large button-down breast pockets are valuable cargo carriers (numerous butane lighters, cord, and other small tools are hard to overestimate—you never know).

Socks

There's an old axiom from the Korean War that warns that dry socks are more important than clean underwear. Again, avoid cotton—in one instance, a close friend and I were camped in March; we wore identical boots, yet he complained of cold toes. Sure enough, he was wearing wet cotton "athletic" socks. I gave him my own spare pair of woolen socks, and his feet were not cold again.

Gloves

Gloves are often overlooked as a tool of survival, but during rugged times, a good pair of gloves is likely to save your life, because fingers are critically important to almost every facet of human life. I've always recommended that survival students bring with them a pair of working-class leather gloves. Few of them have understood the importance I placed on these hand garments, until we got into the woods. Digging into rocky soil, breaking dead branches from standing trees, and more, can damage hands.

In warmer weather, a tough working glove is necessary to protect vital fingers.

Liner Gloves

In winter weather, it may become necessary to add a knit liner glove—available for a few dollars at department stores—inside a tougher shell glove. This outfit is *not* warm enough for Arctic conditions, where a dedicated extreme-cold weather glove or mitten should be worn.

The measure of a warm, multi-layer glove system is that it can ice-over on its outer layer while a hand inside stays warm, indicating virtually no loss of body heat.

Boots

Once, while backpacking a section of the North Country Trail in Mackinaw State Forest, I stopped at an overgrown bank along the Carp River to refill my canteen, where I spotted a pair of abandoned hiking boots, sitting neatly together on the sands, that had probably been there for about a year. Like many garments, it's likely that you won't be wearing survival-quality boots when a catastrophe occurs, but be certain to include them in your home, auto, or bug-out survival outfit.

In cold weather—if there is snow on the ground—this fine hiking boot is not adequate footwear in a survival situation.

There are many good warm-weather boots on the market. A Gore-Tex bootie liner makes them mostly waterproof (dry feet are, in fact, a chimera). Aggressive lug soles provide needed traction, ankle-high uppers give that joint support against sprains, and long laces permit them to be wrapped once around the ankle—woodsman style, to increase ankle support—before tying them. Good boots will cost about $75.

When snow covers the ground, you need a pac-boot, with thick insulation, rated to at least -40 Fahrenheit.

Like every garment, the measure of a boot's warmth is whether snow melts on its outside, indicating heat loss.

If there is snow on the ground, you need an insulated *pac-boot,* rated to keep its wearer warm to a minimum of 20 degrees below zero. Fahrenheit ratings have always been tongue-in-cheek, at best. Again, soles should have aggressive lug soles, for traction on rubble, mud, and other debris, and uppers should be at least ankle-high. Good pac-boots, ironically, cost about the same as their warm weather counterparts.

A traditional winter boot, the mukluk is a bit less rugged.

CHAPTER NINETEEN

SNOWSHOEING AND SURVIVAL

Snowshoes

No one travels very far without snowshoes.

No one can wade through hip-deep powder very far without being entirely exhausted, and people have died trying. A hard wind can transform four inches of falling snow into four-foot drifts that can trap most cars and trucks. If you have any reason to believe that your survival might entail dealing with snow, you need at least one pair of snowshoes, preferably a pair for everyone in your family.

Atlas Snowshoe Company claims that carrying a pound on your feet equates to carrying six pounds on your back, so weight is important. The weight of traditional and new-age snowshoes is equitable for models rated to carry the same mass, but snowshoes with solid decks of tough fabric have more flotation—the ability to support a load based on surface area and weight distribution—and can offer the same load rating in a smaller snowshoe. One myth is that webbed decking of rawhide or neoprene provides more flotation than tube-frame models with solid decking. Think in terms of two canoe paddles, one with a solid wooden blade, and the other with a webbed flow-through blade, like a traditional snowshoe. Per square inch of area inside their frames, solid decks support 27 percent more weight than webbed decks. Tubbs Snowshoes rates its 10-inch by 36-inch *Mountaineer* model with *ArcTec* decking to 300 pounds.

Today you can step into the fastest, most secure and glove-friendly snowshoe bindings yet conceived and be bound for the backcountry in a matter of seconds. Gone is the sloppiness that permitted snowshoes to flop around under your soles, which eliminates the need for ungainly "tracking" tails like those that drag behind tennis-racket-like Michigan snowshoes. From the ratcheting-strap boot harnesses that revolutionized snowshoe bindings to Tubbs' 1-click Bearhug model, new bindings have improved and simplified the snowshoeing experience.

In generations past it was often necessary to remove one's snowshoes to climb steep hills, and coming down was an adventure in sliding. Today, crampons provide traction sufficient to climb any grade your legs can push you up, and are an excellent brake for sure footing on steep descents. If your path leads across the sun-warmed surface of a frozen lake, crampons will keep you on your feet in places where you'd otherwise make frequent hard contact with ice.

Northern tribes of old knew March as the "Moon of the Broken Snowshoes," a time when warming days "rotted" hard-packed snow. Surfaces that had been hard as concrete in February became treacherous with voids hidden below and sun-softened layers that would suddenly cave in for several feet all around, sending a snowshoer crashing downward into tangled brush. It was common to "bridge" a snowshoe across two solid points; when that happened, and with all of a wearer's weight on the unsupported center, wood frames were prone to snap in two. A broken snowshoe could be life-threatening if you've broken trail a mile or two through hip-deep powder that won't support a snowmobile, because you might not be able to get back without two snowshoes. Bridging doesn't appear to be a problem with the latest generation of aluminum, plastic, or carbon-fiber frames, all of which have proved to be much stronger than wood.

When snow covers the ground to a foot or more, you need snowshoes.

Whichever snowshoe you select, be sure to get one with adequate surface area to support the load you intend to put on them. In the softest powder a large enough snowshoe should only sink three or four inches, and having too much snowshoe is erring on the side of caution. Too small a snowshoe may be worse than no snowshoes, because they might let you sink eight or ten inches into a hole that you then have to lift your foot and the attached snowshoe back out of before repeating the process. Generally speaking, the smallest off-trail qualified snowshoe is in the 9-inch by 30-inch range.

Too small a snowshoe is a very common mistake; the minimum adult-size working snowshoe is 9 × 30.

Make certain that the bindings of the snowshoe you choose will fit the boots you intend to wear. A common gripe among long-haul dogsled racers who are required to have snowshoes strapped to their sleds is that many snowshoes have *trail bindings* that are too small to fit the full-size pac-boots that are needed in subzero temperatures.

Too, be aware that snowshoeing is the most energy-intense exercise on the planet. Breaking trail in fresh powder can burn in excess of 1,000 calories per hour—or about twice as much as swimming, biking, or running. A big concern of snowshoers is having enough calories on hand to complete the trek.

Price-wise, both modern and traditional snowshoes cost about the same, starting at around $70 and increasing as features and materials become more sophisticated.

Snowshoeing is not a difficult skill to learn, but if you suspect that you might one day need to do it, by all means, get familiar with the fundamentals.

CHAPTER TWENTY

EMERGENCY MEDICAL PROCEDURES

First-Aid

Today's backcountry first-aid kit can be better equipped than any medic's in WWII.

Emergency medical procedures are a fact of life when dealing with post-disaster scenarios. Television made an almost shameful effort to hide injuries extraneous to the actual attack on the World Trade Center. In the six years following, firefighters were retiring in record numbers with Chronic Obstructive Respiratory Disorder (COPD), after running heroically into a rolling maelstrom of hot particulate matter. These numbers disregard the respiratory and other injuries that befell onlookers who always inexplicably try to get a closer look at the very catastrophe that injures them.

Every experienced paramedic can (but probably won't) relate to you the hard decisions that must be made in the minutes after a bus crash, chemical train derailment, or multi-car pile-up. Medics call it *triage*, which means that living humans are coldly categorized into those who can be saved, and those who would be a waste of time that would best be devoted to others without fatal injuries. Triage is a microcosm of the type of difficult choices that might face you during any multi-victim disaster. Just imagine the scenes that led to city streets lined with corpses, and the nightmarish images of bodies being bulldozed into mass graves.

No one wants to see those things, or even to think about their possibility, but the likelihood of such things happening to you in the future— if they haven't happened already—is greater than any of us would like. You can do nothing to prevent it; what you can do is mediate how badly it impacts your world. Medical equipment and knowledge is essential to doing that.

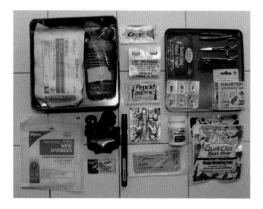

The homespun first-aid kit from the author's own backpack.

Burns, lacerations, sprains, and broken bones are some of the more common injuries that you need to be prepared for, whether the disaster is a small plane crash or Hurricane Sandy.

Blood on the Snow

The temperature was −7 Fahrenheit, falling toward an overnight low of −16. A pale sun settled behind the evergreens, bringing nightfall to the swamp an hour before the rest of the world. My breath condensed in thin white vapors as I knelt atop hard-frozen snow, hacking wedges of meat from a frozen whitetail neck with my field knife.

The neck was bait for a pack of gray wolves that had recently migrated south across the Straits of Mackinaw, to the tip of Michigan's Lower Peninsula. The notches in it would secure a noose that suspended it from a half-down spruce, four feet above the snow. The idea was that carnivores attracted to a free meal would leave paw prints I could cast in plaster. That was looking doubtful so long as subzero temperatures kept the snow hard as stone.

Then the M9's heavy blade skipped off, and slammed, edge-first, into the index finger of my opposite hand. Air hissed through my clenched teeth as steel honed sharp enough to shave whiskers sunk into the first knuckle, embedding the big blade halfway through my finger. When I yanked it free, a fountain of bright blood erupted to contrast almost beautifully against the snow. I immediately pressed hard against the wound with a thumb to stanch the blood flow, but the finger of my woolen glove liner was sliced as neatly as if it had been scissored. This was a bad one.

With my good hand, I finished hoisting and tying off the venison, then headed for camp—and my first-aid kit—two miles away. Lightened of its load, my cargo saucer trailed effortlessly behind me, so I hooked its tow rope over the hilt of my holstered knife to keep both hands free. The thumb of my right hand locked against the wound of its own volition, maintaining a constant blood-stopping pressure, even though the exerted muscles cramped into painful spasms.

Because that wasn't the first time I'd inflicted a potentially serious injury onto myself in the woods with a bonehead stunt, I anticipated the shock-generated nausea, chills, tunnel vision, and sweating that always accompany bone-deep wounds. Knowing what to expect didn't make enduring it less unpleasant, though. I pressed harder toward camp, hoping that added physical exertion would force the more unpleasant symptoms of shock to subside.

At camp, I slipped the first-aid kit from its pocket in my backpack, tore open a roll of self-adhesive safety finger tape with my teeth, and dumped out a single-application packet of antibiotic ointment. With those items at the ready, I stripped off the slashed glove liner in one quick motion. Blood spurted outward as soon as the pressure was released, but in the eyeblink before the gash was obscured I was able to confirm visually that muscle, bone, and cartilage had been damaged. The blade had penetrated halfway through my knuckle joint, into the cuticle at the bottom of my fingernail. It was tough to feel fortunate just then, but I was happy that the blow had been glancing.

My first concern was to stop the bleeding. With sunset the mercury had dropped another five degrees, and ice popped like gunshots from the frozen river that ran past my camp. I was alone, ten miles from civilization, and I wasn't scheduled to be picked up for another three days. It wasn't an optimal time or place to be leaking important body fluids.

I wrapped the injured finger with several turns of safety tape, gently squeezing both sides of the cut together and staunching the flow of blood completely—like taping a ruptured automobile radiator hose. It throbbed a bit that night, but two ibuprofen tablets helped to ensure a restful night's sleep. By morning the gash had closed sufficiently to be washed in a nearby spring, smeared with triple-antibiotic ointment, then rebandaged less tightly, with no further blood loss.

Gangrene is a real concern in temperatures cold enough to kill exposed skin, and with three days left before my scheduled pick-up, there was some reason for concern. Because blood flow through my damaged finger was already inhibited, it was imperative that I keep the digit at body temperature until the blood vessels could reconnect. Exposure to cold would kill off more of the injured flesh, inducing "necrosis," a blackening of dead flesh that, once begun, can spread like a cancer. More than a few old-timers have lost parts of their anatomy—or their lives—proving that.

Because a glove no longer fit over my bandaged forefinger, I switched to the gauntlet-length leather mittens that I carried for those long, cold times when I needed to remain behind camera for hours. I experienced a blackening of dead flesh at the wound's edges, but I trimmed away the necrosis with toenail clippers from my first-aid kit, kept the wound clean, and retaped it each day. Aside from tending my near-amputation for a few minutes each day, I was able to follow my planned itinerary until I broke camp to leave.

I'll always have a scar from that experience to remind me of what can happen to any woodsman who forgets where he is for even a moment. But it could have been a lot worse. The injury might have been more severe—an amputation—and I could have been farther from camp.

Worse, I might not have had the advantages of a well-provisioned first-aid kit. With it, a wound serious enough to make sensible people in civilization seek medical attention had been reduced to a relatively minor inconvenience under conditions that didn't favor the injured.

Still, I did have to hike two miles with a mild case of shock in subzero temperatures before I reached that first-aid kit. I learned my lesson. Now I make certain to have a basic first-aid kit in my daypack wherever I go.

Treating Shock

One of the most basic medical skills is to treat injured victims against *shock*. Put simply: This is a body's reaction to injury that causes it to concentrate resources on organs needed to keep a body alive. Extremities, skin, and brain are among areas of a body that are normally deprived of blood flow, warmth, and oxygen.

Treating for shock is not a complicated process, but it does save lives. First, lay a victim down, flat on his back—unless he vomits or otherwise expels fluids from the mouth (then you should turn him onto one side to prevent "aspiration"—inhaling vomit into the lungs). Elevate feet about

15 degrees, to lessen the load on a victim's heart. A rolled towel placed under the base of the skull forces the neck to bend slightly backwards, and keeps a victim's airway open.

It's a myth that victims can swallow their tongue, but a person who is seizing or convulsing needs something to keep them from biting their tongue—a paperback book has sufficed.

Cover a victim with blankets, more than one, if possible, to keep his body from having to work so hard to maintain normal warmth. Administer first-aid for bleeding, etc., as needed.

Dental Problems

Legalities prohibit me from giving medical advice. But dental problems are a part of everyone's life, and if the services that make life civilized are disrupted, a lost filling can become a bona fide medical emergency. While I cannot tell anyone what to do about that, I can relate to you how I dealt with a ruined tooth when there was no dentist available.

I'd been in the woods for about two months when I bit down on a mouthful of peanuts, and my left bottom molar split in two. After four days the broken molar began to ache from its roots.

The pain was tolerable with an assist from ibuprofen from time to time, especially at bedtime, but then the gum became inflamed and sore. I continued to chew with the broken tooth, hoping to loosen it from its moorings, and kept it brushed clean, but after a few days my jaw began to swell from an infection at the molar's roots.

Having grown up under conditions that have been described as abusive, I'd nearly died when I was twelve when an abscessed tooth ate completely through my mandible. My parents, fearful only of having to explain why their kid had died of neglect, had finally driven me to a hospital emergency room. The doctor who took my temperature cussed aloud when he looked at the reading of 107 degrees, then injected a thousand milligrams of penicillin into my buttocks. I recovered when a putrid abscess drained through the bottom of my jaw, but I knew what could happen.

Most critical was preventing the abscess from becoming a closed infection, because if pressure were allowed to build under the molar, the trapped poisons might be forced into my bloodstream, causing fatal *sepsis*.

Local anesthesia has been around for less than two centuries, but dentistry dates back to the Neolithic Period (around 7,000 B.C.), so, despite its modern over-complexity, it can be performed in a survival scenario.

I first localized the infection using a wash cloth saturated with boiling hot water, placed into a Ziploc bag, then wrapped inside a dry towel. I held the makeshift heat pack against my jaw, directly on top of the abscessed molar, where it created an artificial fever to bring the poison to a head.

The heat caused a blister to form on the outside of my gum, making the skin there taut like a balloon, I took a large-gauge carpet needle from my sewing kit. With an index finger crooked into the side of my mouth to expose the gum, I felt around for the most swollen spot. I didn't sterilize the needle, because I reckoned it couldn't carry anything worse than the germs that were already there. I didn't have a mirror, either, and that might have made the operation less hit-and-miss.

Predictably, the most blistered spot was directly over a root, and I figured that was probably a good place to lance the infection. I steeled myself, then shoved the carpet needle directly into that spot, perpendicular to the gum. Tears came to my eyes as I drove the needle inward until I felt the tip scrape solidly against a root. I wiggled the needle in a circular motion and felt the electric shock of a pus sac bursting from around its still living nerve, followed by an immediate relief as pressure was released from that sensitive area.

With thumb and forefinger, I squeezed the infected gum around the hole I'd lanced. I wiped away a copious amount of yellowish pus with tissue paper, which reduced the swelling considerably. When the tissue came away bloody, I figured the infection had been purged—for now.

I hadn't solved the problem, but by lancing the gum I'd ensured that the molar wouldn't become more than a painful distraction.

Now came the hard part. The abscess had killed the tooth, and the socket would keep infecting, trying to push it upward, as long as the molar was there. I had no choice but to extract it. Dentistry wasn't one of the contingencies I'd prepared for, so I didn't have many tools suitable for pulling teeth. I'd have to make do with my cabin-building tools. I took the big lineman's plier from my tool bag and wiped its jaws clean with alcohol pads. I snapped its disinfected jaws together a few times, trying to envision how they'd work as tooth extractors. I doubted a dentist would approve, but the pliers would have to do.

By feel alone I managed to get the pliers' jaws locked around the molar. Tooth enamel is hard, and the pliers slipped a couple of times before I got a grip strong enough to twist against. When I did, I rocked and twisted the molar back and forth in the steel jaws. The pain was blinding as I heard the cracking sounds of flesh tearing away from tooth. My vision narrowed and bright spots danced in front of me as I channeled the energy of this powerful stimulus to twist the molar even harder.

It came free with a crunching sound, and I was holding the dead tooth before me, still gripped in the pliers' jaws. The good news was that I'd extracted the roots completely on one side. The bad news was that the other roots had broken off at the molar's base. I rinsed my mouth with salt water and spat blood until the hemorrhaging stopped. With my tongue I could feel the remainder of the tooth still embedded just below the gum line, where I couldn't get at it with tools.

The dead root wasn't a danger to my health, but it was a constant irritation. The gum healed nicely around what was now essentially a sliver, but there was an occasional jolt of pain when I was chewing. If I ignored the pain, I'd awaken the next morning with the gum around it feeling tender and swollen. The root had to be extracted too.

With some trepidation, I honed my Spyderco folding knife to shaving sharpness and prepared to perform oral surgery on myself. I laid the tip of its blade against the outer gum, directly over where the dead root lay trapped, and pushed the cutting edge inward through the soft tissue until it stopped against the harder root. I could only imagine what was happening as I operated by feel alone, but I felt the gum separate from around the embedded root.

With the root exposed, I went to work with the big lineman's pliers. Blood was flowing, causing me to spit bright red from time to time as I felt around for a grip with the pliers, but my endorphins were apparently working because the pain was negligible. When I felt the jaws close securely onto the broken root from above and below, I gripped the pliers' handles firmly and twisted hard. A spotlight of pain formed in front of my vision as the root rocked free of my jaw, finally coming free in the jaws of my pliers.

Like an iceberg, the extracted root was larger than it had seemed from the surface, measuring roughly half an inch square by almost a quarter-inch thick. I rinsed my mouth with salt water, glad to have that irritating chunk of bone removed, but a little concerned that the incision I'd made might not heal properly. A dentist would have stitched the severed gum together, but I doubted I could perform that operation by feel alone, so I left it to heal on its own.

As it turned out, I needn't have worried. The incision and empty socket healed quickly and without secondary infection. I kept the damaged gum brushed regularly to keep out food particles and to toughen it, and in two weeks' time I was healed enough to chew on that side.

Maybe I am the masochist I've been told I am, but I prize this experience for the insight it provided. Because of it, I had genuine empathy for a part of life that has been endured by every feral human, and by every animal unlucky enough to survive beyond its prime. I can imagine what an aging bear must go through as every tooth in its mouth progressively becomes the same affliction I'd suffered with just one molar. It was enough to change one's perspective of life and death.

Again, no part of this experience is intended to advise anyone as to how they should handle their own dental problems.

Hypothermia

It was November 14, the day before Michigan's firearm deer season began. I was deep within the Skegemog Swamp, where I would be camped for the duration. Air temperatures had been in the mid-forties all day, and a hard, cold rain had been falling since morning. As day edged into nightfall, temps plummeted to 20 degrees, and everything was sheathed in a glaze of ice.

When all was in order, I hiked two miles up to the gravel pit where I'd arranged to meet my friend, Dar, who'd be staying with me from time to time. He was three hours late when the headlights of his old Dodge 4 × 4 turned off the road toward where I waited at the forest's edge. Following behind him was a bus-size motor home.

The two men in the motor home were Dar's uncle and cousin, who had driven north from the city to try their luck at deer hunting. I did my best to provide them with details of some of the more promising deer trails, but they were reluctant about venturing into lowland woods where they were most likely to find deer. I imagined Dar had exercised his flair for dramatic storytelling to terrify them with tales of killer bears, Sasquatch, and chupacabras.

And because I knew my friend, I wasn't surprised to see that his pickup carried four heavily laden frame packs, a GI duffel bag, a cased Coleman lantern, a catalytic heater, and two gallons of fuel. I reminded him that camp was more than two miles away through untracked cedar swamp. He countered with an argument about having a few comforts.

We were still arguing when Dar backed his truck around—and buried the rear tires axle deep in loose sand. He couldn't extricate himself because he'd disconnected the front drive shaft to increase mileage from the full-time 4 × 4 drive train, and the one-ton pickup was far too heavy to push. The shadowed forest was darkening rapidly when Dar crawled under his truck with U-joints, wrenches, and a Mini-Maglite clenched between his teeth. I resigned myself to making at least two more round trips to camp hauling in his luxuries. Dar's cousin offered to carry a pack in with me, and we set off toward a vague trail through inky dark cedar swamp, guided by the beam of a small flashlight.

On our return, Dar had just finished bolting-up the front drive train. The big V-8 started with a rumble, and freed itself with a mere press of the accelerator, which somehow just made the situation more irritating to me. Finally, the three of us shouldered the last backpacks, while the uncle retired into the motor home behind locked doors to watch a football game. We'd have to make another round trip to guide his cousin back to the motor home, but at least I wouldn't be humping a pack on that last lap.

The trail leading to our secluded deer camp began with a half-mile of long-abandoned farmland with a small but still productive apple orchard. From there we went steadily downhill, crossing numerous springs that flowed directly out of the hillside to merge into some of the best brook trout streams in the state. The next half-mile was across open, soggy lowland marsh. The last mile was through mature poplars bordering a dense forest of cedars and pines that lay in eternal shadow. Finally, there was a quarter-mile of slender footpath that wound through deep swamp, across four streams, to terminate at our camp.

Ice-coated grasses crunched like glass underfoot, and rough-barked trunks glistened with a glaze of ice. That may have contributed to Dar's misstep while crossing a natural footbridge comprised of massed tree roots that time and decomposition had covered with a foot of grassy soil. Four feet to one side of the shoulder-wide bridge was a pair of mature cedars whose trunks actually grew upward from the center of the stream, supported from either streambank by an arch of barked roots. Between the footbridge and the arching cedars, currents had formed a chest-deep hole that was a favorite spot for brook trout.

In the lead with a large flashlight, I wasn't aware of what was happening behind me until I heard a loud splash and felt water wash onto my booted ankles. From solid footing on the opposite bank, I turned and played the beam of my flashlight onto the hole. Dar's boots were still atop the footbridge, but his body was submerged, folded at the waist between root bridges, his butt against the stream bottom.

In summer this might have been funny, but right now my friend's head was under four feet of near-freezing spring water, carried there by a fifty-pound backpack, and snowflakes accumulating against the ground emphasized that this was a bad time to be wet and cold. When Dar's head popped up again, his eyes were bulged wide, and his jaws were working, but the only sound he made was a prolonged, raspy inhalation. Using the weight of my own pack as leverage, I grasped one of Dar's shoulder straps with a gloved hand, and dragged him onto the streambank.

I quickly rolled him out of his backpack while his cousin gaped uselessly, but he refused to take off his sodden down-filled parka.

It was two miles, uphill, back to the motor home, or two hundred yards to camp, where wet, ice-glazed wood meant that making fire would be challenging. Dar needed warmth now, so camp it had to be. He was already curled into a fetal position, a victim of involuntary abdominal spasms that force hypothermia victims to ball-up in an instinctive effort to keep internal organs warm.

I don't recall much of that last leg to camp, except that it was hard work dragging my incapacitated, semi-conscious friend that distance. When we arrived I forced him to trade his saturated down coat for my dry synthetic-fill sleeping bag—wet hypothermia victims often fight relinquishing saturated garments that are, in fact, sapping body heat, because they fear getting colder than they feel. Then, I steered him to a roughhewn bench while I built a fire.

Pine needles, birch bark—every natural tinder was sheathed in ice and wet. I placed a platform of iced-coated dead sticks at the bottom of the fire pit, and dug a pill bottle filled with *fire wicks* from my backpack. The origin of these simple twisted lengths of paraffin-saturated cotton string is unknown, but they have never failed me in the decades I've used them. I lighted the end of one fire wick, then laid it atop the kindling platform, and used its flame to ignite a half-dozen more fire wicks. Then I built a teepee of very thin twigs around the base of the flames, leaving a small opening through which to insert more fire wicks as needed. It was slow going, because the kindling twigs tended to burn through without drying, but a combination of shredded birch bark and mostly-dry needles dug from the thick carpets of them that fall around the bases of white pines finally generated enough heat to dry and fire the kindling teepee.

Seated a few feet away, Dar was shivering uncontrollably, and he'd lost awareness of his surroundings—another symptom of progressing hypothermia that occurs when the body's involuntary energy-saving measures shut down voluntary mental functions. The sleeping bag had stopped further loss of body heat, but he needed reheating immediately. His body, like the wood that was slowly beginning to blaze, needed to be warmed to an operating temperature that enabled it to be self-sustaining.

Because every piece of wood had to first be thawed, then dried, before it would burn, the fire was fed a continuous supply of finger-thick twigs that passed through those stages as quickly as possible. When a good, red bed of coals had developed, I added larger pieces of wood and set a covered pot of water on them. With a steaming canteen cup of hot cocoa gripped between my friend's trembling hands, I went to get his backpack.

Being old school, Dar had waterproofed everything that might be harmed by an immersion. His synthetic-fill sleeping bag, wrapped in a Mylar blanket and inside a heavy-mil trash bag, hadn't absorbed any water. Stripped down to his long underwear and seated next to a crackling fire, he sorted through the wet pack while his body reabsorbed the heat he'd lost.

An hour later, dressed in dry clothing and wearing a Thinsulate-fill field jacket, Dar was recovered sufficiently to accompany me when I took his cousin back to the motor home. Only then did it begin to dawn on him that he'd just had a too-real taste of what happens when you freeze to death. The experience left an impression on both of us.

The moral of this story is that hypothermia is hands-down the most dangerous environmental threat that anyone is likely to face in the out-of-doors, and being prepared to meet that threat is crucial to any survival strategy.

Human body temperature is 98.6 degrees Fahrenheit. As UDT Swimmers and SEALs in the US Navy have known since their inception, prolonged exposure to any temperature below that robs a body of critical heat. A windy rainstorm on Waikiki beach in summer can cause hypothermia, and, while that might not kill you directly, it can weaken your immune system enough for you to contract pneumonia—*that* can kill you, especially when an environment demands as much strength as you can muster. Drop the temperature of the strongest man's internal organs to 85 degrees, and he'll not only be helpless, he'll probably be in a coma.

Shivering is the first stage of hypothermia; it's the body's attempt at regaining external body heat by working muscles to generate heat. Be aware that hypothermia may occur gradually, even inside a heated home, among elderly and infirm individuals whose metabolisms have slowed. In this initial stage, a victim can recover rather easily by being covered with a warm jacket or a blanket.

When shivering stops in a hypothermia victim, the condition has gotten to the critical level. Cognitive faculties will become impaired to a point where victims are incoherent, unable to respond to spoken words, and their speech becomes slurred. They may try to do nonsensical things, like remove warm clothing. Most important at this juncture is to warm a victim's core, to bring warmth in internal organs back to normal levels. Temporarily, disregard restoring warmth in arms and legs; cold fingers won't kill.

Most important is that a victim be laid flat, and his core insulated with blankets, or piled jackets. *Do not massage any portion of a victim's body, as this may induce cardiac arrest.* Warm compresses, like a hot water bottle help, but do not use electric heating pads. The old movie remedy of sharing your own body heat with a hypothermia victim is still a valid, useful strategy. If a victim quits breathing, or if breathing becomes very shallow and weak, begin chest compressions (CPR) immediately.

Another, seldom covered, because little is known about it, version of hypothermia is called "creeping hypothermia." With this condition, a victim, usually the smallest and least strong member of a group, very slowly loses internal heat, becoming progressively weaker, until he or she goes to sleep one night and just never wakes up. Personally, having faced the hazard with friends and survival students a few times, creeping hypothermia terrifies me. The surest prevention is to keep potential victims as warm as possible, and well fed, especially just before bedtime.

Hyperthermia

In the northwoods, we don't see a lot of hyperthermia, but when I lived in the farm belt, we sure did. Picking cherries was a way to make money for school clothes in summer, and cherries ripen in the hottest months of the year. Hyperthermia is generally not a problem if temperatures remain below body temperature (nominally, 98.6 degrees Fahrenheit), but when the mercury tops 100 degrees, whether actual, or inside a building or a vehicle, heat stroke is a very real danger.

The very first defense against hyperthermia, which is not, in itself, a physical condition, but a description of the state that leads to dehydration, heat exhaustion, and heat stroke, is to keep your body hydrated.

When I was building the log cabin for my book of that name, I monitored daily calorie expenditures, and water intake. Periods of heaviest labor coincided with summer's hottest months, and there were days when maintaining normal bodily functions required drinking in excess of 4 gallons of water per day. Forget urination, water was streaming out of my pores, and humidity was so high that my laundry wouldn't dry, so sweating didn't do much to cool me. It was like Burma in July (hard to believe that in 6 months it would be 20 below zero).

It has never happened to me personally (that's a lesson I learned vicariously), but I saw what heat exhaustion can do to a thousand tough, physically fit young sailors the day I graduated from boot camp, in Orlando, Florida. As our battalion stood there in ranks, wearing our woolen winter blue dress uniforms, while an Air Force general droned on about how proud America's politicians were to have more meat for the Vietnam War grinder, young men (and women, from a few segregated female companies) were dropping in significant numbers under a merciless sun.

That's how it starts: You get woozy and light-headed, probably nauseous, maybe lose consciousness, altogether. That's heat exhaustion.

The next step is heat stroke. Your body begins shutting down noncritical systems, including some organs that feel pretty critical. One of the first systems to go is higher thought processes, an instinctive reaction that is not in sync with modern survival requirements. When your internal temperature reaches 102 degrees, Fahrenheit, you'll probably go comatose.

Symptoms of either can include swollen tongue, cessation of sweating, and an incongruous feeling of cold. Victims of heat stroke are typically unconscious.

Treatment for either includes cooling victims. This can be done most effectively by immersing a victim in water, but, if possible, water that is no less than 70 degrees F—ironically a drainage ditch or storm sewer might be the most ideal choice, whereas a bathtub full of ice or icy-cold water might induce a coronary arrest.

When a victim of either heat exhaustion or heat stroke is able, give them brackish-warm water to drink, only a few sips at a time. It's a good sign when a victim starts sweating.

In the field, beware the practice of just falling face-first into a stream, like you see in movies. Thirsty people who have done so have often passed out from the shock of cold water. And if you're face-down when you lose consciousness . . .

This is why you've always heard that if you must travel in hot weather, it's best to lay up in a shaded spot during the heat of the day (a la the traditional Mexican *siesta*), and walk during the comparative cool of night.

Hypoglycemia

It was the fifth morning of an eight-day backpacking excursion at the northwest tip of Michigan's mitt, and it had been raining hard since our arrival on March 26. Not a gentle rain, but a hard, cold deluge that pounded through leafless branches with a sound like sizzling bacon. And it never stopped, not even for a moment.

My fourteen-year-old nephew, Josh, and I were there because we'd been taking a weeklong backpacking trip over his spring break since he'd grown enough to carry his own gear. We'd come to the same area last year, when we'd found a small pack of gray wolves, and had returned to track their activities. Last year at this time there had been four feet of snow on the ground, and snowshoes were required wear; that would have been preferable to this incessant rain.

Our tent doors faced one another, and I'd draped the weighted ends of an ultralight tarp over both to form a covered porch between them, where we kept our gear. Our synthetic-fill bags and closed cell foam pads kept us warm at night, and our shelters were watertight, but there is no way to stay dry during prolonged exposure to such conditions. Woolen long johns and socks, augmented as needed by light, loose layers of wool or synthetic, kept us from becoming hypothermic in weather conditions that demand more from your body than any other.

We'd banked our fire from the night before with three large dead logs, and when we rolled them over, placing the heat-dried, unburned sides directly against the coal bed, they burst into flames. By adding small, then progressively larger wet twigs and branches, we soon had a crackling blaze. There was no need to get water for coffee; I just set one of our rain-filled cookpots next to the fire.

Josh was standing with his back to the fire, where rising heat waves actually pushed falling raindrops away from its perimeter, creating a dry warm shell in the midst of constant deluge. But while the side facing the fire warmed and dried, the outward side got wet and cold. At one point Josh looked at me, water streaming from the brim of his narrow bush hat, and with creative use of colorful metaphors likened our situation to the action of a vacuum cleaner. I felt much the same way, myself.

I'd just taken the hot water from the fire when Josh's eyes suddenly rolled back into his head, showing white, and he collapsed. I watched in horror as he sat down heavily, directly on top of the bed of orange hot coals that covered our fire pit. In slow motion, I saw his right hand, clad only in a fleece-covered glove and knit liner, drive into those coals until it was embedded to the wrist into a place hot enough to melt copper.

I grabbed the hefty youngster by the front of his jacket and yanked him onto his feet. I guided his unsteady legs to a makeshift bench facing the fire. Then I began stripping off his gloves and checking for burns while my heartbeat returned to normal. If his burns were bad, I couldn't be back with medical help in less than five hours.

It was a miracle; there wasn't so much as a red spot anywhere on the boy. Even his clothing wasn't burned, saturated as it was under rain that fell faster than it could run off, and the overlap between jacket and glove cuffs had kept his wrists from touching live embers.

The cause of this near disaster was hypoglycemia—Josh's reaction to having available energy in the form of blood-borne sugars depleted by the increased demand of keeping warm. When blood sugars are gone, the body is designed to switch over to using fat reserves as energy, but the first several times hypoglycemia occurs can literally come as a shock.

Panicked by loss of readily available fuel, the brain can react by shutting down systems needed to power the body. Symptoms range from nausea, tunnel vision, and overpowering fatigue to outright loss of consciousness. Long distance runners call it "hitting the wall," and anyone who participates in heart-pumping activities that demand stamina, from mountain biking to cross-country skiing and—especially—snowshoeing, can expect to experience hypoglycemia.

The cure in every instance is as simple as amping-up a victim's blood sugar to normal operating levels. In Josh's case, it was a cup of hot cocoa for quick energy and warmth, followed by a starchy, slow-burning breakfast of rice and raisins. He was back to normal after about ten minutes, with only a vague recollection of having fallen into the fire.

Conventional wisdom places feeding oneself low on the list of priorities for staying alive in a survival environment, based on a belief that it takes about three months for a typical human to die of starvation. In reality, the greatest danger is likely to be more immediate, stemming from symptoms of hypoglycemia and the loss of function they cause. Slipping off a rocky or icy trail is one more serious secondary hazard of reduced efficiency from having low blood sugar. Falling into a blazing fire is right up there, too.

From helping to keep you warm during an unplanned night in the woods to helping you to feel more positive and energized, having a pocketful of snacks rich in sugars, fats, and proteins can make a difference. Quickly assimilated sugars and fats from chocolate are great for cutting off hypoglycemia at the first signs; slower-burning carbohydrates from cheese, peanut butter, and dried fruit act like slow-burning hardwood in the metabolic furnace; summer sausage can provide both proteins and fats.

Tourniquets

In most instances, a tourniquet is not recommended, because to apply a ligature—a noose—around a limb tightly enough to restrict blood from pumping out of a severed high-pressure artery also means that you must cut off blood flow to the flesh below a wound entirely. While it is true that a tourniquet might save a victim from bleeding to death in as little as four minutes, that comes at the cost of killing, and probably requiring amputation of, the injured limb.

The importance of arteries are signified by their locations, deep within a body, where they are less likely to receive injury. A ruptured artery is identified by copious amounts of bright red. (Oxygenated) blood pulsing from a wound in time with a beating heart. Like a tire, pressure decreases with loss, but an arterial bleed is always identifiable, because blood doesn't just flow from the wound, it spurts.

Apply a tourniquet only when necessary. Field-expedient tourniquets can be made from rope (a lumberjack's timber, or choker, hitch is especially effective), from belts, even extension cords.

If possible, ligature-type field-expedient, even conventional rubber first-aid, tied tourniquets should not be used; best are manufactured strap-type tourniquets, which provide a broader area of compression that is less likely to damage constricted tissue.

According to the Mayo Clinic: "For both adults and children, the tourniquet should be placed just above the wound—not necessarily on the thigh or upper arm only—and the time of application recorded and submitted to the receiving hospital. If transit time is less than an hour, the tourniquet normally remains in place until the patient is in the operating room. When the transit time is longer and the patient is stable, it may be possible to gradually loosen a tourniquet and leave it unfastened as long as bleeding is completely controlled. Use of another hemostatic bandage may be necessary to augment hemorrhage control, however. If bleeding occurs, the tourniquet is simply re-tightened."

Diphenhydramine

Diphenhydramine, probably most recognizable under the brand name Benadryl, is an over-the-counter antihistamine that has a place in every first-aid kit.

Just as ingestion of very small amounts of tincture of (liquid) iodine—2–3 drops per quart of water—or iodine tablets is a good home remedy for cleansing a body of radiation, so is diphenhydramine an effective over-the-counter treatment against the effects of the most common nerve agents, like Sarin, or Agent GB. No reliable dosage has been determined, so following directions on the box the drug came in is probably safest.

Diphenhydramine is also an effective substitute for prescription anesthesia. According to the National Institutes of Health (*nih.gov*) people with an allergy to conventional "caine" anesthesias have good results from, typically, injectable 1 percent diphenhydramine. NIH states: "*Diphenhydramine hydrochloride (DPH) has numerous pharmacological uses in medicine. It is a first-generation, sedating, oral antihistamine. When topically applied, DPH has excellent anesthetic and antipruritic effects. DPH has also been shown to be an effective injectable drug for local anesthesia."*

Anti-Hemorrhagic Products

Quik-Clot. Quik-Clot Sport Anti-Hemorrhagic Bandages are an example of one of the most lifesaving medical innovations of the past decade: the anti-hemorrhagic blood-clotting agents, which can staunch blood loss from a severed artery, without need of a tourniquet that can kill an entire limb, necessitating amputation. First used in combat and on animals (including our own sled dogs), products like Z-Medica's Quik-Clot were available only to medical professionals until 2010, when the civilian-approved Sport line of pre-treated Quik-Clot four-by-four (3.5 × 3.5 inches, actual) bandages became over-the-counter items. Removed from their vacuum-sealed foil envelopes and taped directly over a severed artery, gunshot wound, or any profusely bleeding injury, either Quik-Clot Sport or the new antiseptic Sport Silver has a battle-proven ability to save life and limb when a wound is bad and help is far away. Available in 25- or 50-gram sizes, prices for Quik-Clot Sport 25 average about $10 per envelope, around $12 for Sport Silver.

Sutures

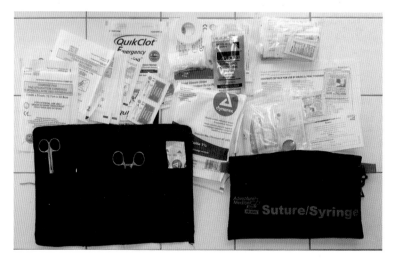

Approved by our twenty-year veteran paramedic, this Suture/Syringe Kit is ready-made for everything from closing wounds to starting an I.V. drip.

I once knew a truck driver who, while dropping his cargo at a loading dock, sustained a gash to his leg from brushing against a sharp piece of metal. After applying a quick pressure bandage, he retired to a motel room with a spool of ordinary cotton/nylon-blend thread, and a large darning needle. Gritting his teeth against the pain, and fortifying himself with a few slugs of whiskey, he stitched the wound closed.

He'd done a good job of sewing, and was quite proud of himself—until he awoke the next morning with the repaired wound red, puffy, and with the striated red marks that indicated the onset of gangrene. The trucker very nearly lost his leg.

In the chaos of a post-disaster environment, you might have time to bleed to death before a doctor becomes available, and it just might be necessary for you to suture yourself or a loved one back together.

Butterfly sutures, available in most pharmacies, are adhesive-backed cloth strips designed to adhere to skin, and hold the sides of a laceration together until it can heal shut. In real life, the best of these has delivered unacceptably poor performance in the field, under actual conditions. In my book *The Log Cabin*, I described an incident in which I laid my knee open with a hand saw that was sharp enough to just zip through double-layer ripstop material, and leave a 4-inch laceration. The butterfly sutures held for just seconds before pulling loss, and allowing the gash to reopen.

I applied a generous layer of triple-antibiotic ointment, and re-closed that wound with the good old boy's cure-all: Duct tape. Duct tape has worked to pull and hold together wounds many times. It is not, however, sterile, and no medical professional would recommend that it be relied upon for that purpose.

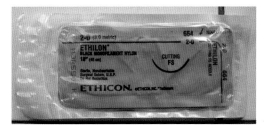

People have almost killed themselves by stitching up their own wounds, a la Rambo; a sterile suture kit should be part of every post-disaster first-aid kit.

Unless a wound is too ripped-open—like some of the injuries we've seen caused from the tearing action of a canine's teeth—traditional stitches should be avoided, because puncturing skin with a needle increases trauma to the area. But, as with the above-described injuries from animals (I've dealt with more wolf- and dog-inflicted bite wounds than I can relate here), sometimes it becomes necessary to close large wounds by sewing skin back together—like darning a hole in a sock.

If you must sew a wound, use a medical suture kit made for that purpose, available at this moment for about $8. Also, it is very important to stitch-in a drain tube, beneath the skin, where the stitches are applied, to permit escape of fluids until healing is well under way.

To apply a drain tube, use a hard—the best choice, because it won't collapse—I.V. (intravenous) tube, about 2 inches longer than the area to be sutured, so that an inch extends from either end of the closed wound. Fold the tube over on itself to create a flat end, then clip-off one corner of the folded-over flat at a 45-degree angle, to make a drain hole in one side of the tube when you unfold it. Make a drain hole like this every inch, down the length of the tube, to ensure that fluids produced from the wound will migrate into, and out the open ends of the tube.

Lay the prepared tube into the wound channel, ensuring that it is long enough to extend from either end. Then, stitch the skin closed over the tube. It's best not to drive thread through the tube, as doing so introduces an occlusion point in the tube, but hold the tube from sliding in a wound channel by wrapping several turns (including at least one timber-hitch choker knot) around each end of the tube before applying the final closing stitch on that end.

Drain tubes should be flushed at least twice daily with liquid antiseptic (we use *Furacin* for our dogs, and it has worked equally well for me, personally), to keep tubes clear and draining freely. After 10 days, sutures holding tubes in place at either end can be snipped, and tubes pulled free; there is minimal pain associated with this tube removal. Do not clip and pull out stitches until 2 weeks have elapsed.

Cutting holes in an I.V. drain tube, before it is stitched into a deep wound.

If you'd prefer to avoid the trouble of putting together your own comprehensive suture and I.V. (intravenous) kit, Adventure Medical Kits offers a nice outfit. Designed for paramedics and medical professionals, this kit has more than most laymen will ever need, but, ironically, needs to have I.V. tubing added to ensure a good supply of drain tubes. The kit is currently priced at $80.

Building a First-Aid Kit

Like any kit, for any purpose, you cannot cover every possibility. Just as I cannot, for legal reasons alone, dispense much at all in the way of medical advice. There are numerous variations of ready-made First-Aid Kits on the market, but, as I've said in my other books, not one of them is complete enough for my tastes. Some do a pretty fine job, however. That said, if you choose a ready-made medical kit, feel free to add to it as you see fit.

Personally, I like to build my own first-aid kit. For example, I'm a big fan of Quik-Clot–type antihemhorragic products. From the first powder-form clotting agents, we've had very good success with such products with our sled dogs—a dog's teeth can do immense harm in a short period of time, and fights between huskies are often vicious and bloody. The first powder-form antihemhorrhagics were infamous for generating heat, from a chemical reaction with the moisture contained in blood, and for leaving a crusty residue that made cleaning deep wounds troublesome. Quik-Clot does stem an arterial bleed, though, and it has saved the lives of many a combat soldier since it was first used in Iraq and Afghanistan. Today's "sport" sponges are pre-moistened, to keep them from getting hot, and they're self-contained to keep bleeding wounds from being contaminated when they clot.

Several varieties of Quik-Clot antihemorrhagic sponges, engineered to stop arterial bleeds that used to require a tourniquet.

Paramedic-approved First-Aid Kit

Put succinctly, based on advice from paramedics whose livings are made from rendering first-aid, unless you have an ambulance, there's no such thing as an ideal first-aid kit. There are some good tries, but if you want as close to perfect as you can get for your situation, you have to build it. Following is the basic first-aid kit recommended by seasoned paramedics. Build on to it as you see fit:

1 bottle ibuprofen, 50 count.

1 4 × 4 gauze sponge.

1 large roll gauze.

1 roll 1" wide self-adhering tape.

1 elastic wrap.

1 sterile suture kit.

1 chewable Pepcid AC heartburn tablet.

2 alcohol prep pads.

2 Quik-Clot antihemorrhage sponges.

6 sealed diphenhydramine HCI (Benadryl) capsules.

6 loperamide HCI antidiarrheal capsules.

1 triple-antibiotic ointment, tube or envelope.

1 miniature LED headlamp.

1 penlight.

1 toenail clipper.

1 tweezer.

1 bandage scissor.

1 small magnifying glass.

1 first-aid manual, Emergency First-Aid (American Red Cross, Adventure Medical Kits).

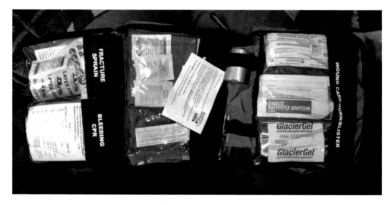

This ready-made first-aid kit from Adventure Medical Kits (AMK) contains everything you could need.

CHAPTER TWENTY-ONE

BUILDING A SURVIVAL KIT

Survival Kits

A winning philosophy in terms of survival gear is to think in terms of kits. Everyone, in any world, carries a survival kit, even if they choose not to call it that. Probably the simplest, and most recognized, form of survival kit is a man's wallet. Inside it are a drivers' license that gives him the ability to operate a motor vehicle in the civilized world he lives in, without being hindered by those who could, and might, prevent him from going about the daily affairs of life in an efficacious manner. Also within its leather or fabric walls are insurance and road service cards, credit or debit cards that enable him to get whatever goods or services he might need to continue functioning.

More comprehensive yet, and a hot topic for some stand-up comedians, is a woman's purse, whose arcane contents might include almost everything the lady of today needs to survive in the modern world of shopping malls, gas stations, and supermarkets. Said to be a dark place of mystery to most men, a purse has been known to carry just about anything from food to tools to weapons.

In many instances, the correct response to a nuclear, biological, or chemical attack, volcanic fallout, or derailment of a railroad train carrying toxic chemicals, may be to simply stay where you are, and wait until the air clears, so to speak.

The Federal Emergency Management Administration (FEMA), a division of the Office of Homeland Security, calls this a "shelter-in-place" strategy. Sheltering-in-place means to seal off doors, windows, any access to the outside, as tightly as possible, to prevent whatever harmful contaminants are outside from getting into the air occupants are breathing.

Preparing a building against outside contaminants isn't rocket science, but it can be a lot of work. Windows are most easily and effectively sealed with storm window kits, consisting of polyethylene sheets and tape—plastic sheeting should be heavier than plastic food wrap; typical storm window kits are minimal. Doors, too, should be sealed with strips of duct tape (no household ever has too much duct tape). Do not overlook vents, including kitchen range hoods, or dryer vents. If you think that you're being too meticulous, too paranoid, you are not. A mere crack can let in an army of viruses, and some nerve agents are terrifyingly deadly. The Occupational Safety and Health Administration (OSHA) recommends covering openings with a sheet that is several inches larger than the opening it covers, so that it lays flat against the wall.

Because the objective is to seal a shelter-in-place building entirely, there's some concern about having sufficient air to breathe. FEMA's rule of thumb is to have 10 cubic feet of air space for every person for every five hours spent sheltered. If you experience the first symptoms of hypoxia (blurred vision, gasping, severe headache), and it becomes necessary to allow in some fresh air, let the air in from as high above ground as you can—here's where people in high-rises have an advantage.

During your wait, monitor a local radio station for at least 10 minutes every hour. Presuming that electrical services are available, save your batteries, and watch television, or listen to AC-powered radio. As with the Mackinac Bridge and tornado anecdote, stated earlier, you might get your best, most truthful information from a foreign news agency on shortwave, because, the worse the situation, the more you can count on government censorship of broadcast news.

It also pays to have a spray or spritz bottle of antiseptic, like Lysol on hand, in the event of a biological threat. After sealing windows and other openings (not before, because it might inhibit tape adhesives from sticking), spray all around sealed openings with antiseptic.

The SERE Pack

One of the ready-made Bug-out Packs offered by ASAP.

The Bug-out Pack from FoodInsurance.com.

Gerber Gear's GO Bag, a shoulder bag survival kit.

Variously called the bug-out bag, the grab-and-go kit, the five-minute pack, or whatever moniker seems to be coolest at the time, the function of this comprehensive do-it-all survival outfit is what the US military's special forces troops term *Survival, Evasion, Resistance, and Escape*, or SERE. Survival is just one of the needs this outfit addresses, because, as the name implies, it, ideally, suits every need, whether that need is avoiding a marauding gang, employing superior force to convince predators to prey elsewhere, eluding capture from an unbeatable force, or, as in the WWII Philippines, mounting a resistance army to harass and sap the strength of an occupying enemy.

This book, as you should have noted already, is far from being paramilitaristic. The phrase "combat survival," coined long ago by an anonymous desk pilot, is an oxymoron. But it has, historically, become necessary to sometimes use the hurtful, often lethal defenses that almost every wild species possesses for defense of itself and its progeny.

The construction of an ideal SERE pack is fluid, dependent entirely on its intended use. In more temperate locations, it has been as simple as a khaki vest with lots of spacious button-down pockets that contain everything from a fire starter and compass to granola bars and fishing gear.

GI-style compass pouches with snap-down flaps had been affixed with all-purpose individual carrying equipment (ALICE) clips. Inside these snap-down pouches, I packed an impressive assortment of tools, including several dozen feet of nylon string, needle-nose pliers (this was before multi-tools had been invented), an array of fishing, navigational, and fire-starting gear, even an ink pen and a waterproof-paper notebook in a plastic Ziploc bag. For extended trips, I clipped on a three-day fanny pack, containing a light blanket and a small tarpaulin. In winter, I had to loosen the belt a little to fit over a heavy coat, but this outfit served amazingly well for over a decade.

Pocket Kits

A pocket-size Soapdish Survival Kit.

Most mobile, even to the point of forgetting that you have them, are pocket survival kits. These can take an almost infinite number of forms. Some have been put together in pill bottles, Altoids tins, even in Ziploc plastic bags. The objective is simply to put as many useful items, chosen in descending order of importance, into an elements-resistant container that fits into a jacket or trousers pocket.

Like every survival kit of any size a pocket kit should begin with *The Basic Three*—Compass and map, fire starter, and knife. If a knife sports a sheath with a gear pocket, these can all be carried as part of the knife.

My personal favorite pocket kit begins with a two-piece (top and bottom) plastic soap dish. Most soap dishes (not those with hinged lids) fit almost perfectly into a GI Compass Pouch, with a snap-down flap. A gear loop sewn to the back of the compass pouch accommodates an *All-purpose lightweight individual carrying equipment* (ALICE) clip that attaches securely to a waist belt, or any strap.

You can get a number of small items into a soap dish—things that would fall out of a compass pouch alone. Carried in a jacket pocket, or clipped to a belt, the little kit can be a stand-alone survival kit, or several compass pouch kits can be combined.

Survival Harness

A step further than the soap dish/compass pouch kits is the survival harness that I carried for decades and thousands of miles in wilderness areas. It started as a heavy GI pistol belt with a standard Vietnam-era super harness. To this was attached numerous dedicated compass-pouch kits, several ammo (magazine) pouches, and other useful tools and items that I could clip, tape, or otherwise fasten to it.

A survival harness can carry almost as much survival gear as a daypack.

The main difference between my survival harness and its combat-type configuration lay in its contents. Mine carried a comprehensive fishing outfit, any-weather fire-making tools, binoculars, numerous small hand tools (this was before the advent of multi-tools), a sewing kit, folding and fixed blade knives, space blanket and small tarpaulin—almost everything I'd need to survive a forced stay in a survival environment for as long as it took.

Today, that old threadbare, worn harness has gone by the wayside, but it has been replaced with a lighter, custom-made version, because the harness configuration is just too useful. This new one incorporates an ultralight bivvy shelter and a light bedroll, and is more comfortable to wear under a backpack. For disaster survival, as part of a modular system that includes, but is not solely reliant upon, a fully stocked backpack, it's nearly ideal.

Automobile Kits

The automobile survival kit is far from new. The practice has become forgotten with today's unwise reliance on technology and Big Brother, but growing up in the northern forests, no one drove anywhere, especially in winter, without having a trunk packed with a big cardboard box containing winter boots, warm coat, gloves, and all more likely tools of survival.

To emphasize why doing that could be as critical today as it ever was, a few years ago a man on a remote but relatively well used highway was driving alone in a blizzard when he lost control and spun off the road.

His car slid down a slight grade to the tree line and the motorist was injured.

The driver was, of course, reported missing, but before anyone could find him, his car was buried beneath the 200-plus inches of snow that fell in that region each winter. I personally drove by him numerous times in the next four months, until melting snow revealed the roof of his car. It's likely that having an emergency survival kit wouldn't have saved this man, but being 20 miles from the nearest village didn't detract from the severity of his situation.

What you'll need depends a lot on where you might be needing to bug-out from. In Florida, it's not likely that you'll be needing snowshoes, don't make the common mistake of loading yourself down with superfluous stuff. Stick to the basics, water (in a wide-mouth metal container that can be heated in areas where it might freeze), a blanket or sleeping bag, high-energy snacks that have a long shelf life, cordage, a tarp, tire-plug repair kit, manual air pump, water filter, a working-size axe, definitely a shovel. Think about it; should you have kitty litter, to provide traction on an icy road? Should you carry a lot of water?—you need more in Arizona than in Minnesota. Don't think in terms of right or wrong, but rather in terms of necessity and priority.

Recreational Vehicle Survival Kits

Whether used for recreation or for bugging-out, every snowmobile and ATV needs to be equipped with a comprehensive survival kit.

I once wrote an article on the topic of snowmobile survival kits for *Michigan Snowmobiler* magazine. I've been riding one of these machines since 1968, and although the urge to drive one recreationally never appealed to me, there's a tuned-up Arctic Cat 580 in my barn at this moment.

I was surprised at the mail that article generated, not from readers who agreed or disagreed with content of the feature, but from snowmobilers who were actually offended at the very suggestion that the particular brand of machine that they'd chosen to buy—usually emblazoned garishly across every article of their clothing—could experience any sort of mechanical failure. Like any veteran of all-terrain vehicle (ATV) riding, I have too many experiences to even entertain such a preposterous notion. But the feedback was real, and there was evidently a fair percentage of aficionados who believed in their own invulnerability.

In many instances, a wheeled or tracked ATV in the garage might be your ideal means of escaping from a disaster zone. When roads are backed-up with cars and trucks so thick that a like vehicle cannot squeeze around them, a smaller, more nimble machine could be the answer to getting yourself and your loved ones to proverbial high ground.

With the exception of carrying extra fuel, motor oil, and tire repair kits, the survival outfit for an ATV is not remarkably dissimilar to any other type—it must provide for a user's most crucial needs, in order of importance. But the kit must be man-portable, because to believe in the infallibility of a machine is pure foolishness. Be prepared to abandon it at any point, and continue onward afoot.

The Bug-Out Boat

You hear about Bug-out Bags, but seen here is a Bug-out Truck, equipped with much more gear than a man can carry; the same can be done with a compact car or motorcycle.

It may have started with the Cold War, when Americans lived with the knowledge that just one multiple-warhead nuclear missile from any of a dozen nations that had them could effectively halt civilized life in America for a long time. Or maybe it began during WWII, when there was legitimate reason to fear enemy assaults against either coast. Some Americans built bomb shelters, and a few counted on having the luxury to buy more of any manufactured goods. Nearly everyone kept grab-and-go survival kits in closets or car trunks. Wintertime in Maine demands that the ability to make fire be absolute, and extra tinder is a necessity. As with any survival kit, regardless of its complexity or size, contents should always be weighted to match the environment in which a kit is most likely to be needed.

For decades, pocket survival kits have taken the form of Sucrets and Altoids metal boxes, with hinged lids (these have typically been too small), ibuprofen and other pill bottles, or Ziploc bags. Best of these has been a two-piece soap dish (available in most pharmacies), placed into a GI compass pouch, with an ALICE clip. Sometimes quick evacuation is a necessary plan of action.

Throughout history, many small boats have been pressed into service as bug-out platforms. Folks dwelling along riparian flood plains have been using river boats, pirogues, and canoes as just-in-case getaway vessels for as long as people have made permanent homes on river banks. Johnny Cash sang about getting his family to safety via a rowboat in his song "Five Feet High and Rising" and no bottom-land farmer would be without a functional boat close at hand in springtime. Since the time of Noah, whenever the threat has been too much water, a boat has often been part of the solution.

When a boat is the best option for a rapid-egress vehicle, a lightweight molded kayak may be the ideal choice. Powered only by muscle and a double-blade paddle, it slices easily through water faster than a racing canoe, and a kayaker doesn't need to be athletic, or even fit. Another potentially invaluable advantage of the kayak design is its very shallow draft, which draws so little water that it spawns axioms like, "If you spit on the ground, you can kayak across it."

As demonstrated by whitewater competitions at the Summer Olympics, the closed-cockpit kayak pattern also handles rough waters more nimbly than other small craft. Because it pivots from amidships, as opposed to turning more slowly from the stern, a kayak can turn on the proverbial dime. Its low center of gravity—like a sports car—is the result of its paddler's lower body actually sitting below the water line, where it provides an almost amazing combination of stability and agility. The shorter the boat, the more abruptly it can be made to change direction. For guiding on rivers and inland waterways, most of the pros prefer boats in the twelve- to fourteen-foot category.

Longer kayaks, fifteen feet or more, provide the spear-like "tracking" needed to carve through rolling swells that would delight a surfer, and terrify a casual angler. With rudder down, spray skirt sealing the cockpit around its paddler's waist, "thigh braces" that enable paddler and boat to move as one, and an approved PFD, experienced sea kayakers frolic in waves and whitewaters that send even power boats scooting for harbor. Combine the seaworthiness of the kayak design with high-performance hull and deck materials that can be molded to precise configurations and are all but indestructible, and it's not surprising that kayakers have conquered some of the roughest big waters on Earth.

If stealth is an issue, a kayak shines there, too. Covert military units have discovered that a kayak can infiltrate backwaters almost silently, and travels at roughly twice the speed of the canoe that still remains a part of US Army Ranger training. Its low profile makes a kayak hard to spot, while its trademark light weight enables a single paddler to portage a boat overland, or to conceal it from wary eyes. Those same attributes appeal to birdwatchers and backcountry explorers, and some waterfowl hunters like that they can retrieve their own birds.

A kayak can't contain the season's worth of supplies or trade goods that a canoe, that original pickup truck of the back waters, was designed to transport, but most can carry more than enough food and equipment to spend a week away from civilization in relative luxury. A twelve-foot kayak, my own ideal compromise between agility in fast water and tracking over rolling waves, can easily haul more than a hundred pounds, and still cruise easily at better than three miles per hour.

Speed, handling, and storage capacity have led to the popularity of kayak-camping, especially for weekend adventurers who have to be back to work on Monday morning. Roll-top vinyl "dry bags" keep vulnerable items and clothing from getting wet—or sinking to the bottom—even if the boat should capsize. The watertight hatches and bulkhead storage spaces found in most kayaks permit even ten-foot boats to be outfitted as outstanding floating survival kits. With tent, sleeping bag, cookset, water filter, and other mainstays of wilderness life packed into its recesses, a twelve-foot kayak has more than enough space left to stash more than a week's worth of food, a comprehensive first-aid kit, extra batteries, and other items that would be too heavy to carry in a grab-and-go backpack.

If you're among the growing population of forward-thinking Americans who've decided that having an exit strategy in the event of a disaster is a smart idea, and if those escape plans might involve traveling over water, the kayak-based outfit merits consideration. Base prices for extra-stable starter boats, like Pelican's Pursuit models, begin at under $500, including paddle, ranging up to several thousand dollars for super-light composite hulls and carbon-fiber paddles. Broader-beam boats are more stable and beginner-friendly, but a little slower and with slightly less performance in rough seas.

Every government and Hollywood disaster scenario that might demand mass evacuation from urban areas also predicts roadways choked with traffic jams. But most large cities sprang up around navigable waterways; if a survival-outfitted kayak can be transported to water (several manufacturers offer folding two-wheel carts for towing laden boats over rough terrain) there will likely be little to impede a rapid egress. And when you're not using it to escape disaster, it can provide a lot of good times fishing, birdwatching, or just paddling quietly on a lonely backwater.

Ready-Made Bug-Out and Home-Survival Kits

Because I've written for a number of magazines that address the topic of survival, I've performed field evaluations of numerous ready-made survival systems. For many who want to be prepared to survive, but know little about what that might entail, and who are simply not interested in devoting the time and learning needed to gain expertise (some people just want the ability to make water safe to drink, they don't want to make a study of it), these may be the best answer.

ICE Pack

Ashbury International's ICE (In Case of Emergency) Pack takes the survival-kit concept to a new level with its fifteen integrated Emergency Sustainment Systems modules. Packed into bright-yellow 6-gallon buckets with airtight covers, each module is a comprehensive stand-alone kit in itself, but all of them together form an interlocking shield against most of the survival challenges that might arise during an extended period without public utilities and services.

The philosophy behind Ashbury's ICE Pack system is to provide not just for the needs of its users, but to enable them to endure life-threatening disasters in relative comfort. Module 3 provides 3 freeze-dried meals, with sufficient water to prepare them, per person per day; Module 4 holds 2 liters of water per person per day, with a 5-gallon collapsible bladder, and Crystal Light–flavored drink mix. Module 6 encases medical items needed to manage bleeding, wounds, bone fractures, and other common first-aid problems. To help keep things clean, Module 7 is a hygiene kit that converts its own bucket into a bag-lined commode, complete with sterile wipes.

Should a disaster include airborne hazards like radioactive dust, lung-abrading volcanic ash, or chemical toxins, Module 14 is a complete shelter-in-place outfit, with duct tape, heavy plastic sheeting, a 12-inch by 16-inch tarp, corner lips, bungees, cable ties, 100 feet of light rope, work gloves, empty sand bags, and even a smoke, fire, and carbon monoxide detector. Module 13 carries a Victorinox Rescue Tool and Leatherman Crunch multi-tool to help make home or office impregnable to windborne agents. Module 5 carries a whistle, orange HELP flag, and a strobe flashlight for making it known that you need assistance. Should circumstances dictate moving to a more hospitable location, Module 2 contains a hooded Space Blanket, vinyl hooded poncho, and a kayaker-type dry bag to protect documents and other items that might be damaged by exposure to the elements. Threats from people and abandoned pets that might become aggressive are handled by a large can of Guardian-brand pepper spray in Module 12.

Ashbury recognizes that people who shelter-in-place during or in the aftermath of a disaster have more than just bodily needs. There is a real need to know what the outside world is doing, so module 8, the Communication module, includes dynamo-charged or battery-operated AM/FM radio receivers. Module 9 is dedicated to lighting, because there are situations where an ability to see in darkness could be a life saver. Module 15 carries the batteries needed to keep lights on and electronics operating. For those long, inevitable hours of idle time, Module 10 is dedicated to mental exercises, with mind-occupying board games, a deck of playing cards with survival tips printed on their backs, and a survival manual to read. Module 1 includes disaster-survival books and a 16-page instructional booklet from the Department of Homeland Security titled "Preparing Makes Sense." Module 11 addresses the need to keep a record of events with an all-weather marker, notebook, and a disposable camera.

ICE Pack Emergency Sustainment Systems are available in various sizes. Largest is the 16-person workplace size, followed by an 8-person office system, a family-size 4-person home outfit, and smaller sizes for couples and individuals. All can be customized to meet specific needs, but the factory-assembled system is quite adequate as is. An ICE Pack system avoids spending time and money trying to guess at which items might be needed to weather a disaster, and that by itself is welcome peace-of-mind.

Foodinsurance.com's Emergency Plus Pack

Your wristwatch says that it's well after midnight when you're awakened by a shrieking wind. Suddenly the bedroom windows blow inward with a thousand shards of glass and you hear the freight-train rumbling of an approaching tornado. With cold rain and debris pounding inside through the broken pane, it's clear that you need to get outside of a house that's collapsing around you.

After spending several miserable and hypothermic hours in a half-flooded culvert beneath the road, the storm blows over and you emerge into a surreal alien world. The devastation that crushed your house took many of your neighbors' houses as well. Governmental help is on the way, but their services are so overstretched that you can't expect assistance for days.

How well you weather this emergency will ultimately be determined by how well prepared you've made yourself. I evaluated this kit for *New Pioneer* magazine, and here's what I found:

Freeze-Dried and Dehydrated Food Pack

The centerpiece in foodinsurance.com's numerous offerings is food. The sealed Mylar/foil pack in our kit contained fourteen pounds of individually sealed foil pouches, enough to feed one person three meals per day for two weeks. Rounding out the dehydrated and freeze-dried meals are large pouches of powdered electrolyte-rich drink mix. Some Ziploc resealable envelopes can be prepared by adding boiling water directly into the packet, which then serves as a convenient bowl.

The proof of the pudding is taste. My family ate six assorted meals and deemed them all good. Reconstitution was excellent, and portions were sufficient to fill up a large man. Even the large main bag has uses beyond containing food packets; it can be used to collect rainwater, and the highly reflective foil can serve as a signal mirror.

Squeeze-Bottle Water Filter

Regardless of how fit, tough, or skilled a person might be, no one survives more than a few miserable days without water. Bottled water is the first emergency supply to be trucked in after every disaster. As demonstrated by the epidemic of cholera, typhoid, and other waterborne diseases that sapped medical resources in the wake of Hurricane Katrina, it's unwise to drink untreated water—even when too much water is the problem.

There exists a medley of different tools to make water potable, but the squeeze-bottle filter in the Emergency Plus Pack is perhaps ideal for real-world survival. Just fill the bottle with untreated water, screw on the filter cartridge and cap, and squeeze clean water from its top. Its EPA-approved Aquamira CR-100 filter cartridge is rated to remove 99.9 percent of cysts like Cryptosporidium, flagellates like Giardia, and bacteria like Typhoid. Filter life is 100 gallons (460 refills), and cartridges are replaceable.

NIOSH N95 Particle-Filter Masks

From the lung-corroding ash of a volcano to airborne radiation spread from a terrorist's dirty bomb, a filter between your respiratory system and the air you breathe might be a life saver. Add in perhaps more imminent threats from super-flu, anthrax, or industrial pollution, and you can see why some people in urban settings wear respiratory filters in daily life.

There are two *N95 NIOSH* (National Institute of Occupational Safety and Health)-approved disposable respirator masks in the Emergency Plus Kit. Rated to remove 95 percent of airborne particulates from inhaled air (not resistant to pneumonia-causing oil), the masks feature padded adjustable nose clips, non-latex synthetic straps, and fold-flat design.

First-Aid Kit

Medical troubles are a reality that need to be guarded against; when there's no 911 to call, a first-aid kit becomes as imperative as any component of a working on-your-own kit. When a simple skin laceration can become gangrenous in an unsterile environment, and amputation or death are real possibilities, an ounce of prevention is worth a ton of cure.

The first-aid kit foodinsurance.com includes with their Emergency Plus Kit is as smart as I've seen, and my paramedic wife concurs. Among the usual Band-Aids, gauze, and alcohol pads are scissors, a rescue-breathing mask, and Nitrile gloves. These and many other of the most important tools of first-aid are contained in a red zippered 7-inch × 10-inch × 2-inch fabric case.

Tommy Cooker Folding Stove

A favorite among British ground troops (Tommies) since WWI, the folding Tommy Cooker stove has been used from the trenches in France to the jungles of Indochina for the past hundred years. Fueled by solid Hexamine (a derivative of paraffin) tabs, the Tommy Cooker is smokeless, odorless, and its flame is so muted as to be almost invisible.

The Tommy Cooker has never been a good substitute for a real fire, but a single fuel tab will heat 2.5 cups of water to a boil (212 degrees Fahrenheit) in about five minutes. Tabs ignite at the touch of a flame in the wettest environments. When not in use, the stove folds into a convenient square, with fuel tabs inside.

Waterproof Safety Matches

The ability to make fire is an important aspect of any type of survival situation. Warmth, water purification, cooking, even medical needs can be served by fire; without fire you might suffer more than necessary.

Foodinsurance.com addresses the need for fire with a good old-fashioned 40-count box of reliable wooden safety matches. Varnished heads make them resistant to water that can powder ordinary match heads. The equally retro wooden matchbox makes an excellent fire-starting kindling in an emergency.

Bale-handle Stainless Drinking Cup

Any survival kit needs a vessel for boiling water, cooking, drinking from, or just containing berries and the like. It should be metal, preferably stainless steel (aluminum has been linked to Alzheimer's disease), single-walled so that it can be heated directly over flame, with a folding handle that enables it to be handled safely when filled with a hot substance.

The heavy-duty two-cup stainless steel mug in the Emergency Plus Kit is built tough enough for survival. The cup comes in its own plastic bag to help keep it clean, and a rolled lip makes it more sip-friendly. Its folding bale handles are spot-welded on in six places for strength, and just the right size to accommodate insertion of a knife blade to lift the cup off a fire when it's too hot to handle.

Dynamo-Crank Flashlight/Radio Combo

I've always had a radio receiver in the backwoods for the same reasons that you need one in a survival situation. If there's a radio station in operation—and if there isn't, things are really bad—then news of what's happening in the world will be carried over the airwaves. News that could not only help you to save your own life, but remind you that civilization still exists.

Dynamo-powered radios are nothing new, but the unit included with our kit takes the concept further with FM and AM reception, LED flashlight, siren, and strobe. Two co-axial 6-volt ports—one input, one output—enable the unit to run or charge from a wall adapter (not included), and a 4-piece adapter set allows it to charge cell phones and other devices. One hundred cranks deliver up to an hour of usable flashlight, or about five minutes of radio. Performance is enhanced by precharging dynamo batteries.

Stainless Steel Multi-tool

It might be argued that humankind began with the appearance of Homo habilis, the toolmaker, more than two million years ago. With poor running speed, little climbing ability, and almost no natural tools or weapons, the earliest humans were forced to be inventive. They learned to manufacture knives and hammers from stone, and kept improving on those until they'd evolved into the multi-faceted toolboxes of today.

Foodinsurance.com recognizes that a bare-handed human is severely restricted, and they've made a stainless steel multi-tool part of the Emergency Plus Kit's survival system. Modeled after the most common multi-tool designs, the tool unfolds to become pliers with seven on-board tools folded into the handles, and six hex head wrenches broached into either handle. A black Cordura holster unsnaps to reveal ten additional tool bits that mate with those wrench cut-outs.

Backpack

I've been carrying a backpack for forty-five years, so I'm a stickler for a good one. It's your toolbox, and what it contains largely determines how capable you'll be in a given situation. There are alternate methods for accomplishing most things, but even a skilled survival expert will have a tough time whittling out an LED flashlight or fashioning a pair of scissors. If you have tools, you need a toolbox.

The 3,600 cubic-inch pack Emergency Plus Kit is of survival-level quality. Four zippered external pockets, roomy main sack, sleeping bag compartment, dual compression straps on either side, and carrier straps top and bottom enable it to carry everything listed above, with room for a sleeping bag, bedroll, bivvy, and more. Its suspension proved to be remarkably comfortable with padded shoulder straps and waist belt, load lifters, and sternum strap—all the things you'd look for in a backpack.

Gerber GO Bag

Just as Davy Crockett carried more in his shoulder bag than he needed to just keep his rifle shooting, Gerber packs real versatility into their new

GO Bag. The outfit begins with Maxpedition's super-functional Mongo Versipack shoulder bag. Made from Teflon-coated 1,000-denier black Cordura, the Mongo Versipack is MOLLE compatible, and then some— if you want to fasten something to this bag, you probably can. All seams are double-stitched and taped, with reinforced corners and stress points. Straps are adjustable, and an over-size quick-release buckle on the front is glove-friendly. A quick-release waist strap keeps the bag from flopping when you run.

The main bag boasts six large pockets, four of them with heavy-duty YKK zippers. There's a polyethylene clip inside one for keeping frequently needed items, and a drawstring closure for the largest inside pocket. Three of the pockets are backed with the loop half of hook-and-loop (Velcro) fabric for attaching patches and more. At either end of the shoulder bag are a water bottle pocket with drawstring closure, and 2 clip-closed pouches for the included MP600-ST multi-tool and a cellphone (or an extra pistol magazine). A stainless steel carabiner on the shoulder strap accepts any small tool with a compatible loop or ring. A large D-ring on the front of the satchel accommodates tools with their own 'biners, and a crosspiece allows it to be used as a buckle in its own right.

MP600-ST Multi-tool

Touted as Gerber's new standard in military issue multi-pliers, the included MP600-ST multi-tool is a must-have for any survival kit, especially for the AR shooter. With its non-reflective black-oxide finish needle-nose pliers, replaceable wire-cutter/crimper jaws, and 9 fold-out locking work blades, the tool isn't remarkably different than its counterparts at first glance. But this one is specifically designed for weapon maintenance in the field. Especially useful to AR owners is the M16/M4 front sight post adjuster wrench. By customer demand, its Philips-head screwdriver is extra-long, and the modified Spey blade offers both serrated and fine edges. Overall length of the multi-tool (pliers extended) is 6.61 inches, 5.04 inches closed; weight is 8.2 ounces. An instruction fold-out for maintenance and use of the tool is included. If your outfit includes a rifle, the MP600-ST is a complete maintenance toolbox. Lifetime warranty.

The main difference between a hunting knife and a survival knife is that the latter is designed to be a self-contained survival kit in and of itself.

FrogLube Weapon Treatment

Completing the GO Bag's weapons maintenance functions is a 4-ounce bottle of FrogLube cleaner/lubricant/protectant (CLP) from Audemous, Inc. Developed by Navy SEALs and made in the USA by a disabled-veteran-owned company, this USDA-certified biobased weapon treatment is actually food-grade, with a pleasant wintergreen scent. Swabbing a rifle bore with it has been shown to improve inherent accuracy, and it retained its lubricating qualities even in the sub-freezing temperatures of our field evaluations. It can be used to maintain working weapons in the field or to treat them for long-term storage, and being non-toxic, FrogLube is also an ideal cleaner/protectant for high-carbon knife blades. Be warned that the bottle's snap-cap can come open with the activity the bag will likely see in field use, so opened bottles are probably best carried sealed inside a zip-lock plastic bag.

EZ-Out Folding Knife

A good knife is a defining component of any survival kit, and Gerber covers that base nicely with its patented EZ-Out DPSF (Drop-Point, Serrated, and Fine) one-hand opening lock back folder. Its 3.5-inch Spey-style blade is crafted from razor-sharp S30V stainless steel (my personal favorite alloy), half serrated, half fine edge, and coated with non-reflective black oxide. A trademark hole at the bolster end enables the knife to be deployed with either hand. The blade is set in the traditional 4.5-inch EZ-Out handle of Zytel with Kraton inserts for superior grip. A tip-down, right-hander pocket clip allows multiple carry options, but isn't detachable or reversible. Open length is a working size 8 inches, but a weight of just 2.8 ounces makes it almost unnoticeable. There have been some complaints about the clip bending or breaking (we haven't experienced a failure with three EZ-Outs in fifteen years), but the knife has a lifetime warranty.

Recon Task Light

Because sometimes survival situations happen in the dark, the GO Bag includes Gerber's outstanding—and nearly indestructible—Recon Task Light. Housed in Gerber's Type III anodized 6061aluminum body, it measures 3.75 inches long, and turns on with a clockwise twist of its tail cap. Its 1-inch diameter rotating DIAL (Diode Illumination Adjustable Lens) head offers a choice of brilliant white light, red light that preserves a user's night vision and is invisible to most animals, a green light for reading maps, and a blue light that highlights blood trails. Despite being powered by a single AA battery, the Recon Task Light can light a trail for more than a dozen hours, depending on ambient temperature and what type of batteries you use. A spring pocket clip allows the 2.6-ounce light to be mounted to any strap or pocket, but we found it especially useful as a hands-free headlamp when clipped to the bill of a ball cap. It comes with a lifetime warranty.

Stainless Steel Water Bottle

Every survival kit needs water, and the last piece of equipment included with the GO Bag is a 1-liter stainless steel H2Go water bottle. Coated black except for a golden Gerber logo, the bottle's wide mouth seals tightly, but doesn't freeze shut in cold weather like narrow-mouth conventional canteens. Being steel, the bottle can be used to boil parasites and microbes to death in suspicious water (Gerber recommends against heating or cooking in the container), and is rugged enough to stand up to extended field service. A carabiner built into the polyethylene screwtop enables the bottle to be secured to a strap or belt loop. A Velcro strap retainer ensures that the bottle won't fall out when the going gets rough.

Maxpedition Pocket Reference

In real-world survival, knowledge is strength. Gerber addresses that need laudably with a compact *Pocket Ref* (3rd Ed.) by Thomas J. Glover. Already well known among tradesmen as a ready answer guide, topics include everything from Boyle's Law to the Beaufort scale to Magnetic Declination to floor joist standards. In today's world where survivability might require a basic knowledge of electricity, carpentry, or plumbing, this is an invaluable reference. Measuring 5.4" × 3.25" × 1.0", the 768-page book fits into a breast pocket. Its only flaw is that it's a standard paperback book, and subject to damage from the elements. We solved that dilemma by sealing it into a Ziploc sandwich bag.

Maxpedition All-Weather Notebook

One survival advantage that the first pioneers of the New World had over native tribes was an ability to efficiently transfer information to one another through detailed written messages. History is replete with instances where knowledge and news from notes have helped to save the day, from the Battle of Lake Erie to Afghanistan, and the folks at Gerber acknowledge that by including a weatherproof spiral flip pad in the GO Bag. Unlike ordinary paper, the 50 lined Rite in the Rain pages can be written onto with pen or pencil in heavy rain, and seem no worse for wear after water has dried from them. Plastic covers are also waterproof, and the back is printed on either edge with 4.25 inches and 11-centimeter scales.